EMPIRE AIRWAYS
EGYPT

NEW YORK
the WONDER CITY

Russia
PAN AM

CHINA

MEXICO

PARIS

AIR FRANCE

Antarctica

Antarctic Flights
7th, 14th, 21st, 28th November 1979.
See your travel Agent
air new zealand

ALASKA

FLY
PACIFIC NORTHERN AIRLINES
The Alaska Flag Line

ASABLANCA

PORTE
DU MAROC
SYNDICAT D'INITIATIVE & DE TOURISME

JAPAN

CHEMINS DE FED ALGÉDIENS

AFRICA
TWA

THE NORTH POLE

ALGÉDIEN
hartenne

THE
MOON
ONLY 230,000 Miles Away!

Fly By Mail
VISIT INDIA

ISTANBUL

GALAPAGOS

BRAZIL

D0951939

ORIGINS OF A JOURNEY

Berdoa
Hair
Targa
Digir
Albaili
AFRICA.
Agi:
lymba.
Borno
Cano
Guan-
guara
Tombotu
Cago
Benin
Alafar
Nubia
Gago
Antonio
C. Bonę Spei
Tristan de
NW
NE
W
E
SW
SE
S

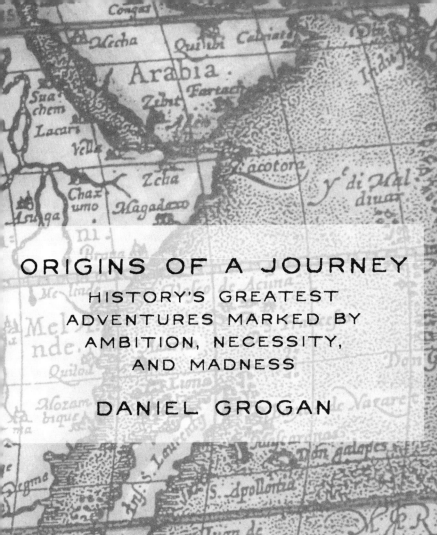

ORIGINS OF A JOURNEY

HISTORY'S GREATEST ADVENTURES MARKED BY AMBITION, NECESSITY, AND MADNESS

DANIEL GROGAN

APPLESEED
· PRESS ·

· BOOK ·
PUBLISHERS

KENNEBUNKPORT, MAINE

For Regan

13-Digit ISBN: 978-1-60464-153-0
10-Digit ISBN: 1-60464-153-3

Appleseed Press Book Publishers
68 North Street
Kennebunkport, Maine 04046

Visit us online!
www.appleseedpressbooks.com

Typography: Garamond, Policy
Gothic, Clarendon, Gotham

Printed in Singapore

1 2 3 4 5 6 7 8 9 0

First Edition

Contents

Introduction

Growing up, a trail ran through my best friend's property: an old railroad track, long abandoned, that had been reclaimed by nature as a forest path. Snaking through trees and underbrush, my friend and I spent countless hours exploring that woodsy passage. For us, it became a tool with which our imaginations could create adventures. Our mundane suburban life required the occasional escape into the forest; in there we had purpose, we were on a journey. And we knew that if we walked far enough, we would reach a waterfall, and our own personal journey would be at an end.

Everyone knows this sort of thrill: the thrill of discovery. It has called to adventurers—some bold, some reluctant—since the dawn of time. In the beginning, it was typically out of necessity; resources would grow scarce and the tribe would move. As society developed, we began to travel for political reasons: to discover new lands, to conquer foreign people, to expand power, to amass riches. In the name of science we have gone to the depths of the sea and to the heart of the jungle. Rivals have raced around the world and tried to climb the highest mountains just to be first, or fastest. We travel to expand our awareness and gain perspective. We do these things because to sit still would be, well, practically inhuman.

As I began writing this book, my idea of what merited inclusion changed drastically. At the beginning, I focused my research on the Age of Exploration. After all, some of history's most famous adventures took place between the 15th and 18th centuries. But as my research approached the modern day, I realized that a journey does not need sinking ships and bloody battles to be worth retelling. Sure, not all adventures have the same impact as others: Ernest Hemingway's African exploits may not be as significant as Neil Armstrong's first steps on the moon. In the same vein, not all journeys are for the good of mankind. Some have tangibly negative effects, others are solely for the traveler's benefit, and some don't even require actual travel! But one fundamental truth emerged from my research: the simplest journey, from crossing a river to taking a road trip, contains the potential for an amazing story. At that moment, no longer restricted to lost lands, hidden treasures, and daring escapes, this book finally began to take shape.

With such a worthy pool of candidates, I had to create a system for selecting the very best. I ended up with an algorithm of sorts, assessing each individual's story based on three criteria: historical significance, unique circumstances, and ability to captivate. Historical significance was the easiest to measure. I simply asked myself, "Did this adventure have an impact on others?" If the answer was yes, in any respect, I knew I was on the right track. Registering the uniqueness of each trip was easy as well: when you're reading hundreds of adventure stories a week, the truly distinct ones tend to stand out. That only left me to figure out which stories were the most captivating. This was typically the hardest to quantify, since the answer largely depended on how I framed the narrative. But generally speaking, if I found myself unable to resist diving into more research, I knew I had a worthwhile journey on my hands. The result was a diverse list of stories from all walks of life—with its fair share of storybook adventure, of course.

If one thing can be gleaned from this collection, it's that one's journey is never really complete. The call to act, to move, to experience something new will always be there. Perhaps that's why we do it: to chase that beautiful freedom only uncertainty can bring.

My friend and I only ever made it as far as the waterfall, but there is always more walking to do.

IN THE AIR

Arabia.
Mecha
Vasco de Acuna
S. Francesco
Adarno
Baixos de Nazaret
Mascarenas
S. Apollonia
Iuan de Lisboa
Pomeri
Los Romeros
Mel inde.
Quiloa
Punta de S. Maria

WILBUR AND ORVILLE WRIGHT

1867-1912; 1871-1948 (RESPECTIVELY)

-

*These American brothers invented, built, and piloted
the world's first operational airplane.*

Today, everyone knows the Wright brothers, but in 1899 the most famous aviation pioneer was Samuel Pierpont Langley, a Smithsonian astronomer who had begun toying with flight earlier in the century. While Langley worked under the public's curious gaze, the Wright brothers toiled away in obscurity.

Since 1893, the duo had worked as successful bicycle manufacturers before moving to North Carolina in 1900. This likely played a significant role in their success; both bikes and airplanes require durable but light components, have similar transmission systems, and utilize a design that accounts for wind resistance. After six years of bicycle work, the Wrights turned their attention from the street to the sky.

Like many before them, the Wright brothers started off with gliders. Where they differed from most, though, was in their philosophy. Some of their contemporaries believed that planes would have to be manned from the ground, but the Wrights understood that any proper plane would need to be controlled by a passenger. And so their first order of business was to master the art of flying.

The brothers would take their glider to the top of Big Kill Devil Hill and jump off time and again. By the end of their trials, they had glided off the hill over a thousand times. Despite a few blunders along the way, the brothers came out of the experiments as masters of powerless flight. With this vast experience under their belts, they began work on their true objective: powered flight.

They knew gasoline could effectively power the plane, they just didn't have the engine for it. Any existing engine would be too heavy for a plane that relied on lightweight materials to stay in the air. So like any great innovators, the Wrights decided to build their own engine. They also designed the propellers for their plane, which had a diameter of 8½ feet and were inspired by ship builder's designs from that time.

At last, on December 14, 1903, the Wright brothers made their first attempt at powered flight. Wilbur won the coin toss and thus the honor of piloting the first trial of the *Flyer*. Unfortunately, he oversteered; the plane climbed steeply into the air only to stall before diving into nearby sand. Wilbur was not injured, but the aircraft needed repairs.

The Wrights took three days to make sure the plane was suitable for another attempt. Having watched his brother, Orville was careful to learn from the mistakes of the first trial. Using a great deal of finesse, he swung his hips in order to control the cradle that had warped the wings. At 10:35 a.m., Orville released the restraining wire and the plane moved down its track, leaving the ground moments later.

The plane flew somewhat wildly as Orville overcompensated with the *Flyer*'s controls, but he still managed to stay in the air for about 120 feet and reach an airspeed of 34 miles per hour.

With their first successful flight under their belts, the brothers spent the rest of the day taking turns in the sky. The day's best run was also its last: Wilbur flew for 59 seconds and covered 852 feet.

The Wrights, fathers of flight, are still celebrated today for their aeronautical innovations. Even more amazing is that many of the ideas they had in the 19th century are still used today—with a few modifications, of course.

AMELIA EARHART

1897-1939

-

This American pilot completed a number of history-making flights before mysteriously disappearing somewhere over the Pacific Ocean.

Amelia Earhart's prolific aviation skills are often overshadowed by the events surrounding her mysterious disappearance. While the story of her final flight is quite intriguing, it is truly a shame that Earhart's considerable achievements get glossed over.

Born to a hardworking mother and an alcoholic but well-meaning father, Earhart exhibited a tough exterior from an early age. She had little interest in the activities associated with womanhood at the time and instead gravitated toward independence and adventure. Her first brush with the sky came in 1920, when she attended an air show in Long Beach,

California. From that moment, Earhart knew she had to learn to fly.

Earhart worked various jobs so she could afford flying lessons, cut her hair short in order to resemble other female aviators, read all the available books on the subject, and even worked hard to establish an appropriately worn look on her new leather jacket. By the summer of 1921, she had saved enough money to purchase an old yellow Kinner Airster biplane. She called it *The Canary*.

On October 22, 1922, she flew *The Canary* to an altitude of 14,000 feet, breaking the world record for female pilots. About seven months later, in May 1923, she became the 16th woman to be issued a pilot's license by the Fédération Aéronautique Internationale. Earhart then took a short break from flying, taking time to study at Columbia University and do social work. She stayed away until 1928, when she received a life-changing phone call.

After Charles Lindbergh's transatlantic flight in 1927, everyone was waiting to see who would become the first female pilot to complete the journey. Captain Hilton Railey reached out to Earhart and asked her to be a part of the mission, along with pilots Wilmer Stultz and Louis Gordon. Shultz did the majority of the flying, and Earhart would later admit that she felt like little more than a passenger. Four years later, Earhart would complete another transatlantic flight, on her own this time, becoming the first female pilot to make the flight and solidifying her status as a renowned pilot and feminist hero.

Still, Earhart wanted to keep making history. She decided that she would be the first person to circumnavigate the globe along the equator. An experienced crew was put together, and on June 1, 1937, they departed from Miami, Florida, in a Lockheed Model 10-E Electra. Things looked good at first, but eventually their luck turned.

After departing Miami, Earhart flew south toward Central America, then east toward Africa, before touching down in New Guinea on June 29, 1937. The crew had covered 22,000 miles of their journey, leaving only the 7,000-mile stretch of the Pacific Ocean. With few options for pit stops along the way, Earhart decided to land the Electra on Howland Island, a small, remote island that was 2,556 miles away from New Guinea. The landing would be difficult, as the island itself was but a sliver of land and thus hard to distinguish from cloud formations. However, using celestial navigation and radio transmission, the crew believed they could make it.

> **"The most difficult thing is the decision to act. The rest is merely tenacity. The fears are paper tigers. You can do anything you decide to do. You can act to change and control your life and the procedure. The process is its own reward."**
> **—Amelia Earhart**

Nobody knows exactly what went wrong that day. It has been said that one of the plane's antennas may have been damaged during takeoff; it is also possible that Earhart was using inaccurate maps. Whatever the case, the last coherent transmission Earhart sent stated, "We must be on you, but we cannot see you. Fuel is running low. Been unable to reach you by radio. We are flying at 1,000 feet." Amelia Earhart, her crew, and the Electra were never seen, or heard from, again.

CHARLES LINDBERGH

1902-1974

-

*This American was the first pilot to successfully
complete a solo transatlantic flight.*

During the 1920s, humanity pushed the boundaries of
possibility; the Wright brothers had barely gotten their plane
off the ground just two decades earlier, and now the prospect
of transatlantic flight was real. In fact, so great was the public's
desire to see someone fly across the Atlantic Ocean that the
wealthy Raymond Orteig offered $25,000 to the first pilot who
could fly from New York to Paris without stopping. Aviator
Charles Lindbergh felt he was up to the task. The real question
was: was his plane?

Lindbergh already had extensive piloting experience when
he decided to attempt to cross the Atlantic. He had worked for
many years as a barnstormer, or stunt pilot, and an airmail pilot,
and had served in the United States Army Air Service for one
year. But when Lindbergh received word of the competition, he
felt he had found his true calling. Though several others had tried
and failed to make the journey, Lindbergh's confidence didn't
waver. Lindbergh chalked up the past failures to insufficiently
sized fuel tanks, so he teamed up with Ryan Airlines out of San
Diego, California and built a plane specifically designed for the
3,600-mile journey. It had a longer wingspan and fuselage than
a typical aircraft, plus additional struts to support the weight

of extra fuel tanks. They placed the extra tanks in the plane's nose, in the wings, and between the engine and cockpit—an inconvenient spot, as it obstructed Lindbergh's view for the duration of the trip. The special airplane was dubbed *The Spirit of St. Louis*.

Just 25 years old, Lindbergh took off from Long Island's Roosevelt Field on May 20, 1927. Immediately, the extra fuel tank in the cockpit started giving him trouble. In order to deal with the obstructed view, Lindbergh utilized various instruments to get a complete sense of his surroundings. He would lean out of his left-side window and use a retractable periscope to observe everything he couldn't see from the cabin. Surprisingly, this was not his only reason for keeping the window open: Lindbergh later explained that he relied on the cold air, wind, and rain to keep him awake for the entire 33½-hour flight. The strategy worked, but it did not stop him from experiencing hallucinations caused by sleep deprivation.

Finally, after 3,600 miles and nearly 34 hours in the air, he landed at Le Bourget Field near Paris without incident. A crowd of over 100,000 people waited for Lindbergh in Paris, along with the $25,000 prize, which amounts to about $335,000 today. When he returned to New York, a ticker-tape parade attended by an estimated three to four million people was held in his honor. Needless to say, Lindbergh was officially a legend. Unfortunately, his time in the public eye was just beginning, as his family became embroiled in what famed journalist H. L. Mencken would describe as "the biggest story since the Resurrection."

Lindbergh, now a wealthy and famous man, married the already prominent Anne Morrow. Together they sought out a quiet life away from the spotlight on a large estate in Hopewell, New Jersey. But in 1932, their first child, Charles Augustus Jr., was kidnapped at just 20 months old. The perpetrator anonymously demanded that a ransom of $50,000 be paid, and the Lindberghs readily complied. Tragically, their son's body was found in the woods near their house weeks later. The family became the subject of constant media attention as the nation waited with bated breath for more information to surface.

The money was eventually traced back to a man named Bruno Hauptmann, who was arrested and later executed. Throughout the trial, the media frenzy continued to escalate. In an effort to regain a semblance of privacy, the Lindberghs moved to Europe, where Charles continued his aviation work. He went on to assist Henry Ford in the World War II efforts, as well as to act as a test pilot and adviser for United Aircraft, cementing himself as one of America's most famous aviators ever.

NEIL ARMSTRONG

1930-2012

-

*He was the commander of the first successful trip to the moon
who never lost his cool—even during the rarely discussed
panic just moments before the lunar landing.*

On July 16, 1969, an estimated 530 million people watched on television as the Apollo 11 spacecraft launched from Cape Kennedy with Neil Armstrong in command. As the entire world knew, the objective of the mission was monumental: to successfully perform a manned lunar landing.

Within four days of blastoff, Apollo 11 had entered lunar orbit, and on July 20, Armstrong and copilot Buzz Aldrin exited the command module *Columbia* and entered the lunar module *Eagle*, at which point they separated from *Columbia* and began to pilot the *Eagle* toward the lunar surface.

Even as Armstrong and Aldrin approached the moon on July 20, 1969, tensions were high. It was still very unclear whether or not America would win the Space Race. As the *Eagle* prepared for landing, "Error Code 1202" appeared on the monitor in front of Armstrong and Aldrin. The unexpected message meant that the *Eagle* was being overworked. As they were already descending quite rapidly toward the moon's surface, options were limited. Hesitantly, mission control gave Armstrong the go-ahead to make a powered descent. Armstrong and Aldrin complied, but as they made their approach they quickly realized their troubles were far from over.

During the descent, the *Eagle* had flown outside of the intended landing zone. Fuel was low, communication with mission control was spotty, and the surface over which the lunar module hovered was nothing but craters and boulders. Adjusting rapidly, Armstrong began flying just above the landscape in search of an area smooth enough for landing.

Just as Armstrong located a suitable landing spot, the *Eagle* alerted its pilots that it had just 60 seconds of fuel remaining, and it was unclear if they would have enough to land. Mission control considered aborting the mission despite being so close to success, but that might have been just as risky as letting it play out. With 30 seconds of fuel left, the *Eagle* hovered about 10 feet above the surface of the moon. There was absolutely no turning back. After a tense moment of silence, Armstrong reached out to NASA. "Houston, Tranquility Base here. The *Eagle* has landed."

It is safe to assume that mission control, NASA, and the many people following along let out a collective sigh of relief. By the time the men were ready to step onto the moon, there were hundreds of millions watching the broadcast on television, and even more listening on the radio. Neil Armstrong exited the lunar module and uttered the now-iconic: "That's one small step for man, one giant leap for mankind."

YURI GAGARIN

1934-1968

-

Though the Americans get most of the credit,
this Soviet man was the first person to enter space.

In 1969, Neil Armstrong was the first man to step on the moon. But Armstrong and the rest of the Apollo 11 crew were not the first men to enter space. That honor belongs to Yuri Gagarin, a cosmonaut whose voyage secured a great Space Race victory for the Soviet Union in 1961.

Born to a long line of peasants in the Smolensk region of the Soviet Union, Gagarin always dreamed of being a pilot. He excelled in school, and as soon as he was old enough he enrolled in the Saratov Industrial Technicum to study smelting. After graduating in 1955, his destiny began to take shape. He was accepted to the Orenburg Aviation School and studied there for two years, after which he became a fighter pilot with the Soviet Armed Forces. When Gagarin learned of the Soviet cosmonaut program, he put in a request for consideration and was quickly accepted. Once he completed the necessary training, he was selected for the Vostok 1 mission: to become the first human to enter space and complete an orbit of Earth.

The flight was relatively uneventful. Totally alone, Gagarin was launched into space aboard the Vostok 1. The vessel completed one full rotation of Earth, a journey that took only one hour and 29 minutes. As smooth as the flight was, the landing nearly ended in disaster. As the spacecraft descended toward Earth's surface, the cables connecting the descent and service modules did not disconnect as they were supposed to. The vessel began shaking uncontrollably, but, acting quickly, Gagarin ejected from the spacecraft and parachuted safely to the ground.

Gagarin's name is rarely mentioned alongside the likes of Armstrong and Aldrin, but his journey's long-term impact is immeasurable. Human beings were determined to reach outer space, and Gagarin's mission proved that it could be done. And without the Soviets striking the Space Race's first blow, there's no telling whether the U.S. would have gotten a man on the moon so quickly, if at all.

Sadly, Gagarin died in a tragic plane crash during a 1968 training mission. His untimely demise has likely contributed to his relative lack of fame, but space lovers the world over know his name and know that Gagarin was the first man to ever leave—and return to—Earth.

VALENTINA TERESHKOVA

1937-PRESENT

-

This Soviet was the first woman in space.

Tensions were high between the United States and the Soviet Union for the majority of the 20th century, to put it mildly.

And while it may not have been at the center of the feud, the Space Race was certainly one of its most visible components. Though the U.S. won in 1969 by first putting men on the moon, the Soviet Union was still able to reach some major milestones in the field of space exploration. Among them was the achievement of Valentina Tereshkova, who became the first woman in space.

Before turning 16, Tereshkova decided to leave school and work at a textile mill to support her family and widowed mother. However, still recognizing the importance of education, she continued taking courses on the side. In addition to work and schooling, Tereshkova expressed great interest in parachuting and began taking classes on how to complete successful jumps.

Following the Soviet Union's success in sending Yuri Gagarin to space in 1961, Tereshkova was inspired to apply for the space program. Though she had no experience flying whatsoever, her 126 successful parachute jumps were enough to convince the program to accept her as a cosmonaut-in-training. After 18 months of training, the decision was made to send her into space.

In 1963, Tereshkova launched into space aboard the Vostok 6. "Hey, sky, take off your hat. I'm on my way!" she shouted as the spacecraft took flight. Once the rocket left Earth's atmosphere, it completed 48 orbits of the planet. Tereshkova was in space for about 71 hours, which was more time than all prior American astronauts combined.

Due to the classification of the story by the Soviet government, for 40 years the public never knew that Tereshkova's historic mission almost ended in tragedy. While she was orbiting, Tereshkova noticed that her ship was slowly drifting away from Earth due to an error in the navigation software. Had she not noticed it, and had the Soviet ground team not rapidly developed the algorithm to correct it, the spacecraft would have left Earth's orbit, meaning certain death for Tereshkova.

Fortunately, this did not occur, and she returned to Earth in one piece. Upon arriving back on terra firma, Tereshkova was dubbed a hero of the Soviet Union. It would be 19 years before another woman went into space.

JIM LOVELL

1928-PRESENT

-

His calm and experience helped NASA
avert disaster on the Apollo 13 mission.

Commander Jim Lovell, the most experienced astronaut in the world at the time with 572 spaceflight hours under his belt, might have been confident at the start of the Apollo 13 mission on April 11, 1970. But two days and 200,000 miles later, he and his crewmembers were staring their demise in the face.

The spacecraft was made up of two separate vessels: the *Odyssey*, which was an orbiter, and the *Aquarius*, which was a lander. These two separate crafts were connected by a tunnel. The plan was for the men to occupy the *Odyssey* until they got close to the moon's surface, at which point they would use the *Aquarius* to land. Unfortunately, things did not work out that way.

It started when a low-pressure alert went off on one of the *Odyssey*'s hydrogen tanks. This was not a certain sign of trouble, just an indication that procedural maintenance was required. However, when Command Module Pilot Jack Swigert attempted to fix the problem, the alarms went off. Oxygen levels were falling and power was failing. The *Odyssey* had been irreversibly damaged. Swigert quickly contacted mission control and uttered the now-famous words "Houston, we've had a problem here."

With no other options, Lovell and the crew aborted the mission. The *Odyssey* was unable to make the return trip home, so they went over to the *Aquarius*. Once aboard, the crew had to drain a substantial amount of power in order to turn the lander toward Earth. Once this was complete, it was essential to conserve as much power as possible, so they powered down every piece of equipment that was deemed a luxury. The conditions became far from comfortable; temperatures in the cabin dropped close to freezing, and water had to be conserved in order to cool down the *Aquarius*'s hardware. Once they were close enough to Earth, the three men returned to the *Odyssey* and hoped that it had enough life in it to make the landing.

On April 17, Jim Lovell, Jack Swigert, and Fred Haise landed safely in the Pacific Ocean. Each man had lost a considerable amount of weight and Haise had a kidney infection, but they were safe. NASA learned valuable lessons as a result of the mission, and the story has since been dramatized numerous times.

JULIANE KOEPCKE

1954-PRESENT

-

Approximately 40 minutes into a trip, a plane carrying Juliane Koepcke and her mother suddenly began to plummet.

From the day she was born, it seemed that Juliane Koepcke was destined to have an interesting life. Her parents were both famous zoologists who established Panguana, an ecological research station in the Peruvian rain forest., and they would often take her with them on expeditions. She did end up being the subject of an astounding story, but, unfortunately, it is steeped in tragedy.

On December 24, 1971, a day after Koepcke's high school graduation, she and her mother boarded an airplane in Lima, Peru, to fly back to Panguana for Christmas. The flight was only supposed to be an hour long, and the first half of it passed smoothly. But approximately 40 minutes into the trip, the plane flew directly into a thunderstorm. As lightning flashed all around them, the plane began to plummet. The next thing Koepcke knew, she was free-falling while still strapped in her seat.

Miraculously, she survived free-falling nearly two miles out of the sky, landing safely on the plush jungle floor below. As soon as Koepcke regained her senses, she began searching for her mother and the other passengers. She was unable to see clearly without her glasses, so she tested the ground in front of her with a shoe. When it became clear that her mother was nowhere to be found, Koepcke began to focus on her own survival. All of her previous jungle experience came back to her in an instant.

One of the first things the young woman did was pick up a bag of candy she found near her crash site. These sweets would end up being the only sustenance she had during her 10 days in the wild. Creek water kept her hydrated, and she was able to keep maggots out of her wounds by using gasoline that she syphoned from a motor found near a large boat, a trick she had learned from her father. Still, despite Koepcke's expertise, the nights were frightening, and the loneliness was getting to her.

At last, on her 10th day in the jungle, a group of men found her by the boat she had discovered. At first they were amazed by her presence and thought her to be some sort of mystical being. But after some conversation, the situation became clear and she was rescued. Koepcke managed to be the sole survivor of LANSA Flight 508: 91 people died in the crash, including her mother.

BESSIE COLEMAN

1892-1926

-

Despite severe institutional prejudice against African Americans, Bessie Coleman never gave up her desire to become a licensed pilot.

Career opportunities were few and far between for African American women in the early 1900s. The nation was still racially divided, both socially and legally. For these reasons, it may have seemed absurd when Bessie Coleman made known her desire to become a licensed pilot.

At the time, aviation was all the rage in America, and Coleman became interested in the subject while working various jobs in Chicago. But no aviation schools would accept a black woman. Learning of her interest, the African American millionaire Robert Abbott took it upon himself to sponsor Coleman. With Abbott's advice—and his money—Coleman decided to go to France, where she would be permitted to earn a pilot's license.

She began studying French in 1918, and by 1920 she was fluent enough to make the journey. Coleman was the only African American student in the flying school, and she proved herself as capable as anyone. Despite witnessing the death of a fellow student, and occasionally being saddled with a faulty plane, she was undeterred from pursuing her dream. After just seven months, Coleman became the first black woman to receive her pilot's license.

Coleman returned to America, where she was lauded for her courage by people of all colors. From that point on, she was a celebrity, participating in air shows, doing interviews with local papers, and using her platform to advocate for equality. So committed was Coleman to advancing civil rights that she would not perform anywhere that didn't admit black people, regardless of what she stood to gain.

Unfortunately, Coleman's life ended in tragedy in 1926. During a routine preparation flight in advance of an air show, a wrench managed to lodge itself into Coleman's control gears. The vessel nose-dived instantly, causing the unfastened Coleman to fall to her death. Over 10,000 people showed up to her funeral, lining the streets in tribute to the cultural icon.

NETA SNOOK

1886-1991

-

Behind every famous innovator is someone who put them on the map. In Amelia Earhart's case, that person was Neta Snook.

There are only a handful of names the average person associates with aviation: the Wright brothers, Charles Lindbergh, Amelia Earhart, and Chuck Yeager. And while those individuals have earned their fame, they are by no means the only stars in the sky. Neta Snook, who helped put Earhart on the map, is another.

Snook never made any daring, record-breaking flights. She

never landed a plane before a mob of cheering fans. No parades were ever thrown in her honor. She ran a modest business, offering simple aerial tours of Ames, Iowa. But that modest business eventually led Earhart to her and changed the course of aviation forever.

In 1918, after having trained as an aviator for three years, Snook finally received her pilot's license. However, she was restricted to solo flights, a stipulation by which she refused to abide: "I ignored it, as did my pilot friends, and erased the first 'n' in 'none' and carried passengers until I sold my plane."

For less than a year, Snook offered passengers 15 minutes in the air for $15. Her business provided her valuable savings and experience, but by the fall of 1920, Snook had arrived at two important realizations: Iowa winters would impede her ability to fly, and, more than anything, she wanted to become an officially licensed pilot with no restrictions. And so she contacted the Fédération Aéronautique Internationale, who appointed three men to observe Snook's capabilities. After a short test, she was awarded the license she desired.

Shortly thereafter, Snook packed up and moved to California, where she became the first woman to run a commercial airfield. Just a few months later, in 1921, a young Earhart walked onto the airfield, strode right up to Snook, and said, "I want to fly. Will you teach me?" From that moment, Earhart was her star pupil.

It is bittersweet that Snook is primarily remembered for her association with Earhart, who is arguably the most famous pilot in history. Snook was a brilliant flier in her own right. She was headstrong and brave in a time when women were discouraged from acting independently. But it is also a testament to her abilities that her finest student was able to achieve such notoriety. Without Snook, there would likely be no Earhart. From offering 15-minute trips across Iowa to running her own airfield, Snook's personal journey is inspirational from any perspective.

ON WHEELS (CARS, BIKES, AND TRAINS)

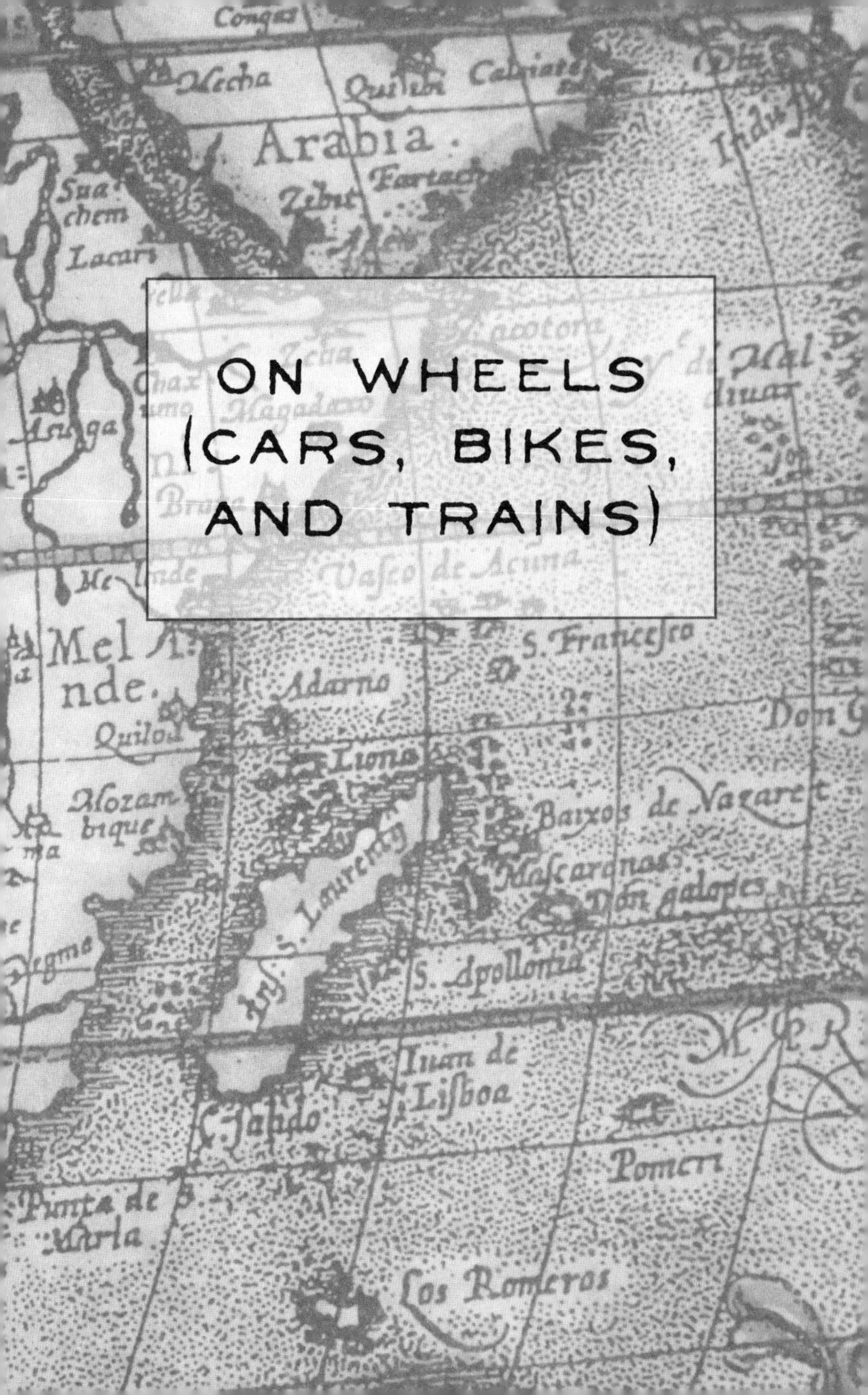

KEN KESEY &
THE MERRY PRANKSTERS

1935-2001

-

These counterculture pioneers set out to
enlighten America, one "trip" at a time.

On June 17, 1964, Ken Kesey and 13 of the Merry Pranksters boarded their bus in California and set off for New York. Named *Further*, the bus would be their mobile home for the next 12 days. Dubbed "the Pied Piper of the psychedelic era" by the *New York Times*, Ken Kesey was already a prominent writer and countercultural figure before he began his famous journey east. His first novel, *One Flew Over the Cuckoo's Nest*, was influenced by his time working the graveyard shift at a mental health facility, where Kesey often worked under the influence of psychoactive drugs. He obtained those drugs through his involvement in Project MKUltra, a CIA program designed to test the effects of drugs like LSD and mescaline on the human mind.

After *Cuckoo*'s release, Kesey divided his time between homes in Oregon and California. Both locations served as communes for Kesey and his friends—a group that would come to be known as "The Band of Merry Pranksters"—to share ideas and experiment with psychedelics. When the writer learned that he would need to be in New York City for the release of his second novel, *Sometimes a Great Notion*, he recruited 13 of the

Pranksters and organized the now-famous road trip.

The goal was simple: get to New York, and expand Middle America's minds along the way. Throughout the journey, passengers on the psychedelic bus took copious amounts of LSD, marijuana, and amphetamines. Occasionally, they would make stops and organize small parties or simply engage with the locals. *Further* was decked out with a roof platform, from which the Pranksters would blurt out notes on their flutes, trumpets, and horns. It also had a public address system: Kesey's megaphone for the flyover states. Drugged-up stream of consciousness poured from the PA, walking the line between utter nonsense and provocative insight. The Pranksters made sure to film all of these escapades, but the resulting footage was predictably incomprehensible.

Further's main driver was a man named Neal Cassady, who was the inspiration for the protagonist of Jack Kerouac's 1957 novel *On the Road*. In a particularly shocking bit of footage from the trip, Cassady can be seen driving the bus while high on speed, shouting into the PA system, and flailing his arms, only looking up to check the road every so often—not that this was a cause for concern for any of the passengers. Novelist Robert Stone once described Cassady as "the world's greatest driver, who could roll a joint while backing a 1937 Packard onto the lip of the Grand Canyon."

By the time they arrived in New York, the group's perspective on the country had changed significantly. Kesey told *Publishers Weekly* afterward, "The sense of communication in this country has damn near atrophied. But we found as we went along it got easier to make contact with people. If people could just understand it is possible to be different without being a threat."

ANNIE LONDONDERRY

1870-1947

-

She was a married mother who accepted the challenge of cycling around the world in 15 months without a single dollar to her name.

In 1894, two men had a disagreement. Though their identities were never confirmed, it is believed they were Bostonians named Dr. Albert Reeder and Colonel Albert Pope. Regardless of who they actually were, it is certain that they were wealthy. One of the men believed that no woman could travel around the world on a bicycle in 15 months, while the other had faith that it could be done. And so a wager was placed: $10,000 at two-to-one odds. As if the task were not difficult enough, one more caveat was added: the woman chosen to settle this bet would have to start the journey without a dollar to her name. She would have to earn money along the way.

At the time, bicycles were hugely popular in the United States and abroad. They became a primary mode of local transport, but their popularity did not just stem from the convenience they offered. For women, bicycles were a vehicle for social and political change. These new vehicles allowed them freedom of movement, something that had never been so readily accessible before. They also encouraged women to abandon the oppressive garb society had expected them to wear in favor of more aerodynamic clothing. On a bike, a woman was liberated.

Annie Cohen Kopchovsky was an unlikely choice for this challenge. After all, she was a married mother of three and she had never ridden a bicycle in her life. To this day, it is unclear exactly what led the two men to choose Annie as the subject of their bet. Annie's motivation was more straightforward: it likely had to do with the substantial cash prize of $10,000 if she succeeded, plus the attention she'd bring to the suffrage movement.

After a handful of cycling lessons, Annie was ready to begin her journey. On June 25, 1894, in front of a crowd of suffragists, supporters, and curious pedestrians that had gathered in Boston, Annie began her adventure not with a little push, but with a lucrative business plan. In exchange for $100, Annie placed a "New Hampshire's Londonderry Lithia Spring Water Company" placard on her bicycle. On top of that, she agreed to go by Annie Londonderry for the duration of the journey.

With a pearl-handled revolver and little else, Annie traveled west, making it as far as Chicago before turning back to New York City in order to sail to France. For most of her trip, she garnered advertisements of all kinds in order to earn the income necessitated by the wager's guidelines. The significant amount of attention her story received made it impossible for Annie to go through a city unrecognized, and by the time she arrived in Marseilles she was mobbed by exuberant well-wishers.

With just eight months left to make it back to Chicago, Annie pedalled through France and boarded a ship to Egypt. From there she made short stops in Jerusalem and modern-day Yemen before sailing to Sri Lanka and Singapore. Her time in Asia is not well documented, but she is believed to have pedalled near Port Arthur during the first Sino-Japanese War. According to Annie, she sustained a minor gunshot wound in China, and then rode to Siberia before boarding a ship to San Francisco.

It was on the last leg of her journey that Annie faced the most obstacles. Soon after leaving San Francisco, a horse and buggy knocked into her, flinging her off her bicycle. The injuries were not too severe, and she exaggerated their significance while recounting the events later on, but they certainly made the trip more difficult. Perhaps the worst hardship came when Annie's bicycle blew a tire outside of Yuma, Arizona. She was forced to carry her bike through the intense desert climate. Passing train crews gave her milk so that she would not dehydrate. Although Annie claims she did not accept a ride on any of the trains, some say that she did in fact use the rails for part of her journey. Either way, Annie reached Chicago on September 12, 1895, thereby completing the challenge and winning a victory for women everywhere.

ANNEMARIE SCHWARZENBACH

1908-1942

-

*This hard-living photographer yearned
to capture some of humanity's darker aspects.*

Perhaps it was Annemarie Schwarzenbach's own dark background that fueled her desire to photograph and write about subjects of despair. Her first experience with drugs—specifically morphine—came in Berlin, just after writing her first book in 1931. Following her introduction to morphine, Schwarzenbach's lifestyle changed quite a bit. She often drank too much, drove cars too fast, and slept too little. It was this type of behavior, as well as her condemnation of Nazi practices—practices with which her mother sympathized—that led Schwarzenbach to constantly feud with her family.

Over time, Schwarzenbach developed an interest in travel; in 1936, she visited the United States with photographer Barbara Hamilton-Wright. The country was in the grip of the Great Depression, and the scenes the duo photographed all featured misery. From New York to the Deep South, Schwarzenbach captured images that challenged the idea of the American Dream. Filthy children standing in deserted streets, a clothesline hung with prisoner garb outside a jailhouse—her photos stood in stark contrast to the concept of America many Europeans still held on to. Schwarzenbach returned to Europe and shared her collection, as well as some of the writing she had done on the trip.

In 1937, Schwarzenbach returned to the United States, this time to document the Deep South. The racism, violence, and social problems in the region exceeded any sort of anguish she had ever witnessed. She returned to Europe and, severely affected by what she had seen, became unable to resist the temptation of drugs. For a number of years, Schwarzenbach was in and out of rehabilitation programs. She returned to the United States in 1940, but a suicide attempt led to her admittance to a psychiatric clinic, where she remained for a few months. In the end, tragedy defined her death just as it had her life. After returning to her home country of Switzerland in 1942, Schwarzenbach died in a bicycle accident that same year.

PAUL THEROUX

1941-PRESENT

-

Having already written several stories featuring characters of his own creation, Theroux decided to make himself the protagonist of his own adventure story.

Paul Theroux, already an accomplished novelist, found himself fresh out of ideas in 1973. Frustrated by his writer's block, Theroux decided to take a trip to search for inspiration. His plan was to board a train and simply go for a ride, a tactic he had always turned to when creatively parched. What Theroux didn't know is that this attempt to get his gears turning would result in a creative breakthrough for himself that would revolutionize the genre of travel literature.

At the same time as Theroux began aching for inspiration, he purchased a copy of the 1973 edition of *Overseas Timetable: Railway, Road and Shipping Services Outside Europe*. It was a complete guide to the railways outside the European continent, from departure times to points of connection. This book offered Theroux complete knowledge of what was previously an incomprehensible system. He began to think: what if he turned his simple train ride into a journey and wrote a nonfiction book based on his travels? With that, Theroux's writer's block lifted; he knew what his next project would be.

His trip would take him from London to France, and then on to the *Orient Express*, which traveled through Iran, Afghanistan, India, Burma, Vietnam, China, Japan, and the Soviet Union. Unlike most travel writers, Theroux honed his craft in fiction, and he made heavy use of his narrative sensibilities. While many travelogues would feature endless details of cities and sights, Theroux focused on character moments, specifically his own. He described conversations he had with fellow passengers, ephemeral scenes viewed from his window, and the way both of these made him feel. With his book, *The Great Railway Bazaar*, Theroux shaped fact into a satisfying narrative reminiscent of a fictional story; a style which travel writers would emulate for years to come.

THOMAS STEVENS

1854-1935

-

In 1884, Thomas Stevens decided to up the ante
by bicycling around the world.

Also known as the "high wheeler," the penny-farthing was one of the first bicycle models to hit the mass market in the late 1800s. It was nothing like the conventional trail bikes of today; a massive front wheel made mounting the vehicle quite difficult, and even the most skilled riders had trouble braking at high speeds. Aboard a penny-farthing, even a simple ride around town became a strenuous undertaking. Nonetheless, in 1884 Thomas Stevens decided to ride one around the world.

Without a lot of forethought, Stevens departed his San Francisco home on the morning of April 22, 1884, and just kept riding east. He was in no great rush, stopping in any town that piqued his interest or offered comfort. At various points, Stevens was forced to ride his bike on train tracks suspended high above the ground, and it is said that he even had to dodge oncoming trains on a few occasions, which he did by dangling off the side of the track with the heavy bike in his hand. Thankfully, Stevens always managed to hoist himself back up, and he arrived in Boston on August 4, becoming the first person to complete a transcontinental cycling trip. But he was far from done.

He spent the winter in New York and began making plans to travel across Europe. He gained sponsorship from a travel magazine called *Outing*, and after arriving in Great Britain he began his trip on May 4, 1885. Stevens's journey took him through France, Germany, Austria, Hungary, modern-day Croatia, Serbia, Bulgaria, and modern-day Turkey, thus completing his journey across Europe. He ended in Constantinople—now known as Istanbul—where he spent some time recuperating before beginning the Asian leg of his trip.

Still somehow riding a penny-farthing, Stevens passed through Anatolia, Armenia, and Iraq before stopping in Tehran, Iran, where he spent the winter in the shah's palace. But before he could continue his trip, Stevens realized he had a problem: he would not be allowed passage through Afghanistan. So he rerouted, heading south in order to continue his trip through India. It was inconvenient, of course, but no more so than the rest of the sojourn had been. For Stevens, convenience was hardly the point.

After arriving in Calcutta, Stevens boarded a steamboat to China. He biked the length of the country, hopped on another boat, and then continued his journey through Japan. It was December 17, 1886, by the time Stevens reached Yokohama, completing his circumnavigation of Earth. He'd become the first person to ever do so on a bicycle—and on a high wheeler, to boot. With one last boat ride, he arrived home in San Francisco and continued his life of adventure.

In making this trip, Stevens effectively popularized a new type of travel: recreational exploration. He did not ride to discover lands or find lost treasure, to become famous or rich; he just wanted to see new places and meet new people. And while road trips are still incredibly popular today—even on bikes—it's safe to say few people have the patience, or the stamina, to match Stevens's incredible feat.

ON FOOT (HUMAN OR HORSE)

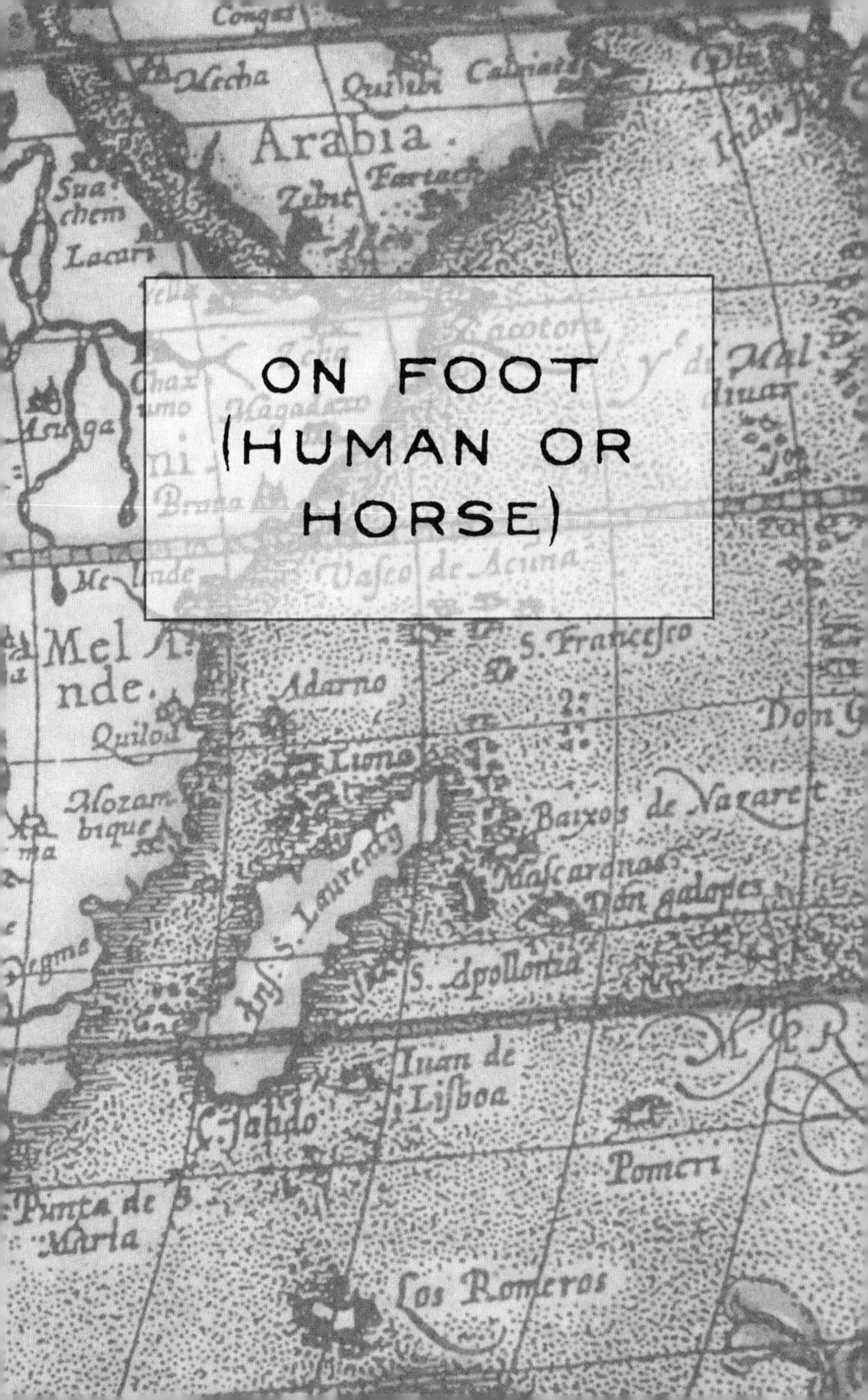

SIR EDMUND HILLARY

1919-2008

-

A New Zealand mountaineer and explorer, he was the
first person to reach the summit of Mount Everest, in 1953.

Mount Everest has always loomed large in the minds of devoted mountaineers. When conquering mountains is your passion, the allure of Earth's highest peak is undeniable. Today, reaching the top of the 29,000-foot summit is still one of the ultimate achievements in the climbing community, but prior to 1953 it was considered impossible.

After serving in the Royal New Zealand Air Force during World War II, Edmund Hillary had little else on his mind but climbing Everest. Many had tried, but their efforts either ended in failure or death. Hillary was a somewhat experienced climber; at the age of 20 he ascended Mount Ollivier in his home country of New Zealand—about one-fifth the height of Mount Everest. He made his second significant climb in 1948, reaching the peak of New Zealand's tallest mountain, Mount Cook.

With a few successes under his belt, Hillary set his sights on the mountain that had been previously deemed unconquerable. His credentials allowed him to join up with the ninth British expedition to attempt Everest, led by army officer John Hunt. After establishing a series of camps along their charted route, Hunt planned to send men up the mountain in pairs. The first duo to set out was Tom Bourdillon and Dr. Charles Evans. They gave up just 315 feet from the summit due to exhaustion and an ominous ice storm, which made the final stretch all the more perilous. The next pair to make the climb was Edmund Hillary and Nepalese Sherpa Tenzing Norgay.

Storms clouded the first leg of their ascent. At 27,900 feet, the two men made camp on a rock ledge that was six feet wide and rested at a 30-degree angle. They weighed down their tent in order to withstand the powerful gusts of wind, but sleeping conditions were poor; the temperature reached 30 below zero. Despite their discomfort, Hillary and Norgay managed to get some much-needed rest. When they rose the next morning, clear skies filled them with optimism.

Despite the fair conditions, the men faced their most daunting obstacle just before reaching the summit: a 40-foot wall made of solid rock and ice. At first, it seemed unmanageable, but Hillary and Norgay managed to find a crack that ran up the entire

> "It is not the mountain we conquer, but ourselves."
> **—Sir Edmund Hillary**

face of the wall and was just wide enough for the men to squeeze into. Using their feet and backs to brace themselves against the sides of the crevice, they shimmied up the 90-degree incline. This particular part of Everest has been known as the Hillary Step ever since, though in 2017 climbers confirmed that it had been partially destroyed.

Upon successfully navigating the Hillary Step, the duo realized they were just a short distance away from the very top of the mountain. Quietly, but excitedly, the pair completed the final leg with no issue.

Their ascent finished, Hillary and Norgay took in a view never before seen by any other humans: the sprawling, jagged peaks of the Himalayas, and clouds stretching below them like a sea of cotton. The men shook hands, but the act proved to be too reserved for the occasion, and so they embraced each other and patted one another on the back. Each man posed for photos with the flag of his country, they left a crucifix for expedition leader John Hunt, and Norgay buried chocolate and biscuits as an offering to the powerful but generous gods of Everest. Just before beginning their descent, the elated men shared a mint cake and took in the heavenly view one last time.

YURI TRUSH

1950-PRESENT

-

A Russian animal activist, he faced a difficult decision:
allow a man-eating Siberian tiger to roam free,
or track it across the hinterlands.

Life in Russia's eastern hinterlands was often quite uneventful for Yuri Trush, the head of an anti-poaching unit called Inspection Tiger. His was one of six teams that the Primorye government had designated to protect the country's diminishing tiger population from poachers. Trush had a simple purpose: maintain a peaceful coexistence between man and nature. On one December evening in 1997, that all changed with a phone call.

Vladimir Markov, a poacher and beekeeper, had committed his profession's cardinal sin: he'd wounded a tiger without killing it. Thinking he had succeeded in killing the tiger, Markov left the scene. But the big cat recovered quickly—and unfortunately for Markov, it wanted vengeance.

In a display of cunning that is as impressive as it is horrifying, the tiger stalked Markov for the next 12 to 48 hours, located his cabin, destroyed anything carrying Markov's scent, and waited patiently for the man to return home. Once Markov arrived, the tiger killed him, dragged his body into the forest, and ate him. "This wasn't an impulsive response," said John Vaillant, who documented the case in his 2010 book *The Tiger: A True Story of Vengeance and Survival.* "The tiger was able to hold this idea over a period of time."

Upon learning of the attack, Yuri Trush set out to investigate with his hunting dog Gitta and two members of his team, Alexander Gorborukov and Sasha Lazurenko. On the way to the scene, they picked up a deputy sheriff named Bush. After a fair bit of off-roading, they arrived at the isolated cabin, where they were greeted by three of Markov's friends: Danila Zaitsev, Sasha Dvornik, and Andrei Onofreychuk.

The seven men followed the tracks of what appeared to be a large animal dragging something into the woods, each step bringing a more horrific scene into focus. The white snow grew pink before they came across the bloodstained cuff of Markov's jacket next to a single glove. Finally, arranged on a snowless patch of earth, they came across the final tableau: a head with its face torn off completely.

Gitta ran ahead to investigate. Her behavior had become more and more erratic, indicating to the men that the tiger was still close by. Trush needed to make a judgment call: wait for permission from Moscow to hunt and kill an endangered species, or act on the one chance he'd have. He decided to track the tiger, despite the fact that few of the men were trained for such a situation and suitable weapons were scarce.

In the end, Yuri Trush bested the tiger. He cornered the animal, and as it leapt through the air Trush raised his rifle. The tip of the gun went through the open mouth of the beast and pierced the back of its throat, killing it just in time.

SIR ERNEST HENRY SHACKLETON

1874-1922

-

After a disastrous attempt at making history, this Irish explorer was forced to keep his crew alive in Antarctica's brutal conditions.

On December 5, 1914, Ernest Shackleton and his crew departed for Antarctica aboard the ship *Endurance*. Shackleton's goal was to make history as the first man to cross the continent on foot. This mission, known as the Imperial Trans-Antarctic Expedition, or the *Endurance* Expedition, was conceived by Shackleton after his initial dream of being the first person to set foot on Earth's southernmost point was accomplished by

Norwegian explorer Roald Amundsen.

For the first several weeks of the journey, the *Endurance* made slow progress, but progress nonetheless. They sailed southward, stymied occasionally by clusters of ice but always breaking free to continue on their way. Then, on February 21, 1915, when the *Endurance* reached a latitude of 76°58'S, the ice would not allow Shackleton to venture any farther, and the *Endurance* was caught up in a northbound pack of ice that would prove to be the expedition's undoing.

The ship continued to drift northward as the dark months of May, June, and July rolled along. Shackleton, committed to maintaining morale aboard the ship, encouraged the men to celebrate holidays and put on theatrical performances for one another. They were reminded to appreciate the beauty of their surroundings, despite the fact that nature seemed to be working against them. These exercises in optimism were fairly effective until October 27, when the *Endurance* was squeezed so severely by the ice that Shackleton gave the order to abandon ship.

Immediately, Shackleton abandoned his plan to cross the Antarctic on foot. Survival was his only concern now. He believed the smartest course of action was to march westward to Snow Hill Island, a walk one of the crewmembers estimated to be 312 miles. Despite this daunting distance, they set out on October 30, taking with them two lifeboats and whatever supplies they could carry. Just two miles and three days later, they accepted that they'd have to abandon the mission.

Shackleton decided they would wait for the ice to break up and continue their journey via lifeboat. When conditions failed to improve, the crew attempted a second march on December 23. This attempt brought them about seven miles in seven days. Once again, Shackleton ordered the crew to stop. It was here that they set up what they called "Patience Camp," which would be their home for the next three months.

Rations became scarce, and the crew had to incorporate seal meat into their diet. Eventually, the situation became so dire that they had to kill their dog teams for food. By April 8, 1916, the ground upon which the camp stood began to crack and drift, leaving the men stranded on a small triangle of ice. Refusing to give up, the crew took to the water once more. Using the two boats that the team had brought with them, and a third that had been salvaged from the *Endurance*'s wreckage, the crew set sail for Elephant Island, approximately 100 miles north of their location.

Against all odds, the boats reached Elephant Island on April 14. Still, more drastic actions were required in order to ensure survival. After all, Elephant Island was a remote piece of land that provided little relief and fewer resources. So Shackleton devised a bold plan: they would rig one of the lifeboats to sail to the island of South Georgia, 800 miles north. The men built makeshift tools and materials and, on April 24, 1916, Shackleton and five of his men sailed for South Georgia. The remainder of his crew stayed on Elephant Island and hoped for their captain's speedy return.

After 16 perilous days on the Southern Ocean, Shackleton and his small team reached South Georgia. From there, they traveled to Stromness, a whaling station on the island's northern coast. Shackleton began devising a plan to rescue the crewmembers still stranded on Elephant Island. It wasn't going to be easy; in fact, it took four attempts and more than three months before he was even able to secure a proper vessel for rescue. Using a small steamboat borrowed from the Chilean government, Shackleton returned to Elephant Island on August 30, 1916. All of the men were still alive.

Although Ernest Shackleton was unable to make history by crossing the Antarctic on foot, he is still recognized as a principle figure of the Heroic Age of Antarctic Exploration, and his ability to keep his entire 28-man team alive over a period of almost two years is still considered an astonishing achievement to this day.

JOE SIMPSON

1960-PRESENT

-

This English mountaineer faced certain death after his history-making climb in the Peruvian Andes.

Joe Simpson and climbing partner Simon Yates were in a less-than-ideal situation. The previous afternoon, June 8, 1985, Simpson, then 24 years old, and Yates, 21, completed the first-ever summit of Siula Grande's West Face in the Peruvian Andes. Shortly after completing their climb, things went bad.

Simpson was introduced to mountain climbing at the age of

14, when he read the book *The White Spider*. "The stories in the book were enough to put the willies up anyone," Simpson said in a 2007 interview with *The Telegraph*. "But then, when I thought about it, I kept coming back to the idea that these climbers were intelligent people and that there must be something really good to be had from mountaineering if they were prepared to take risks like that."

Ten years later, Simpson was fully immersed in the mountaineering world. He and Yates had taken on the West Face of Siula Grande because they believed it to be the most difficult route that could be taken. They wanted a challenge; they wanted to make history.

Ironically, the climb became the least interesting part of the story: it was a walk in the park compared to the descent. As the two men began to climb down the mountain, Simpson took a bad fall and completely shattered his right leg. Yates now had to get both himself and his severely injured partner down the approximately 21,000-foot mountain.

Using a rope tied securely to his body, Yates lowered Simpson a few hundred feet at a time. After about nine hours of this process, Yates lost control of the rope and Simpson began to quickly slip down the mountain. As the angle of decline grew steeper, Simpson's body slid faster until he flew off the side of a cliff and was left dangling over a deep crevasse.

Yates, still safely on the mountain, struggled to hold Simpson's weight, and had no slack to work with. For an hour Yates sat with no idea how to proceed. He was unable to hear Simpson's voice, the wind was picking up, and the snow on which he sat felt as if it were losing hold. He had no choice but to cut the rope. Yates then proceeded to make his way down to base camp, certain that his actions had resulted in his friend's death.

Cutting the rope, however, ended up being the action that saved Simpson's life. Rather than plunging into the darkness of the crevasse, Simpson fell onto a narrow ice shelf. He waited on the small ledge through the night and managed to climb up the side of the cliff the following morning. With a shattered leg, Simpson began dragging himself toward base camp. It took 60 excruciating hours to cover the six-mile journey back, and he arrived just as Yates was preparing to leave.

For three days, Yates took care of Simpson, slowly nursing him out of dehydration and starvation. They then traveled to Lima by donkey and by truck, a trip that took another three days. At long last, they were able to find an orthopedist who operated on Simpson's leg and saved his life.

XUANZANG

602-664

-

This Chinese Buddhist monk risked everything to travel to India in pursuit of knowledge.

It is said that Xuanzang had a vision. This vision would convince him to undertake a seemingly impossible journey to India in order to obtain information regarding key Buddhist texts. Before all that, though, he was just a young student of Confucianism.

At the time of Xuanzang's birth in AD 602, China was in a state of political strife. His father, a devout Confucianist, originally served as magistrate of Jiangling County before abandoning his position to escape the government turmoil. Young Xuanzang developed an interest in his father's Confucianism, but after his father's death in 611 he was forced to look elsewhere for guidance. Xuanzang's brother, Chensu, had been living as a Buddhist monk in the monastery of Jingtu at Luoyang. Before long, Xuanzang began visiting the monastery and studying the sacred texts of Buddhism.

In 622, Xuanzang was officially ordained as a Buddhist monk. Still deeply invested in the sacred texts, he was determined to figure out why there were so many discrepancies within the passages. When it became clear to him that the Chinese monks under whom he studied couldn't answer his questions, he decided to seek answers in India.

Unfortunately, the Chinese government denied his request on the grounds that national security might be compromised. It was then, in 629, that Xuanzang had a vision. It told him he had to find some way to get to India, and so he set off to learn more.

Traveling exclusively under the cover of night, Xuanzang risked severe punishment by embarking on this journey. His success was largely due to aid provided by Good Samaritans and fellow Buddhists along the way. During his travels, Xuanzang continually preached the Buddhist practice of *Yogācāra*, which uses meditation to promote inner peace and clarity. Despite his discretion, word of his pilgrimage got around. Eventually, he was invited to the Chinese city of Hami by King Qu Wentai of Turfan. Being that the king was a practicing Buddhist, Xuanzang did not object.

Unfortunately, the king's intentions were not entirely benevolent. He wanted to hold Xuanzang against his will and make him serve as his court's ecclesiastical head. Xuanzang protested by way of hunger strike and eventually a deal was struck. The king would release Xuanzang if he promised to return when his journey was complete and serve under him for three years. Xuanzang, finally in a king's good favor, continued his journey in 630 as an authorized pilgrim.

When Xuanzang reached the Nalanda Monastery in India, he studied amongst over 10,000 likeminded monks. In 636, Xuanzang became a disciple of the abbot of Nalanda, Silabhadra, who was contemplating suicide before a dream convinced him to await the arrival of a Chinese monk who would preach the Mahayana Buddhist tradition abroad.

Xuanzang spent much time learning Mahayana practices and scriptures, and studying logic, arithmetic, and medicine. He would go on to debate many representatives of other religions who opposed his teachings. Eventually, in 645, Xuanzang decided it was time that he return to China in order to continue his mission of studying, establishing, and preserving Buddhism.

ALISON HARGREAVES

1962-1995

-

*Scaling Mount Everest is hard enough, but this English
mountaineer did it without supplementary oxygen;
then she set her sights on K2.*

On August 13, 1995, Alison Hargreaves succeeded in reaching
the peak of Pakistan's K2, bringing her one step closer to
achieving her goal of becoming the first woman to summit
Earth's three tallest mountains. That same day, however,
Hargreaves learned that the descent posed more of a threat than
the climb.

Exactly three months prior, on May 13, Hargreaves had
become the first woman to reach the top of Mount Everest
without wearing an oxygen tank and without the support of
a Sherpa team. K2 was the second mountain that Hargreaves
needed to climb in order to achieve her goal. The third would
be Kangchenjunga, which straddles the border between India
and Nepal.

Before Hargreaves began her ascent of K2, Pakistani army
officer Captain Fawad Khan urged her not to make this attempt.
The weather conditions were becoming severe and the mission,
Fawad Khan believed, would be suicidal. Despite the warning,
Hargreaves decided to make the climb.

After spending about six weeks at base camp waiting out
storms and a four-day journey upward, Hargreaves reached

Camp Four, approximately 25,000 feet above sea level. From there, the summit was about 12 hours away. On August 13 weather conditions appeared fair enough to make the final ascent. The climb proved less treacherous than expected, and at around 6:45 p.m. Hargreaves and fellow mountaineer Javier Olivar reached the summit. Shortly after they reached the top of K2, four more mountaineers arrived. Between 8 and 10 p.m. that night, the weather turned from benign to hostile. All six climbers died while descending the mountain.

The details of the descent are somewhat ambiguous. Whether or not the climbers decided to leave the summit at the same time is unknown, and even the causes of death are not entirely clear. It is presumed, however, that the climbers were swept to their deaths by wind that may have reached 260 miles per hour.

As word of Hargreaves's tragic death spread, many were critical of her decision to summit despite being told it was an unwise decision. Much of this criticism revolved around the fact that she was the mother of two young children. The fact that this same condemnation is not lodged at men who continue pursuing their dreams despite having children sheds light on an all too familiar double standard. Hargreaves's family certainly does not fault her for attempting to make history. In reference to her death, her husband, James Ballard, stated, "How could I have stopped her? I loved Alison because she wanted to climb the highest peak her skills would allow her to. That's who she was."

SACAGAWEA

1788-1812

-

Without her, Lewis and Clark are just a couple guys who got lost.

Every year, grade-school children across the United States learn of the heroic journey undertaken by Meriwether Lewis and William Clark. Their story, featured in a later entry, has been told and retold in countless books, with varying degrees of accuracy. One aspect of their tale that is always included, but never detailed, is the role of the Shoshone woman Sacagawea. She is typically portrayed as an entirely willing participant in the adventures of these two lauded men and their party of explorers. The truth is, however, that Sacagawea had most of her decisions made for her from the time she was a young girl.

In 1800, Sacagawea was living amongst her people, nestled in the Rocky Mountains of present-day Idaho. She was about 12 years old when a group of Hidatsa Indians, enemies of the Shoshones, kidnapped her and took her to present-day North Dakota. This abduction was the first in a series of events that led to Sacagawea joining the Lewis and Clark expedition.

After some time living as a slave of the Hidatsa Indians, Sacagawea was sold to Toussaint Charbonneau, a fur trader who he claimed Sacagawea and one other enslaved Shoshone woman as his "wives." It was in 1805 that Sacagawea gave birth to Charbonneau's son, Jean-Baptiste, who would go on to become just as legendary as his mother. Sacagawea, Toussaint

Charbonneau, and their son were soon hired by Lewis and Clark, with Sacagawea serving as a guide and Toussaint serving as her interpreter.

The image of Sacagawea confidently pointing westward with a papoose strapped to her back is a fairly accurate representation of her role in Lewis and Clark's journey. Despite being coerced into the position by her husband, whom she was forced to marry, Sacagawea seemed to take great pride in her work. She gathered indigenous berries and plants for the group to eat, she navigated through territories only she was familiar with, and, most importantly, she kept Indian tribes from interfering with the expedition's progress, all while caring for her infant son.

For their part, Lewis and Clark held Sacagawea in very high regard. They were extremely fond of her child as well, whom Clark nicknamed "Pompy" or "Dancing Boy" in reference to his showy dancing performances. Sacagawea's suggestions and guidance were always met with appreciation. But for the majority of her life, Sacagawea was indeed a slave. This detail is often omitted from the Lewis and Clark story. However, the positive relationship between Lewis, Clark, and Sacagawea is not exaggerated. They truly did care for each other, and when Sacagawea died six years after the expedition, Clark adopted her son, and the daughter she gave birth to shortly after returning home from the journey.

SWAMINARAYAN

1781-1830

-

*This Indian yogi developed a new branch of Hinduism
and came to be viewed as a manifestation of God.*

Every now and again, a person achieves a level of existence beyond the mortal plane; their time on earth is so remarkable that they live on forever in the minds of others. Swaminarayan is such a person. Recognized as the central figure of Swaminarayan Hinduism, his followers believe him to be a manifestation of God.

Born in India, Swaminarayan's original name was Ghanshyam Pande. Those who practice the religion of Swaminarayan Hinduism believe that when Swaminarayan was just three months old, a sage astrologer studied his signs and claimed that "he will establish Dharma on earth and remove pain and misery from people. He will be famed all over the land. He will also induce people with *samadhi* (a state of spiritual trance). He will lead people to the path of God." When he turned 11, the boy set out on a journey that would ultimately result in the fulfilment of that prophecy.

Swaminarayan's pilgrimage lasted seven years, and its purpose was somewhat ambiguous. He simply wandered, stopping whenever he believed his assistance was required. His charitable journey came to an end when he settled in the West Indian state of Gujarat, where he met his guru, Ramanand Swami, and was given the name Swaminarayan.

Before Ramanand Swami's death in 1802, the two men worked together to develop a new religion, based on ultimate devotion to God. Swaminarayan's belief in nonviolence greatly impacted the formation of this new religion, and he instituted a new kind of *yajna* (sacrificial offering) that did not require suffering of any human or animal. He also vehemently opposed two common practices in the Hindu tradition: *sati*, which involved a woman throwing herself on her husband's funeral pyre, and female infanticide—the killing of newborn female children. After developing the foundation for this form of Hinduism, Swaminarayan began to spread his practices, establishing temples that recognized these new customs in cities all over India.

While working to spread his new faith, Swaminarayan continued to directly aid the underprivileged and mistreated. It is suggested that he attempted to deconstruct the caste system, an age-old practice that dictated the social hierarchy of India's population. Some texts claim that he would often eat among members of a lower caste, something unheard of at the time; other accounts indicate that he would not associate with untouchables, the lowest members of the caste system. It's possible that both accounts contain some truth.

Some of the most famous stories surrounding Swaminarayan focus on his ability to convert famous criminals. One such story involved a man named Jogidas Khuman, a greatly feared thief. He would rob entire villages and pilfer their cattle, evading escape each time. Swaminarayan helped to mediate a truce between Khuman and those with whom he took issue, and his calming influence set Khuman on a path of redemption.

Swaminarayan lived his life of charity and faith until his death at the age of 49. He claimed that although he was leaving his physical body, he would spiritually remain in the temples he established, and with the people he influenced.

FANNY BULLOCK WORKMAN

1859-1925

-

A pioneer in the world of mountaineering,
Workman spent a lifetime seeking out danger.

Mountaineering has been a popular sport for centuries. Wherever there is a peak, there will be people trying to reach it. As in many other sports, it wasn't easy for women to achieve acceptance in the mountaineering community, but achieve it they did. And Fanny Bullock Workman deserves a lot of credit for paving the way.

It was on New Hampshire's Mount Washington that Workman discovered her love for the extreme. She summited the 6,288-foot mountain without issue and immediately set her sights on more challenging endeavors. Her newfound passion would have to wait, however, because she and her husband William soon packed their things and moved to Dresden, Germany.

Workman could no longer climb, but she was not about

to stop seeking adventure. The year was 1895, and a new craze was sweeping across Europe: the Rover safety bicycle. Unlike previous designs, this bike had two wheels of the same size, allowing riders to place their feet on the ground while resting. Fanny and William each purchased one of the new bikes and began planning a journey.

Armed with few supplies, the couple set off across Spain. Along the way, they took detailed notes of their travels, which spanned approximately 45 miles a day and 2,800 miles total. These notes eventually grew into the book *Sketches Awheel in Modern Iberia*. The success of their writings and the enjoyment they gained from riding led them to go on similar journeys across Algeria, Italy, and India. But through it all, Workman never forgot about her first love.

While biking through India in 1897, the Workmans became acquainted with the Himalayas. The notion of exploring the intimidating mountain range greatly intrigued the couple. In fact, it became their obsession. They spent a great deal of time surveying the area, and after one failed attempt at climbing, the Workmans prepared for a second try in 1899. With the help of the skilled mountain climber and guide Matthias Zurbriggen, along with 50 hired servants, they began their ascent.

They set their sights on the Skoro La pass, and after traversing a shaky rope bridge across the 270-foot chasm of the Braldu River, they reached the Skoro La. They sat at an altitude of 17,000 feet, debating whether or not to travel through the pass. Zurbriggen urged against it, advising them that it was too early in the season to make the crossing. But they decided to push on.

As altitude increases, so does the expectation of sickness. But both of the Workmans displayed a strong resistance to the typical effects of oxygen loss. This, along with their general fearlessness, enabled them to reach the summit of Koser Gunge just a few weeks later. Fanny stood atop the mountain at 21,000 feet, higher than any woman had ever climbed before.

She would go on to deliver lectures and write books about her adventures, giving the mountaineering community no choice but to pay attention, and proving that women can climb to the same heights as men.

GENGHIS KHAN

1162-1227

-

A ruthless Mongolian ruler, he established the largest contiguous empire in human history.

Genghis Khan, likely the strongest and most deplorable warlord of all time, became the head of his family when he was quite young. He cemented his position when he murdered his half brother over a minor dispute. By the age of 20, he had already amassed a following of more than 20,000 men. With this army, Genghis set out to unite the traditional tribes of central Mongolia under his rule. This objective may have seemed outlandish to rival tribes at the time, but they had no idea what Genghis was capable of.

Perhaps more than anything, the Mongolian ruler is remembered for his brutal war tactics. While fighting the Tatar army, Genghis ordered all men over three feet tall to be killed. In battle with the Taichi'ut army, Genghis and his men killed enemy chiefs by boiling them alive. By the time they defeated the Naiman tribe and gained control of central and eastern Mongolia in 1206, Genghis and his soldiers were feared far and wide.

Following that landmark victory, the Mongol army was comprised of roughly 80,000 extremely well-trained soldiers. Their ability to accurately shoot a bow while gracefully riding on horseback made them devastating in battle. Before long, the remaining Mongol leaders surrendered and Genghis Khan was declared the Supreme God of the Mongols and the rightful ruler of the world. With his destiny in mind, as well as a lack of resources in the Mongolian area, Genghis set his sights on Northern China.

From 1207 to 1209, Genghis waged war against the kingdom Xi Xia, which eventually surrendered. Now with a foothold in China, Genghis began his 20-year assault on the Jin dynasty, an empire whose vast rice fields were essential to the desperate Mongolian army.

In the meantime, Genghis had been attempting to establish diplomatic relations with the Turkish Empire, known as the Khwarizm dynasty, which included Turkistan, Persia, and Afghanistan. However, the governor of Otrar refused the act of civility and attacked the Mongolian caravan sent to discuss relations. Upon hearing of this, Genghis sent another diplomat to the Khwarizm dynasty in order to retrieve the unruly governor of Otrar. However, the leader of the dynasty, Shah Muhammad, had something else in mind. He decapitated the Mongolian diplomat and sent his head back to Genghis Khan.

Of course, the message of defiance was not well received. In 1219, Genghis and 200,000 of his soldiers put their efforts against the Jin dynasty on hold and focused all of their attention on laying waste to the Khwarizm dynasty. They tore through every city, sparing no life in the process. Men were slaughtered, women were raped and killed, children were used as human shields, and skulls were piled in city centers—all with the intent to send a message to Shah Muhammad: Genghis Khan would not be ignored. By 1221, Muhammad and his family had been captured and killed, bringing an end to the dynasty.

The purpose of the assault was retribution, but its effects were much more significant. In bringing European countries under Mongol control, Genghis Khan had connected the significant trade centers of Europe and China and established the largest contiguous empire in human history.

ROBERT FALCON SCOTT

1868-1912

-

*An Arctic explorer whose attempt to reach
the South Pole ended in tragedy.*

The race to the South Pole was in full swing by the early 20th century. Although not an official race, the destination had yet to be reached by man, and explorers everywhere were vying to be the first. In 1910, Robert Falcon Scott, already an accomplished Arctic explorer, decided to make his own attempt at planting his flag at Earth's southernmost point. To some, Scott is viewed as an unfortunate pioneer; to others, he is condemned as a misguided man responsible for the death of his team. It is unclear which side is correct, but it is undeniable that the tragedy ended up making Scott famous.

Utilizing sledges, ponies, and dogs, Scott's expedition set off in October 1911. As they quickly realized that the ponies and sledges wouldn't make it through the horrible conditions, a handful of team members took them back to base camp as Scott pushed onward with the dogs and a handful of men. By mid-December, winter was in full swing and even the dog teams were having a difficult time progressing, so they too were taken back to base camp. Now just Scott and four of his men remained. Had the thought of being the first to reach the South Pole not been so enticing, perhaps they would have turned back when the dogs did.

The men turned reluctantly toward the final leg of their journey: the ascent of the Beardmore Glacier and the polar plateau. The trek was difficult, but on January 17, 1912, they made it to their destination. They had successfully reached the South Pole, but much to their surprise and disappointment, they were not the first. The explorer Roald Amundsen had beaten them there. Scott's journey had been in vain, and the men began their trek back with low morale. Unfortunately, their hardships were just beginning.

Conditions grew worse as the men plodded along the 800-mile journey back to base camp. The first death occurred in February, when team member Edgar Evans fell from a glacier. Dejected, the remaining four men pressed on. Sub-zero temperatures and a lack of supplies made for a difficult journey, but Scott knew that if they just got to the agreed-upon rendezvous point, a team would be waiting with dogs and sleds to transport them the remainder of the way. Or so he thought.

A decision had been made by the men at base camp: instead of going all the way to the meeting point, the dogs were sent only a fraction of the way. Why this occurred is not entirely clear, but it is likely that the men believed they would be putting human lives in jeopardy by going so far into the tundra.

When Scott and his men reached the rendezvous point, they found no dogs waiting for them. Concerned but not entirely hopeless, they decided that the men were running late. However, after waiting for some time, it became clear that something was amiss. Scott gave up hope on the rendezvous point and decided to take his team north on his own, understanding that they would likely die. By March 29, 1912, all four men had died of starvation and exposure to the cold, just 11 miles from where the dogs waited.

The tragic outcome of Scott's expedition saddened many, especially those in the scientific community. Since his death, many have criticized Scott's decisions as a leader, specifically his choice to continue the journey south without dog teams. But today the general consensus seems to accept that Scott and his men all knew the risks involved in the mission, and were pushed forward by their passion for glory.

MERIWETHER LEWIS & WILLIAM CLARK

1774-1809, 1770-1838 (RESPECTIVELY)

-

With the help of Sacagawea, these two men explored the Louisiana Territory and established a route to the Pacific Ocean.

In 1803, the land west of the Mississippi River was an expanse of uncharted terrain known as the Louisiana Territory, which Thomas Jefferson had purchased from France. Jefferson was eager to learn more of the 828 million square miles newly added to the republic. But with unexplored places came daunting uncertainty. Whomever Jefferson selected to chart the new land would have to stand tall in the face of untold dangers, beasts, and obstacles. So Jefferson chose his personal secretary,

Meriwether Lewis, a capable frontiersman and intellectual. Despite his qualifications, Lewis still needed an outdoorsman with more expertise, and so he called upon William Clark.

Jefferson's primary goal in sponsoring the journey was to find a waterway that extended westward through the country and could be used as a new trade route. For that reason, Lewis, Clark, and 33 other expedition members known as the Corps of Discovery traveled via the Missouri River for the first leg of their trip, hoping that it might take them all the way across the North American continent. But when the party reached the Rocky Mountains, they realized that the river would not take them any farther. They set up camp for the winter and prepared themselves for the harsh conditions, but the generosity of Native American tribes such as the Mandans enabled the men to remain comfortable throughout the season.

When the spring of 1805 brought warm weather and high water, Lewis and Clark set off for the remainder of their journey. That November, the expedition reached the Pacific Ocean via present-day Oregon. There, they built Fort Clatsop and spent the winter indoors. When the weather once again turned favorable they began their trek east. This time around, however, Lewis and Clark would split up, each taking a portion of the corps with them. They did so in order to chart more territory than they could have done together, and while Lewis and his men ran into conflict with the Blackfeet Indians, the famous duo was able to reconvene at the Missouri River and travel home together.

All told, the men covered roughly 8,000 miles on their

journey. The trip took two and a half years, during which time Jefferson became confident that the group had perished. When Lewis and Clark triumphantly returned, group intact, they presented their findings: more than 300 plant and animal species, as well as detailed maps of the land they had covered. Their bravery opened the door to the West and changed the course of American history.

OSA & MARTIN JOHNSON

1894-1953, 1884-1937 (RESPECTIVELY)

-

A husband-and-wife team who risked
life and limb to document exotic lands.

A man pointing a camera toward exotic animals and untamed lands, a woman pointing a rifle toward any beast that might prove antagonistic: this was the Johnson couple in a nutshell. Osa married Martin when he was already a full-fledged adventurer, and, determined to keep up with him in all endeavors, she quickly proved herself invaluable to whatever cause the couple pursued.

In their travels, the couple viewed unfamiliar peoples and practices through a prism of cultural superiority, observing different cultures in ways that would be incredibly offensive today. For example, the couple once gave cigars to African tribesmen and photographed them as they choked on the smoke. This type of exploitative documentation was, and is, deplorable. But the Johnsons are still rightly regarded as pioneering filmmakers with a number of intriguing stories.

Their first joint expedition was in 1917, to the island of Malekula in the South Pacific. There was said to be a group of cannibals known as the Big Nambas living there, and the Johnsons intended to film their behavior. They trekked through thick jungle and eventually located the tribe. Osa attempted to communicate with the group's leader, Nagapate, while Martin filmed, but it quickly became apparent to the crew that Nagapate was interested in Osa in a dangerous way. They quickly retreated from the camp as the natives followed in close pursuit. All escaped safely, and the resulting footage became the widely acclaimed *Among the Cannibals of the South Pacific*.

The Johnsons had proven themselves skilled explorers and filmmakers, and they continued to document sections of the world most people would not get to see otherwise. Eventually, their exploits led them to Africa, where the couple's professional chemistry developed even further. While Martin filmed packs of dangerous creatures, Osa would stand at the ready in case of an attack. On one notable occasion, Martin was filming a herd of rhinoceroses when one of them charged directly at him. Unflappable, Osa raised her rifle, shot, and killed the beast. Not only that: the entire ordeal was caught on film.

Osa and Martin continued to produce works that amazed viewers the world over. Sadly, Martin died in a plane crash in 1937, but Osa survived and continued her work as an explorer, writer, and documentarian.

ROBERT O'HARA BURKE

1821-1861

-

*This Australian man attempted to chart a course
from Melbourne to the continent's northern shore, though
it's unclear why he was ever chosen for the job.*

Robert O'Hara Burke's misguided expedition would be described as farcical if it hadn't resulted in several deaths. The objective was fairly simple: chart a course from Melbourne, Australia, to the northern shore of the continent. However, sloppy planning and even sloppier execution resulted in a tragic end.

Victoria, Australia, had come into a surplus of gold in the 19th century. As its inhabitants had become wealthy in a fairly short span of time, they were looking for ways to spend their newfound wealth. The Royal Society of Victoria decided it would sponsor a south-to-north mission across the continent, the first of its kind. There did not appear to be any practical reason for the mission; Victoria's only discernible motivation was bragging rights, so to speak.

Things became even more puzzling when the Royal Society appointed Robert O'Hara Burke to lead the expedition—up until that time, Burke had virtually no experience as an outdoorsman or explorer. They provided him a large group of capable men and a plethora of supplies, including six tons of firewood, horses, wagons, camels, and enough food to last two years.

Burke knew that another man, John McDouall Stuart, was attempting to accomplish the same feat. Unwilling to be bested, Burke made a series of decisions he believed would better his chances of beating Stuart to the north shore. First, Burke decided against taking all of the provided supplies, thinking that traveling light would make his journey speedier. Second, he ditched a significant number of the expedition's members early on in the journey. Third, when they arrived at Cooper's Creek, about 400 miles north of their starting point, he reduced the size of his group even further. He ordered five men to remain at the creek with the majority of the supplies in a makeshift base camp known as Camp LXV. Only four men would make the journey north: William John Wills, John King, Charles Gray, and Burke. They took with them one horse, six camels, and enough food for 12 weeks.

Conditions were pleasant as the four men marched north. Water was readily available, as even the desert terrains were littered with ponds after a season of heavy rain. Every day the men would travel from 5 a.m. to 5 p.m., but these good breaks were still not enough to get them there and back before food began to dwindle. It took four months to cover the entire 1,500 miles, and Gray died of exhaustion before the group made it back to Cooper's Creek. The other three men were in bad shape, but they believed that as long as they made it back to Camp LXV the rest of their party would be waiting with food.

Unfortunately, this was not the case. The men stationed at the camp had departed just hours before Burke's arrival. The three men found a note which stated that after waiting a month longer than instructed, they had decided to return to civilization. Accompanying the note was a small portion of rations. Dejectedly, Burke and his men tried to head toward a police station about 150 miles away, but they did not make it far before exhaustion caused them to collapse by the creek. At one point a group of natives approached the dying men and offered to share food and resources with them. King accepted, but Burke and Wills did not. In fact, not only did Burke refuse their generous offer, he also inexplicably shot at them. King was the only member of the party who lived long enough to be rescued.

In the end, Burke and his team beat Stuart to North Australia, but their mission achieved little else; the men did not keep sufficient notes to contribute anything scientifically meaningful. Still, they had accomplished the strange goal of Victoria's Royal Society, and a statue of Burke and Wills was erected in Melbourne.

ROBERT PEARY

1856-1920

-

An American man who claimed—dubiously—to be the first person to reach the North Pole.

Robert Peary may or may not have accomplished a monumental feat in human history. Until his death, he maintained that he and his crew were the first to set foot on the North Pole, though the validity of this claim has long been a topic of debate.

While his eventual claim to fame may have been false, Peary was certainly someone who was up to the task of reaching the North Pole. He had gained significant experience exploring during his time with the U.S. Navy Civil Engineers Corps, which he joined in 1881. With the corps, Peary was tasked with exploring the interior of Nicaragua in order to map out the land for an inter-oceanic canal project. Though the canal was never built, the project instilled in Peary a love of exploration that would eventually take him far north of Nicaragua, all the way to the Arctic.

Peary first became interested in the North Pole when he ventured to Greenland several times in the 1890s. While there, he determined that reaching the pole via Greenland would be immensely difficult, and so he began developing plans to take an "American route," which would bring him up through Canada all the way to Ellesmere Island.

Peary's first attempt to reach the North Pole, in 1905, failed. Though he got within 175 miles of his destination, the final leg of the journey was blocked by ice. Just a few years later, in 1908, Peary, 24 men, 19 sleds, and 133 dogs made another attempt aboard the SS *Roosevelt*.

Departing from New York City on July 6, the crew reached Ellesmere Island after a few months at sea. They spent the winter near Cape Sheridan, and continued traveling once the coldest weather had passed. On April 1, close to reaching their destination, Peary made a somewhat suspicious move: he ordered most of the crew to stay behind, and brought just five men with him, all of whom were completely incapable of determining geographical position. Of course, he may have had legitimate reasons for doing this, but in hindsight it is somewhat suspicious. By only bringing crewmembers who had no ability to refute his claims, Peary could have pulled up far short of the North Pole and still convinced them that they had reached it.

Nevertheless, on April 6, 1909, Peary claims to have reached the North Pole, writing in his journal, "The Pole at last!!! The prize of three centuries, my dream and ambition for twenty-three years, Mine at last . . ." However, this elation was short-lived, for when he returned to the United States he learned that a man named Frederick A. Cook was claiming to have reached the pole before Peary. Though Cook's claims were eventually proven false, they cast the first shadow of doubt on Peary's story. To this day, experts still cite inconsistencies in record keeping and glaring navigational blunders as proof that Robert Peary may not have actually reached the North Pole.

ALEXANDER THE GREAT

356-323 BCE

-

This king of Macedonia is still considered one of the greatest military tacticians of all time.

With an education that came at the knee of Aristotle and an extensive knowledge of military tactics, it is no surprise that

Alexander became king of Macedonia at the age of 20. His father had served as king before his death, and with the support of the Macedonian army, Alexander ascended to the throne unimpeded.

Alexander improved upon nearly every aspect of his father's kingdom—most notably its military. Already a formidable force, the addition of Alexander's strategic mind made them nearly unstoppable. He convinced, coerced, or forced the rebellious Greek city-states of the Corinthian League to accept him as leader, adding their military forces to his own. By the time he made his push into Western Asia, Alexander's force numbered between 32,000 and 47,000 soldiers.

It was on the outskirts of Asia Minor, in modern-day Turkey, that Alexander faced the forces of the Persian king Darius III. The Macedonians defeated Darius and the Persians quite easily, but this would not be the only time that they came into conflict.

Alexander and his forces took an extended period of rest near Asia Minor's southern border during the winter, and then once again found themselves preparing for battle with Darius. It seemed that while Alexander was occupying the majority of Asia Minor, Darius was amassing a large army near Babylon; he had learned his lesson and decided that he needed more soldiers to defeat Alexander.

In 333 BCE, the Macedonian forces encountered Darius and the Persians at Issus. Darius's army greatly outnumbered that of Alexander, which could easily have affected the morale of the Macedonians. But Alexander rode to the frontline of his force and passionately reminded them what they fought for: the pride of being the world's liberators. Darius was defeated, despite his sizable advantage. He ended up fleeing, leaving his wife and children behind to suffer whatever fate Alexander decided upon. Alexander ended up treating them respectfully, in deference to their royal status.

Alexander continued his efforts in Syria, where most cities surrendered to him without pause. The same thing occurred along the Phoenician coast. Eventually, in 331 BCE, Alexander and his army entered Egypt. There, they were lauded as saviors, for the Egyptians had been living under Persia's oppressive rule. It was ordered that a great city be erected at the mouth of the Nile River in his name as an honor. Alexander's path to global domination seemed clear, but Darius had something else in mind.

While moving toward Babylon, Alexander spotted the campfires of Darius and his military on the plains of Gaugamela in modern-day Iraq. It was a golden opportunity to gain the upper hand, but Alexander refused to ambush Darius. He wanted to face him fairly one final time. He got his wish on October 1, 331 BCE, and was victorious for the third time, thanks in large part to the significant cavalry of the Macedonian army. As the long reign of the Persian Empire came to an end, Alexander was declared king of Asia.

Alexander's ruthlessness in battle and his short temper made him somewhat unpopular in his lifetime, but his legacy is indisputable. His endless pursuit of new conquests inspired future leaders such as Julius Caesar and Napoleon Bonaparte, and his name remains synonymous with power to this day.

BALTO

1919-1933

-

Man's best friend, indeed; the bravery of this
Siberian husky saved the lives of hundreds of Alaskan
children during a diphtheria outbreak.

Diphtheria is an infection that causes a thick coating to form in the back of the throat. The disease is easily preventable through vaccination, but if untreated it can lead to heart failure, paralysis, and death. In 1925, doctors realized that a serious diphtheria epidemic might be imminent in the remote city of Nome, Alaska. The outbreak was poised to affect Nome's youth, and the only way to prevent the deadly illness was to obtain a serum from Anchorage, almost a thousand miles away. There was no aircraft available to deliver the medicine, and so with no other option and time running out, dogs were called upon.

More than 20 mushers bravely took part in the mission. The plan was for one to cover a certain amount of distance with their dog sled team, then hand off the fragile package of medicine to another musher, like a relay. If just one team was unable to complete their leg of the journey, the whole operation may have failed. It was estimated that the entire journey would take 13 days, and potentially more if conditions became worse than expected.

On January 27, the first musher left Nenana with the medicine. One after another, the man-and-dog teams pushed through subzero temperatures and extremely high winds. Finally, the package was handed off to the last team: musher Gunnar Kaasen and his pack of dogs, led by a black Siberian husky named Balto.

Soon after Balto took off toward Nome, a severe blizzard started up. The temperature fell to 50° below zero and wind speeds reached more than 50 miles per hour. Kaasen could barely see his own hands in the whiteout conditions, but the young Balto knew the trail well and was able to keep the sled on course as the team slowly made its way toward Nome.

Miraculously, the sled made it to Nome in just 127 hours: about five and a half days after the mission began. Thanks to all of the mushers who volunteered, and the admirable efforts of Balto and the other sled dogs that took part, a potential catastrophe was prevented.

ERIK WEIHENMAYER

1968-PRESENT

-

Proving that nothing is impossible, this blind mountaineer defied the odds and climbed the Seven Summits.

The term *Seven Summits* refers to the highest mountain located on each of the seven continents. Unsurprisingly, conquering the Seven Summits is one of the mountaineering community's crowning achievements, and has only been completed by a few hundred men and women. Of those few hundred, only one is blind: Erik Weihenmayer.

Weihenmayer wasn't born blind, but he had lost all sight by his freshman year in high school. With the help of his supportive parents and his guide dog, he slowly learned to navigate the world without one of his senses.

Realizing that rock climbing was more about feeling than seeing, he quickly developed a love for the activity. After college, Weihenmayer moved to Arizona, where he practiced rock climbing every weekend and enjoyed the modest climbs. He loved it, but when a friend suggested that they summit North America's tallest peak, Weihenmayer thought he was crazy.

Still, he gave it a try. For preparation, he and his friends participated in team-building climbs so that Weihenmayer's lack of sight would not be an issue. By June 1995, they felt ready, and with the help of seasoned mountaineer Chris Morris, Weihenmayer and his friends ascended Alaska's Denali, a climb of 20,320 feet, in 19 days.

Six years later, Weihenmayer had climbed three more of the Seven Summits, and he felt ready to take on Everest. Though he had already triumphed over many mountains, experts still

> **"A summit isn't just a place on a mountain. A summit exists in our hearts and minds. It is a tiny scrap of a dream made real, indisputable proof that our lives have meaning. A summit is a symbol that with the force of our will and the power of our legs, our backs, and our two hands, we can transform our lives into whatever we choose them to be, whatever our hands are strong enough to create."**
>
> **—Erik Wehenmayer**

advised against him climbing the tallest mountain in the world. They believed that the ice at the top would prove problematic for Weihenmayer, especially if he slipped and needed to use his ax to keep himself from falling. On top of that, they thought that Everest's famously low oxygen levels would be a problem for someone who relied so heavily on his thought process. But Weihenmayer remained steadfast.

With the help of a professional team and funding from the National Federation of the Blind, Weihenmayer reached the summit of Everest in 2001, making him the first blind man to do so, an achievement that landed him on the cover of *Time* magazine. A year later he completed the last of the Seven Summits, expanding his list of incredible milestones.

Weihenmayer's pursuit of the Seven Summits left him with a taste for all things extreme, and he has since climbed the Carstensz Pyramid, white-water rafted through the Grand Canyon, and skied down double black diamond slopes.

YUICHIRO MIURA

1932-PRESENT

-

Age is just a number for this octogenarian, who has climbed Mount Everest three times since his 70th birthday.

For many, the word *retirement* is synonymous with relaxation, reflection, and rest. It is something to aspire to. Not all people are lucky enough to retire comfortably, but those who do cherish their well-earned downtime. However, for Yuichiro Miura, *retirement* is synonymous with high-stakes adventure and death-defying feats of courage.

At the age of 70, Miura climbed Mount Everest. At the age of 75, Miura climbed Mount Everest again. But why stop there? After all, he'd only missed the record for oldest person to climb the mountain—held by Min Bahadur Sherchan, who did it at 76—by one year. So when Miura turned 80, he deemed himself ready for a third attempt.

Though he obviously possesses exceptional health and athleticism, Miura is not without his ailments. He has battled diabetes, suffered a crippling pelvis injury, and undergone three heart operations. Any sensible person would've urged Miura not to attempt a third summit of the tallest mountain on Earth, but he was determined to get it done.

Through extensive physical training and a sensible diet, Miura was able to get his body into a condition he believed to be suitable. On May 16, 2013, Miura and a group of understandably impressed climbers began their ascent from base camp. Filled with adrenaline and good fortune, Miura made the climb without issue and reached the summit on May 23. It was only when he stood atop the mountain for the third time and began contemplating what he had done that the immensity of the challenge finally sunk in: Miura believed he was going to die.

The descent was very hard on him, and Miura made his way down the mountain very slowly. Suddenly, the weather worsened, and Miura's feeling of imminent demise grew even stronger.

His team would walk 10 paces with Miura, then wait as he rested. The descent carried on in this way: 10 paces, then rest. All the while, a daunting storm brewed. At one point the entire group feared that an avalanche would take out everybody. Luckily, after what seemed like an eternity spent inching down the mountain, they reached advanced base camp. Technically, Miura had not completed the entirety of the descent, but nobody was going to take issue with that. Miura took a helicopter the rest of the way down, having successfully become the oldest person to summit Mount Everest.

Conventional retirement is still not in the cards for Miura. He plans on attempting a fourth climb of Mount Everest in 2022, when he is 90 years old.

JOAN OF ARC

1412-1431

-

The "Maid of Orléans," this Frenchwoman was only 14 when she led her countrymen in the Hundred Years' War and only 19 when the British burned her alive for it.

Perspectives on psychological disorders and mental illness have come a long way in recent years, but there is still a lot of work to be done. That being said, we are light-years ahead of where the medical field was in the 15th century. Today, if someone were to claim they were hearing voices, they might be tested for schizophrenia; back then, it was simply chalked up to God or the devil. This is where Joan of Arc's story begins.

Joan was born in France to a peasant family in the year 1412, and the prospects for her future were bleak: her father was a lowly tenant farmer and Joan never learned how to read or write. Beyond her individual challenges, France was in a state of turmoil. The Hundred Years' War was raging on, and Joan and her family feared that English forces might overrun their village at any moment.

While Joan did not receive a traditional education, her mother did raise her as a devout Catholic. This strict religious upbringing likely contributed to a belief that God was speaking to her directly. At the age of 13, Joan began hearing voices. They were somewhat subtle at first but grew more strident with each passing year. Eventually, Joan believed she'd seen the visages of St. Michael and St. Catherine before her, and they prophesied that she would save France and restore Charles VI as its king.

Joan took heed. In 1428 she traveled to Vaucouleurs, where she sought contact with Charles. At first, commander Robert de Baudricourt denied Joan the meeting, but by 1429 he noticed her substantial following and approved her meeting with the rightful king.

Joan, now 17 years old, had her work cut out for her. She had to somehow convince Charles that she'd been divinely chosen to accompany the French army into battle and ensure their victory. Charles was skeptical, but with little left to lose, he gave her a shot to prove herself. After she passed a series of trials designed to test the validity of her claims, Charles granted her permission to ride with the army. He also gifted her a set of white armor and a large white horse, and sent her on to Orléans, which was under siege.

In May and June of 1429, Joan was at the forefront of several assaults that resulted in the French army gaining control of English bulwarks. By the end of June, the French had forced the English to retreat across the Loire River. Joan had made a significant contribution to the victory, and word of her skills in battle and her bizarre claims spread quickly. With each battle her reputation grew stronger. To the French, she was an icon; to the English, she was a target.

In a 1430 battle at Compiégne, Joan was thrown from her horse. English troops were able to surround and capture her, as they had long desired. In captivity, Joan faced charges of witchcraft and heresy. She remained imprisoned for one year until authorities ordered that she be put to death. On May 30, 1431, at the age of 19, Joan of Arc was burned alive in front of thousands of people. Today, she is remembered as a French hero and a Roman Catholic saint.

HUGH GLASS

1783-1833

-

An American fur trader, he survived seemingly certain death
during his expeditions across the western frontier.

Many people who saw the 2015 film *The Revenant* may have been surprised to find out that the story was based on real events. Hugh Glass was a real frontiersman, and although some aspects of the film were exaggerated, his tale is still truly unbelievable.

In 1823, Glass found employment with a group of fur traders. Alongside a crew of 30 men, he entered the St. Louis wilderness in March of that year. After surviving several violent encounters with Native American tribes, which resulted in the deaths of 17 other men, Glass found himself scouting ahead of his group. He was a well-built, capable man who preferred solitude while hunting. But in this particular instance his solitude would prove damning; as Glass trekked ahead of the group in the South Dakota woods, a large grizzly bear viciously attacked him.

Glass eventually managed to fight off the bear, but not before it practically tore him to shreds. When the group caught up to him, they found him mangled and close to death. They carried Glass on a makeshift stretcher until the inconvenience became too great. Believing that Glass would be dead soon anyway, two men were assigned to wait with him until he perished, at which time they would give him a proper burial.

Instead of following orders, the men waited several days and buried Glass while he was still alive. They took his gun and supplies and left him for dead in a shallow grave. What they had not counted on was Glass recovering to where he could dig himself out, forage for food without his equipment, and travel hundreds of miles to Fort Kiowa.

The details of Glass's journey after his arrival in Fort Kiowa are unclear. It is believed that he sought revenge for the actions of the two men who left him for dead, but the figure of Hugh Glass has become too iconic to separate fact from fiction. Whether he exacted his revenge or spared them cannot be known, but the details we are sure of certainly support his legendary status.

ALEISTER CROWLEY

1875-1947

-

This Englishman was mountaineering's most famous occultist.

The name Aleister Crowley is associated with a number of things: Satan, magic, sacrifice, and many other aspects of the occult. His behavior earned him the title of "wickedest man in the world," and his teachings played a large part in the "Satanic panic" of decades past. But one aspect of his life often seems to get forgotten: his mountaineering experience.

Crowley's climbing career began to take shape when he

was a student at Cambridge University. Along with his close friend Oscar Eckenstein, he would take annual Alpine trips between 1894 and 1898. During this time, Crowley successfully climbed Mönch, a substantial Swiss mountain, without the help of a guide. This achievement earned him the respect of the mountaineering community and led to his continued interest in the sport.

In 1900, Crowley's travels took him to Mexico, where he remained for quite some time. He was aware that Mexico was home to several significant mountains, and so he invited Eckenstein down to join him for some climbing. Together, they ascended Iztaccihuatl and Popocatépetl. They began to ascend Volcán de Colima but had to abandon the climb due to an impending eruption.

By 1902, Crowley and Eckenstein found themselves in India, the home of some of the world's most challenging mountains. They first set their sights on K2, which had never before been climbed. Along with several other men, they reached an altitude of 20,000 feet, but they were forced to turn back after several of the expedition's members, including Crowley, were struck by illness.

This was certainly seen by Crowley as a failure, but it was during his next expedition, on Kanchenjunga, that disaster struck. This mission was proposed to Crowley by fellow climber Jules Jacot-Guillarmod in 1905, and Crowley agreed to make the journey. From the beginning, tensions were high. Internal conflict broke out among the team members, but this did not stop Crowley from attempting to warn Jacot-Guillarmod and three others against taking a particularly dangerous route. The men did not heed his warnings, and they were killed in an avalanche. It is rumored that Crowley listened as the men died and made no attempt to save them. Though this story was never verified, it would certainly be in keeping with the man that Crowley grew up to be.

HARRIET TUBMAN

CA. 1822–1913

-

A conductor of the Underground Railroad, her heroism
helped hundreds if not thousands of African Americans.

Harriet Tubman was a slave from the day she was born in Maryland in the 1820s. Despite the circumstances, she never missed an opportunity to stand up for herself or others. In one instance, a man demanded that Tubman assist in restraining a runaway slave; Tubman refused and the man threw a weight at her head. The resulting injuries would affect Tubman for the rest of her life.

By 1849, Tubman had had enough. She resolved to escape from her enslavement. She ran away by night, using the North Star for guidance and garnering aid from a supportive white woman she met along the way. Eventually, Tubman made it all the way to Philadelphia and reflected, "I looked at my hands to see if I was the same person. There was such a glory over everything; the sun came like gold through the trees, and over the fields, and I felt like I was in Heaven." Thus began Tubman's tenure as a conductor on the Underground Railroad.

After raising some money in Philadelphia, she returned to Maryland in order to liberate the family she had left behind, as well as any slave who desired freedom. Tubman traveled at night, armed only with a pistol on her hip and an unflappable disposition. She and her passengers would hide out in sympathetic homes, empty schoolhouses, and churches. As she continued to successfully rescue slaves, the bounty on Tubman's head grew larger and larger, eventually reaching a staggering $40,000 (well over $1 million today). Despite the enticing price on her head, Tubman managed to elude the many bounty hunters who attempted to capture her.

Throughout her time as a conductor she made the perilous trip 19 times and rescued about 60 slaves. Not once did someone die or abandon the mission on her watch. When the Civil War began, Tubman's commitment to abolition only intensified.

At first, she served as a cook and a nurse for the Union Army, but after some time her service brought her closer to the line of fire. She acted as a spy and scout, and even led the Combahee River Raid, an armed attack that led to the freeing of around 700 slaves in South Carolina. After a long life of brave service and charitable acts in the name of freedom, Tubman moved to a farm in upstate New York, where she lived with her family.

Tubman's life stands as one of the greatest contributions to equal rights, not just for African Americans but for women as well.

DAVID CROCKETT

1786-1836

-

An American frontiersman turned folk legend,
Crockett's adventures took him all the way to Congress.

A man commonly referred to as "King of the Wild Frontier" must have quite a story, especially considering that the American frontier was the bedrock for countless adventurers, outlaws, heroes, and capable cowboys. However, as is so often the case, the media called the shots. And it was only after David Crockett's somewhat underwhelming story passed through countless embellishments that he grew into the folk legend he is today.

Westward expansion was constant during the late 18th century, and, like many early settlers of the frontier, Crockett's family moved frequently. By the time young Crockett was 12 years old, he had moved three times. He would continue this pattern all through his life, picking up and moving whenever it felt right or necessary.

Crockett's first real adventure came in the form of an escape. In 1798, he and his family lived near Knoxville, Tennessee. Out of necessity, Crockett's father hired him out to a man named Jacob Siler, who needed help transporting cattle to Rockbridge County, Virginia. Young Crockett fulfilled his obligation, but Siler attempted to keep the boy by force. Already possessing keen awareness, Crockett fled in the night and traveled seven miles through knee-deep snow in only two hours, thereby evading recapture. He continued to journey home and arrived after several months.

After that, Crockett felt quite comfortable on his own. He even voluntarily left his home for over two years, simply to avoid punishment from his father. Crockett ended this stint of independence and returned home in 1802, only to realize that his family no longer recognized him. Once he revealed his identity, however, all was forgiven.

Crockett continued to work and grow in Tennessee, and in 1813 he decided to enlist as a militia scout in the city of Winchester. As a soldier, he participated in the massacre on the Native American town of Tallushatchee, and later worked to expel Native Americans from the swamps of Florida. Following his years of success in the military, Crockett established a career in politics. He was elected to Congress in 1827 and remained a congressman until 1835, when he grew so frustrated that the unverified statement "You can all go to Hell and I'm going to Texas" was attributed to him.

More than anything, it is Crockett's time in Texas that earned him his reputation, though it is unclear why. He was indeed at the famed Battle of the Alamo in 1836, but his reason for fighting is a matter of debate. Some believe that he chose to stand against the Mexican Army because he viewed an independent Texas as something worth defending, while others say that he simply enjoyed battle. In any event, he died during combat.

For decades to follow, stories featuring a fictionalized Davy

Crockett appeared throughout the country. People grew to love the lingo-spouting, superhuman version of the actual man, and that characterization endures nearly two centuries after his death.

WITOLD PILECKI

1901–1948

-

This Allied soldier purposely interned himself in a concentration camp in order to gain military intelligence.

Few incidents in modern history are as horrifying as the Holocaust. People who heard about what was going on in places like Auschwitz either found it hard to fathom or prayed that they would never end up there themselves. No one went willingly into such horror. That is, no one besides Witold Pilecki, a 39-year-old man who purposely got himself incarcerated in the notorious camp.

In 1940, many members of the Allied Forces did not have a clear idea of what was going on at Auschwitz. It was known to be some sort of detention facility, possibly for prisoners of war. This worked against the notion that Pilecki, a member of the Polish Resistance who had fought against the Nazi invasion, had of Auschwitz.

He volunteered to infiltrate the camp as a prisoner in order to gather intelligence for Poland, as well as possibly organize a resistance operation within the camp. Pilecki would go on to spend three years at Auschwitz, and watched it shift from a prison into a death factory.

Pilecki was able to smuggle intelligence out of the camp by sending it with escaped prisoners or hiding it in the dirty laundry that was sent into town to be cleaned. As the years dragged on and word from Pilecki kept coming, the underground Polish army became increasingly horrified at the events being detailed.

Conditions were bad immediately, but nowhere near what they would become. Pilecki told of the unsustainable diet prisoners were forced to adopt, as well as the unbearable physical labor they were ordered to complete. Eventually, the notorious methods of execution were introduced: gas chambers, lethal injections, and the large ovens where countless bodies were burned.

By 1943, Pilecki realized that his time was limited; he knew that he would have to make an escape if he wanted to live. On the night of April 26, while working in the camp's bakery, he and two other inmates escaped through the back door. They ran into the dark as guards fired shots at them, and Pilecki managed to get away.

By the time World War II came to an end, approximately 1.1 million people had been killed at Auschwitz. Though Pilecki's name was kept classified for a long period of time, it is now public knowledge that without the information he provided to the Polish and British armies, the already staggering number of fatalities might have been even higher.

ANNIE SMITH PECK

1850-1935

-

*She broke a number barriers for female mountaineers,
but all the media could talk about was her outfit.*

The dormant volcano Mount Coropuna towers 20,922 feet above Peru. In 1911, this vantage trumpeted its support of the suffrage movement when 65-year-old Annie Smith Peck climbed the mountain and planted a "Women's Vote" banner there.

Peck first became interested in mountaineering when she was 45, and from that point on she dedicated her life to it. Women were still uncommon in the climbing world, and so Peck set quite a few milestones. She was the third woman to ever climb the Matterhorn in Switzerland. Peck also claimed to hold the world altitude record for a woman with her ascent of Pinnacle Peak in India, though another prolific female climber—Fanny Bullock Workman—challenged her claim. As it turned out, Peck's altitude estimation was in fact wrong, and she did not hold the record. However, she did do something that ended up being quite significant not just for mountaineers, but for all women.

Peck's climb of the Matterhorn should have been the subject of news reports, but the achievement was swept aside because of what she wore on the climb: long pants and a pair of climbing boots. The era's social norms dictated that women were not to wear trousers in public, and on a few occasions the breaking of this code resulted in actual arrests. So instead of focusing on Peck's historical accomplishment, people debated over whether she should be placed in jail for her garb.

All of the controversy likely did not faze Peck; in fact, it is safe to assume that it encouraged her to climb more mountains and continue to fly in the face of patriarchal absurdity, since she did exactly that for the rest of her life.

APSLEY CHERRY-GARRARD

1886–1959
-
He risked everything to obtain penguin eggs near the South Pole.

Many consider Robert Falcon Scott's tragic journey to the South Pole to be one of the biggest failures in the history of Antarctic expeditions. Apsley Cherry-Garrard was part of the Scott expedition, but it was not that trek which he described as "the worst journey in the world" in a book featuring that title.

Cherry-Garrard's trip from hell was something of an offshoot of the Scott mission. He, Dr. Bill Wilson, and Henry "Birdie" Bowers accompanied Scott to the Antarctic with the intention of collecting three emperor penguin eggs to establish evolutionary links between reptiles and birds.

The destination was a penguin colony at Cape Crozier, approximately 70 miles away from Scott's base camp. The date was June 27, 1911, during the middle of Antarctica's winter. The three men knew it would be a challenge, but they believed that the scientific potential was worth the risk.

The men learned quickly how unbearable the temperatures could be. Pulling two sleds of food and equipment, they trudged through weather that sometimes reached 60° below zero, and was so punishing that Cherry-Garrard's teeth eventually cracked from the violent chattering. Every night the men had to chip away at the ice forming on their sleeping bags. At one point the team's tent blew away and they simply lied down, accepting death, until a brief stint of relatively decent weather allowed Bowers to retrieve their shelter. All the while, complete darkness forced them to travel by candlelight and the small illumination provided by the stars.

Finally, after days of severe struggle, the three men reached the penguin colony. They gathered up their specimens and returned to base camp 35 days after their departure. Their frozen clothes had to be cut off of them, and Cherry-Garrard appeared to have aged years during the sojourn. He was so tired he ended up remaining at camp as Scott led his team to the South Pole. Bowers and Wilson opted to go with Scott, a decision that ultimately led to their deaths.

To this day, the three eggs acquired by Cherry-Garrard, Wilson, and Bowers are kept in London's Natural History Museum, where they are occasionally displayed to great public interest. They exist as much as a monument to human perseverance as they do to the evolutionary discoveries they provided.

ROALD AMUNDSEN

1872-1928

-

The first man to lead a team to the South Pole,
all without the extra drama of his competitors.

It would be fair—if a little macabre—to admit that the stories of those who *failed* to reach the South Pole first are more interesting than that of the man who did. Roald Amundsen was undoubtedly one of the most important people in the field of early Arctic exploration, but unlike his peers Robert F. Scott and Robert E. Peary, Amundsen seemed to face little to no inconvenience during his journeys.

A 1906 sailing expedition to Nome, Alaska, gave Amundsen a taste of Arctic adventure. Finding that taste to his liking, the Norwegian explorer made a plan to journey to the North Pole. However, upon hearing of Robert Peary's supposed arrival there in 1909, Amundsen decided he would try for the South Pole instead.

Amundsen's firm belief in thorough preparation helped him beat Robert F. Scott to the South Pole, as his research led him to establish his base camp in Antarctica's Bay of Whales: 60 miles closer to the Pole than Scott's camp. Amundsen also made sure to leave caches of food along his route for the journey back.

On October 19, 1911, Amundsen, four men, 52 dogs, and four sleighs departed their base for the South Pole. The trip went smoothly, and they arrived at their destination on December 14, becoming the first people to make it to the planet's southernmost point. Their arrival came more than a month before that of Robert F. Scott, who would tragically perish on his return trip. Amundsen and his men remained at the South Pole for several days, recording scientific data and reveling in their achievement. They began their return trip on December 17 and arrived safely back at their base on January 25, 1912.

Amundsen went on to gain considerable attention and wealth following his historic journey. He used those funds to start a successful shipping business, and continued pursuing his career as an explorer. Most notably, he purchased a new ship named *Maud* and attempted to sail to the North Pole in 1918. Unfortunately, unlike his South Pole journey, the plan did not work out. He attempted to reach the North Pole again, this time by airplane in 1925, but came 150 miles short: two failures that did nothing to sully his legacy.

HERODOTUS

CA. 484 BCE–CA. 425 BCE

-

This prolific historian traveled the Persian Empire in order to document the Greco-Persian wars.

It may be a bit trite to say that history repeats itself, but there's no denying the value of studying the past. We learn from those who have come before us in order to inform the decisions we make today. Few ancients understood this simple truth better than Herodotus, as evidenced by his commitment to keeping a detailed record of historical events.

The Greco-Persian wars occurred from 499 BCE to 479 BCE, so Herodotus was only a child when they came to an end. His home city of Halicarnassus was of Greek origin but had been under Persian rule for some time. Because Herodotus's family openly opposed the tyrannical Persian ruler Lygdamis, they were exiled from the city.

Young Herodotus had no interest in settling down following his exile. Instead he enthusiastically traveled from one Persian city to another, much like a modern backpacker. He went to Palestine, Syria, Babylon, and all of the islands of the Greek Archipelago. In each city, Herodotus spoke with many individuals, recording their personal histories and the local mythology.

He took the many stories he'd gathered and recited them to the people of Athens, where he was met with praise for his dedication to spreading knowledge, and was eventually awarded a substantial monetary prize so he could continue with his scholarly work. Now financially comfortable, he committed the rest of his life to creating a detailed account of the Greco-Persian wars called *The Histories*.

The work focuses mainly on cause and effect: a case study of the Persian Empire's rise to power, their defeat at Salamis, Plataea, and Mycale, and the reasons why these events occurred. *The Histories* was mainly comprised of the personal reflections Herodotus had collected in his travels, as well as fabricated stories that were, in a sense, early examples of historical fiction. The book does indeed contain encyclopedic information of places, but it also contains apocryphal stories about the individuals who inhabited them. Herodotus believed that these stories, which were essentially amalgamations of the many personalities he would encounter in a given area, made the final product much more enjoyable for the average reader.

Though some criticized him for inserting tall tales into what was supposed to be a factual account, his legacy is generally quite positive. Prior to him, nobody had attempted to conduct a thorough study of past events and record them in a permanent manner. Correctly tabbed the "Father of History" by the Roman writer Cicero, Herodotus was the first to show society how to learn from the mistakes and triumphs of the past.

PERCY FAWCETT

1867–1925

-

He scoured the Amazon in search of a hidden city deep in the jungle, which he believed to be a bastion of art and history.

The allure of lost cities has long been a siren song to determined explorers. From Atlantis to El Dorado, fictional utopias are often believed to be actual locations, hidden away for centuries, just waiting to be discovered. Percy Fawcett claimed that his belief in the city known as "Z" was based in logic, but to some, his exploits seemed as foolhardy as the search for Bigfoot.

Fawcett spent a great deal of time exploring the Amazon in order to create maps of previously uncharted territories. Over the course of his several expeditions Fawcett generated some attention, but it was his quest for "Z" that would make him legendary.

Fawcett had heard scuttlebutt of cities stumbled upon by the old European conquistadores. Specifically, he was intrigued by a 1753 document known as Manuscript 512, a Portuguese account of an enormous stone city containing sophisticated architecture, hieroglyphics, and art. The document, however, did not provide a specific location of the city. Fawcett, who had spent considerable time mapping the Amazon jungle, had once stumbled upon what appeared to be the scattered ruins of a once-large settlement. Believing the Amazon to be "the last great blank space in the world," Fawcett determined that Manuscript 512 could only be describing an undiscovered city in the jungle.

By 1925, the 57-year-old Fawcett and his son had become convinced of this great city's existence, and so they and a friend set off for the Mato Grosso region of Brazil in search of the lost metropolis, which Fawcett dubbed "Z." The men struggled through swarms of vicious bugs, dense vegetation, and muggy heat, but Fawcett still insisted that they travel at least 10 miles per day. Once they entered uncharted territory, all correspondence stopped, and neither Fawcett nor the other men were ever seen or heard from again.

Most thought Fawcett was capable of triumphing over any challenge, and so, at first, few feared the worst. Plus, the team had informed their loved ones that communication would cease at some point. But after two years passed, people became worried. In 1928 the first search party was sent into the jungle to find evidence of Fawcett's expedition. They emerged unsuccessful, but were certain that the three men must have perished.

Speculation began to swirl almost immediately, and the mystery continues to intrigue interested parties to this day. An estimated 100 people have died in the Amazon Rain Forest while searching for clues regarding Fawcett's disappearance. Expert opinions vary; hypotheses about the cause of death range from malaria to drowning to an animal attack. Some more fantastical suggestions involve Fawcett taking up residence in the jungle to establish a mystic commune. Whatever the case, his disappearance has inspired almost 100 years of intrigue—and will likely continue to do so.

> **"Deep down inside me a tiny voice was calling. At first scarcely audible, it persisted until I could no longer ignore it. It was the voice of the wild places, and I knew that it was now part of me forever."**
> **—Percy Fawcett**

SITTING BULL

1831-1890

-

This Sioux chief courageously stood against American forces.

In the 19th century, little could be done to stop America from expanding; though well versed in the ways of warfare, Native Americans did not have the same weaponry as American soldiers. Despite their significant handicaps, many Native Americans refused to lie down for their oppressors. Sitting Bull was one of the courageous Sioux chiefs to stand up for his people and oppose the American government.

Sitting Bull's trademark stoicism is best illustrated through one of his life's more famous anecdotes. In an 1872 battle at the Yellowstone River, Sitting Bull and four other men marched into the middle of the battlefield, sat down, and calmly smoked a pipe as bullets whizzed past their heads.

Tensions escalated in the mid-1870s when American prospectors invaded the Black Hills in search of gold. Though Native Americans considered the area to be sacred, the government refused to honor their claims, and instead declared that any Native American tribes who resisted the gold rush would be dealt with through combat. But Sitting Bull made it clear that he would not go down without a fight.

In 1876, he led about 3,500 Sioux soldiers into battle against General George Armstrong Custer at Little Big Horn. The now-famous conflict ended badly for the American troops, who were greatly outnumbered. The defeat was hugely embarrassing for the Army, and they responded by pursuing the Native Americans with unrelenting force.

In an effort to remain free, Sitting Bull led a number of his people north, across the Canadian border and outside of U.S. military jurisdiction. However, after four years it became impossible to maintain a food supply, and in 1881 Sitting Bull reluctantly traveled south to surrender. He was held as a prisoner of war for almost two years before being allowed to re-join his tribe at Standing Rock.

WILFRED THESIGER

1910-2003

-

Seeking to escape the world's increasing modernity, Thesiger set off to the Rub' al Khali, the largest sand desert in the world.

In Saudi Arabia there lies a vast expanse of territory known as the Rub' al Khali, or Empty Quarter. At 250,000 square miles, with dunes reaching as high as 1,000 feet, it is the largest sand desert in the world. And in 1946, it was still unmapped land. Wilfred Thesiger saw this immense desert as an invitation to go exploring.

Thesiger greatly admired the Bedu people who resided in the Empty Quarter. He desired to emulate their hardships—perhaps as a humbling exercise, perhaps for purely sociological reasons.

Though the desert had been crossed before, no Westerner had ever done it with Thesiger's minimalist style. He utilized little else besides a camel for transportation, and relied on a pint of water and a handful of dates for his daily sustenance.

Uninhibited by material possessions, Thesiger found relief during his time in the desert—so much so that he made another journey in 1948 and described his love of the barren lands in his book *Arabian Sands*. Though his travels did not result in many significant discoveries, life in the desert, honest and unadorned, brought clarity to Thesiger. As he would write: "The harder the life, the finer the person." But it was in this desert that he loved so much that Thesiger would encounter the future that he so dreaded. In April 1948 he arrived in Buraimi Oasis, near present-day Abu Dhabi, and witnessed what would come to be an enormous oil drilling operation. The Iraq Petroleum Company was searching for oil in many underdeveloped areas at the time: the very areas that Thesiger had spent so much time exploring. He protested, claiming that the drilling would threaten the lifestyle of the Bedu people, but nothing could be done. And upon consideration, even Thesiger caved: he accepted money from the Iraq Petroleum Company in exchange for information that he had gathered during his years of travel.

> **"For me, exploration was a personal venture. I did not go to the Arabian Desert to collect plants nor to make a map; such things were incidental. At heart I knew that to write or even to talk of my travels was to tarnish the achievement. I went there to find peace in the hardship of desert travel and the company of desert peoples."**
>
> **—Wilfred Thesiger**

Though Thesiger eventually gave in to progress, he still found himself more comfortable living in the past. Toward the end of his life, he found solace among tribesmen in a shantytown in northern Kenya. Through his 70s and 80s, he lived in a small cabin without running water or electricity. Finally, in his late 80s, he returned to the United Kingdom, where he passed away a few years later.

ALEX HONNOLD

1985–PRESENT

-

In June 2017, Alex Honnold became the first person to ever scale Yosemite National Park's El Capitan rock face without using any ropes or protective gear.

Rock climbing is not for the faint of heart; low oxygen, freezing weather, tumbling rocks, and avalanches are all occupational hazards. Perhaps the biggest deterrents, though, are the nearly vertical rock walls that reach unimaginable heights. Even a skydiver would be forgiven a shudder at the prospect of dangling 5,000 feet above a gorge. Still, experienced climbers are able to swallow their fear, secure in the knowledge that their ropes and harnesses will protect them if they lose their grip. That is, unless you're Alex Honnold.

The 33-year-old climber does not use protective equipment of any kind when he makes his ascents. One misplaced foot or slip of the hand is the difference between life and death, barring a well-placed branch or soft aerie. This very dangerous style of climbing is known as "free soloing," and although Honnold is not the only one risking life and limb in this manner, few are as daring—and none as successful.

In June 2017, Honnold became the first person to ever scale Yosemite National Park's famous El Capitan rock face without using any ropes or protective gear. To make the 3,000-foot climb using the typical safety equipment is considered a great accomplishment among professional climbers; to make the climb as Honnold did is one of the pinnacle accomplishments in the history of the sport.

El Capitan offers little relief for those brave enough to take it on. The ledges are barely wide enough to support a toe—and that's when there even are ledges. During one part of the climb, Honnold had to get up a large expanse of rock smoothed over by millennia-old glaciers. Using a technique called "smearing," he pushed his rubber shoes up against the 90-degree rock face and slowly crept upward, distributing his weight with technical brilliance.

Honnold's ability to remain calm in such dangerous situations enables him to plan every step meticulously. No hand, foot, finger, or toe moves without careful calculation, a system that has always brought him safely to the summit.

ANNIE OAKLEY

1860–1926

-

*A sharpshooter so accurate she could shoot
a cigarette out of a person's mouth.*

Annie Oakley, born Phoebe Ann Moses, never had the opportunity to apply her immense talent to something beyond theatrics, but that did not stop her from becoming one of the most renowned marksmen of all time. Standing just five feet tall, Oakley always had a knack for what most considered "masculine" activities at the time. She learned how to trap and hunt at a very young age, and later used those skills to earn money and support her family.

As she got older, Oakley continued to seek out situations that enabled her to profit off of her shooting ability. Eventually, she teamed up with the famous Buffalo Bill's Wild West Show in 1885, where she dazzled the country with mind-blowing feats of marksmanship. She could hit the edge of a playing card from 30 feet away; she shot coins that had been thrown up high in the air; she could shoot the flame off of a candle while skipping across a stage. And, in what was arguably her most famous trick, she would shoot a cigarette out of a person's mouth.

During one of Oakley's many performances, a man challenged her to perform this particular stunt. This man happened to be Kaiser Wilhelm II, the last German emperor and king of Prussia. Not one to shy from a challenge, Oakley complied. As usual, the trick went off without a hitch. However, if she had happened to miss the cigarette that day—if the bullet had instead struck Wilhelm in the head—then it is possible that World War I never would have occurred, and we would have had little Annie Oakley to thank.

In 1887, Oakley, along with the rest of Buffalo Bill's troupe, traveled to London to represent the American Exhibition in Queen Victoria's Golden Jubilee. During their performance, a large American flag was lowered into the arena, the queen bowed out of respect, and the crowd roared in approval; this marked the first recorded instance of a British monarch saluting the American flag.

Following this significant performance, Oakley and the show remained in England for over 300 more performances before returning to the United States in 1888.

By 1901, Oakley had been a member of Buffalo Bill's Wild West Show for over 15 years (excluding a brief departure in 1888). She was 41 years old, and all that travel was catching up to her. On the way to a performance in North Carolina, the train on which Oakley rode collided headfirst with a train traveling in the opposite direction. Oakley survived the accident, but perhaps took it as an omen, because she decided to retire soon after.

DANIEL BOONE

1734-1820

-

Daniel Boone fought alongside the British during the French and Indian War in 1755, worked as a hunter and trapper in the Appalachian Mountains, and eventually made several journeys into present-day Kentucky, which solidified his legacy in that state's—and America's—lore.

When folks think about Kentucky, bourbon and horse racing are probably what come to mind. On the first Saturday of May, those two things go hand in hand; the overdressed masses—sipping mint juleps, big, fancy hats on their heads—watch from their boxes as the fastest horses race for the Kentucky Derby crown. But they aren't the only ones in attendance. On the track's infield, a boisterous crowd also watches the Run for the Roses. And despite his penchant for silly hats, it's safe to say that famed frontiersman and Kentucky settler Daniel Boone would feel far more at home with that rambunctious crowd.

Boone's fascination with the outdoors began at his family's home in Pennsylvania, where he would walk the cattle through the woods each day so they could graze. He liked to linger in the forest, and by age 13 he would spend countless hours hunting for game, eventually becoming so skilled that he was able to provide his family with a steady supply of fresh meat.

As he grew older, Boone applied his knowledge of the outdoors to various pursuits, including fighting alongside the

British during the French and Indian War in 1755, and working as a hunter and trapper. But it was his forays into Kentucky that cemented his place in history.

In 1769, Boone and five of his friends traveled through the Cumberland Gap of the Appalachian Mountains. It was a dangerous route that few colonists had ever used, but the men made it through and built a base camp near what is now Irvine, Kentucky. It was there that the group lived and hunted for several months before Shawnee Indians captured them. Boone managed to escape and return home, though all of his belongings were lost.

In 1775, Boone was hired to help establish a new colony in Kentucky, thanks to his prior experience in the region. With the help of roughly 30 men, he cut a path through the wilderness until he reached the Kentucky River, where a town named Boonesborough was established.

Though life in Boonesborough was quite dangerous, Boone moved his entire family—his wife and 10 children—to the developing colony. At one point, Shawnee men kidnapped his daughter Jemina. Boone was able to rescue her after two days, but the attacks kept coming, and Boone himself was captured once more in 1778. Managing to evade death by impressing the tribe's chief with his hunting abilities, the Shawnee adopted him as one of their own, and he lived among them for several months before escaping.

By 1799, Boone was ready to leave Kentucky. He and several family members moved to present-day Missouri, where he remained until his death. Though his actual life story reads like a work of fiction, there is one key detail the histories consistently get wrong: Boone is famously depicted wearing a coonskin cap, but the truth is he didn't really wear them—he actually preferred one made of beaver felt.

GEORGE MALLORY

1886-1924

-

George Mallory made one of the first attempts to climb Mount Everest, and also played a part in one of the 20th century's greatest mysteries.

George Mallory was an experienced climber who was lauded by his peers for his catlike ability to scale a mountain. He was also a member of the British Alpine Club's first expedition to Mount Everest, in 1921, as well as the second one, in 1922. Both attempts were unsuccessful, though each try provided the club with useful insight.

In 1924, Mallory was asked to return for a third attempt. He was reluctant at first, but eventually he agreed. Along with a less experienced climber named Andrew Irvine, Mallory began the ascent on June 6. The first leg of the journey was particularly difficult, as the winds were stronger and the snows were deeper than expected. Following a brief stay at a camp 26,800 feet up the mountain, the two men began climbing toward the summit as soon as the fog cleared. The date was June 8—the last day either man was seen alive.

Years went by with no indication as to what befell Mallory and Irvine, or if they ever even made it to the top. Speculation swirled regarding their fate. Did they freeze to death? Did a patch of ice cause them to slip and fall? Was a yeti involved? Interest was piqued, not just among mountaineers, but the general public as well.

> **"What we get from this adventure is just sheer joy. And joy is, after all, the end of life. We do not live to eat and make money. We eat and make money to be able to live. That is what life means and what life is for."**
> **—George Mallory**

In 1999, after 75 years, the exceptionally well-preserved body of Mallory was found at an altitude of 26,760 feet. Evidence suggests that his death was caused by injuries resulting from a bad fall. The body of Irvine was never found, nor was the camera the men took with them on the expedition. It was hoped that through photographs experts would be able to determine whether or not they reached the summit of Everest, but alas, it was not meant to be.

WILD BILL HICKOK

1837-1876

-

Prior to Manifest Destiny, "Wild Bill" lived a free lifestyle as an expert marksman and skilled fighter, solidifying his reputation as one of America's legendary cowboys.

Following the Louisiana Purchase in 1803, eager Americans were free to venture west of the Mississippi River and conduct themselves without fear of government prosecution. That is, until Manifest Destiny caught up with the free-spirited cowpokes and the last contiguous state was admitted in 1912. From that point on, all those who chose to settle in the country were required to live obediently under U.S. law. Still, the heyday of America's Old West lasted for most of the 19th century, and few enjoyed that time more than the notorious "Wild Bill" Hickok, who never lived to see the day when man had no farther west to go.

Hickok's reputation began to grow in 1861. No version of the story has ever been verified, but the first known iteration, reported by *Harper's New Monthly Magazine* in 1867, painted Hickok as an expert marksman and skilled fighter. According to *Harper's*, Hickok was leading a group of Union soldiers through Nebraska in 1861 when he decided to stop and visit a friend. Shortly thereafter, a group of Confederate soldiers ambushed Hickok when he let his guard down.

Legend has it that Hickok responded quickly, shooting and

killing six of the soldiers before being tackled by three others. He managed to wriggle out from underneath the men while gouging them with his knife. Though historians would later debate several aspects of this tale, the myth had already spread far and wide, earning Hickok fear and respect.

Hickok went on to lend his skills to the likes of General Winfield Scott Hancock and Colonel George Armstrong Custer. He served as sheriff in a little Kansas town called Hays City, where he shot and killed several men who were foolish enough to engage in a shootout. By 1871, Hickok had seen enough of Hays City, and decided to take his law enforcement career down to the Abilene, Texas. As a marshal, he continued to gun down criminals, his legend growing with each encounter. Everyone knew enough to stay out of Hickok's way—until he took up residence in the famous town of Deadwood, South Dakota.

In 1876, Hickok agreed to become a peace officer of the prosperous mining town. By that time, however, his eyesight had begun to fail him, along with his marksmanship. Word of the great Hickok's diminishing abilities spread, and on August 2 a man named Jack McCall took his shot.

Hickok was playing poker in a saloon when McCall sneaked up from behind and shot him in the head. It is said that Hickok held a pair of black aces, a pair of black eights, and one unknown card, a combination now known as the "Dead Man's Hand."

ALEXANDRA DAVID-NÉEL
1868-1969
–

Armed with an arsenal of "magic spells" and an automatic pistol,
Alexandra David-Néel traveled west toward the "place of the gods"
with her 15-year-old companion, Aphur Yongden.

By the time Alexandra David-Néel decided to sneak into the forbidden city of Lhasa, she already had a firm grasp on all things mystic. David-Néel had previously spent many years in Tibet, despite the region being closed off to foreigners. She studied Buddhism with the local monks and even had the opportunity to meet the Dalai Lama, making her the first Western woman to do so. With the help of these skilled teachers, David-Néel became versed in the ways of mindfulness, to the point that she is rumored to have once summoned a thunderstorm out of the blue in order to scare off a gang of thieves. Having already achieved the supposed status of "the first Buddhist in France," she set her sights on a seemingly unattainable goal: entering Lhasa, the religious capital of Tibet and home to many sacred Buddhist sites.

Armed with an arsenal of "magic spells" and an automatic pistol, David-Néel traveled west toward the "place of the gods" with her 15-year-old companion, Aphur Yongden. Though she had already traveled extensively, few things could have prepared her for the hardships she was about to endure.

The journey required them to don disguises, so they smeared

their faces with soot and wore the traditional clothing of Tibetan pilgrims. Camouflaged to the best of their ability, David-Néel and Yongden set off during the winter of 1923. The route took them across a treacherous 19,000-foot mountain pass, a task made even more dangerous by the freezing, icy conditions.

"Ever since I was five years old, a tiny precocious child of Paris, I wished to move out of the narrow limits in which, like all children of my age, I was then kept. I craved to go beyond the garden gate, to follow the road that passed it by, and to set out for the Unknown."
—Alexandra David-Néel

All things considered, the trip was successful, but it was not without hiccups. On one occasion, David-Néel and Yongden found themselves without any means of sustenance. They were forced to consume strips of leather from their hiking boots, which had been boiled in water to make them more tender. But after four hard months, they finally arrived in Lhasa.

David-Néel and Yongden managed to remain in the city for two months before being discovered and kicked out of Tibet. David-Néel would go on to legally adopt Yongden as her son, and lived to the impressive age of 101, giving credence to the belief that mindfulness can improve physical well-being.

ELLA MAILLART

1903-1997

-

Having established herself as a notable figure in the world of exploration writing, Maillart set out to travel from Beijing to Kashmir, a trip that would take her through forbidden territory and across vast deserts.

Ella Maillart never had any illusions about her skills as a writer. Although some might consider her prose beautifully minimalist, at the time of its publication it was widely condemned for its lack of flourish. But these criticisms did not bother Maillart. In her mind, the writing was always secondary to the travel.

Maillart's interest in leaving her home in Switzerland budded during adolescence. The horrific acts that occurred during the First World War incited in her a strong desire to get out of Europe. Her first substantial journey occurred in 1930, when she obtained a Russian visa in order to study film in Moscow.

While in Russia, Maillart decided to trek across the Caucasus Mountains, and following her return from the region she made her first attempt to enter the world of experiential journalism. Her initial article was rejected based on her lack of writing skills, but she was not discouraged by the criticism. She continued to practice and expand the content of her article, so much so that it would eventually become the basis for her first two books: *Among Russian Youth: From Moscow to the Caucasus* and *Turkestan Solo*, both of which were published in 1932.

Having established herself as a notable figure in the world of exploration writing, Maillart decided that she was ready to take on something of greater significance. She had previously made the acquaintance of Peter Fleming, a fellow adventurer and journalist with whom she believed a particular mission could be accomplished. Maillart suggested that they travel from Beijing to Kashmir, a trip that would cover 3,500 miles, taking them through forbidden territory and across vast deserts. Fleming agreed, and the two set off in 1935, with Maillart carrying little more than two pounds of marmalade, a rifle, writing paper, and her camera.

Maillart's fortitude proved invaluable to the pair, as Fleming had far less survival knowledge. It was Maillart who could build a shelter, find and prepare food, and maintain clean supplies; it was she who was able to withstand freezing winds and walk up to 14 miles with no sustenance; it quickly became apparent that if the two were to survive, they would have to follow Maillart's lead. The seven-month trip provided them with a stark look at early 20th-century life in Turkistan, and both kept detailed records of what they witnessed. Maillart described one particularly resonant scene: a child mingling with newborn lambs on the bare floor of a yurt, both the infant and animals coated in the fluid from the birthing canal.

Fleming and Maillart each developed the records they kept into long-form accounts of the journey. And though Fleming's account was initially lauded as exhibiting more skillful storytelling, it is Maillart's matter-of-fact version that has stood the test of time.

CARL AKELEY

1864–1926

-

A hunter and eventually an activist for wild animals in the Congo,
Carl Akeley pioneered the field of taxidermy.

New York City's American Museum of Natural History famously features lifelike replicas of exotic animals from all over the world. Life-size hippos, lions, and elephants are posed in detailed dioramas of their natural habitats so that visitors can get a glimpse of how wildlife lives. Amazingly, these animal models are created using the actual skin and bones of their real-life counterparts, which required hunters and taxidermists to track down these large, often dangerous creatures. And that's where Carl Akeley came in.

Not only skilled in safari-going, Akeley also pioneered the modern techniques of taxidermy. Prior to his involvement, animal skins were just stuffed with anything that would prop them up, which often resulted in lumpy, unrealistic versions of the original. Akeley entered the field with a deep understanding of anatomy and began creating finely sculpted animal molds. He would then carefully apply the animal's skin so that it rested smoothly on the model. To this day, taxidermists still utilize these methods.

More compelling, though, was Akeley's involvement in the actual gathering of animals. On one occasion, while on expedition in Somaliland in 1896, Akeley was out hunting ostriches for the Field Museum in Chicago. He fired blindly into the high grass and, much to his surprise, came into contact with a large leopard. The big cat pounced on him and they both fell to the ground. A scuffle commenced and Akeley miraculously came out on top: legend has it, he strangled the leopard to death with his bare hands.

Later in his career, Akeley would feel conflicted about his role in the pursuit of wildlife and developed moral objections to what he saw as the senseless slaying of beasts. And so he convinced the Belgian government to establish a sanctuary for wild animals in the Congo.

ARON RALSTON

1975-PRESENT

-

After a boulder landed directly on his arm in eastern Utah, Aron Ralston made a decision that no one else could fathom.

Aron Ralston's story of survival has achieved legendary status since it occurred in 2003, and has since been immortalized in the popular biopic *127 Hours.* Though his tale continues to inspire countless people, the specific details of how it happened are not for the faint of heart.

An experienced mountaineer, Ralston found himself hiking alone through eastern Utah in late April.

As he was climbing down a narrow crevice, a large rock

tumbled down after him. It landed directly on his right arm, pinning it to the canyon's wall. Realizing that the boulder was immovable, Ralston started to panic.

His intended journey was quite short, so he only had one gallon of water with him and few other supplies. Days and nights went by as Ralston became increasingly delirious. By the fifth day, he was forced to drink his own urine to stay hydrated. It became apparent that he only had two choices: die or do something drastic.

He had already considered cutting off his right forearm with the multitool he brought along, but it wasn't until the sixth day that he realized how it could be done. Using the weight of the boulder, he snapped the bone in half. Then, using his small blade, he began the violent process of cutting through his flesh. Before long, Ralston was free of the boulder. He was rescued shortly after climbing out of the canyon, an embodiment of mankind's need to survive.

Upon returning to civilization, Ralston's decision to go out alone without telling anyone else was criticized. After all, had he just informed one person of his planned excursion, his rescue likely would have been expedited.

GEORGE DONNER

1784-1847

-

As was the case with George Donner and the "Donner Party,"
sometimes there is just no other option than cannibalism.

Like many other Americans, George Donner dreamed of the potential wealth that California had to offer. So, in April 1846, he, his brother, and a group of 90 men and women set out west from Springfield, Illinois.

The journey from Illinois to Fort Bridger, Wyoming, was rather pleasant. After all, the trail had been well worn by the many westward travelers who passed over it. However, upon arriving in Fort Bridger, the group decided to depart from the beaten path in order to take a shortcut through the Wasatch Mountains, which they were told would shave 400 miles off of their trip. This route was proposed to Donner by the trail guide Lansford Hastings, who had made the trip before. Hastings told Donner to make camp at the mouth of Weber Canyon and wait for him to return, at which time he would lead them through the rugged mountain pass.

After eight days of waiting and no sign of Hastings, the Donner Party sent a messenger through the pass in search of the trail guide. The messenger returned several days later with a note from Hastings instructing them to follow the trail without him, as he would not be able to meet them for some time. Donner and the party complied, but they quickly realized that the trail was much less welcoming than they were led to believe. Boulders and thick trees made navigation difficult and progress slow. By the time they made it through the mountains they were 18 days behind schedule, and that much closer to winter.

When they reached the Sierra Nevada Mountain crossing, it was already October, and on the 28th of that month, heavy snowfall began. The high mountain pass was blocked, trapping the party in the wilderness. After being stranded for three weeks, they had eaten all of their food. They began to eat the charred bones of their pack animals, along with twigs, leaves, and dirt. But it wasn't until December 25, 1846 that the true horror of their situation set in.

Desperate, the group cooked and ate the remains of one of the fallen party members. They began cutting up and rationing the corpses, going as far as to label the meat so as to prevent a parent from accidentally consuming the flesh of their own child.

After five months, the first rescue party showed up. Three more parties were sent in to carry out the survivors, of which there were 45. George Donner's body was found with his skull split open and his brain removed from the cavity.

MIYAMOTO MUSASHI

1584-1645

-

In order to determine who was the superior warrior, Miyamoto Musashi and Sasaki Kaojiro agreed to a fight that would take place on a small island off of Japan's coast.

In feudal Japan, a *rōnin* was a wandering samurai without a lord, either due to misdeeds on their part or the lord's death. By the 17th century, the number of *rōnins* in Japan had spiked, and most roamed the countryside without a clear purpose. Miyamoto Musashi killed his first man at age 13, en route to becoming Japan's greatest living swordsman. By the end of his life, though, his main quest was not for violence, but knowledge.

Musashi became a *rōnin* in 1600 after losing the Battle of Sekigahara. From that point on, he committed himself to perfecting his fighting technique. He traveled across Japan, engaging in duel after duel, most notably with the members of the Yoshioka clan, a group of swordsmen who worked for the Ashikaga family.

The first duel, initiated by Musashi, was with Yoshioka Seijuro, and took place on March 8, 1604, in North Kyoto. It was at this time that Musashi began developing his strategy of arriving to the fight late, thereby angering his opponent and throwing them off-balance. The strategy worked, and he won the duel almost instantly. The second duel was with Yoshioka

Denshichiro and took place in the Higashiyama district of Kyoto. And once again, arriving late, Musashi easily won. The final duel was with Yoshioka Matashichiro, and this time his opponent had something else planned for Musashi.

The duel was, per Matashichiro's request, to take place at night, an unusual choice. Somewhat suspicious, Musashi decided to show up early and watch the rendezvous point from a hidden location. He witnessed Matashichiro arrive, followed by a party of well-armed soldiers who hid in various spots surrounding the duel location. Quickly, Musashi sprung from his hiding spot, ran toward Matashichiro, and chopped off his head before fleeing through a rice field.

By this point, he had established himself as one of the land's best swordsmen. However, in 1612, there was one other whose skill was said to equal Musashi's: Sasaki Kojiro.

In order to determine who was the superior warrior, the two agreed to a fight that would take place on a small island off of Japan's coast. In his usual fashion, Musashi showed up late in order to throw off his opponent. Kojiro was enraged when the duel began, and his technique greatly suffered. Musashi, using the skills and knowledge that he had attained in his travels, quickly killed Kojiro. In doing so, he had an awakening. Musashi vowed to no longer be a dealer of death in one-on-one combat. With the exception of his participation in the Shimabara Rebellion of 1637, he spent the rest of his life living peacefully as a teacher and writer.

HANNIBAL BARCA

247 BCE–UNKNOWN

-

*During the Second Punic War, Hannibal Barca led a massive
Carthaginian army of soldiers and elephants across the
Alps in order to meet Roman forces in battle.*

Considered by many to be one of the greatest military minds
of all time, Hannibal Barca had no shortage of war stories.
However, one always seems to stand out: the time he led his
troops and elephants over the Alps.

The move was something of a preliminary strike. The
Carthaginians had considerable control over regions in Spain
and North Africa, and Hannibal wanted to make sure that
the Romans were unable to conquer those strongholds. The
Roman naval power was unparalleled, and they supplemented
that power with fortifications all over the roads approaching
modern-day Italy. Hannibal circumvented those roads by
bringing his elephants over the frozen mountains, rousing other
conquered groups along the way.

The question of where exactly Hannibal procured the
elephants has been a topic of debate; some historians believe
he used Indian elephants while others claim that African
elephants were more likely. Regardless of the species, the big-
eared beasts were certainly effective in combat. The very sight of
them frightened enemy soldiers, and once they engaged in battle
their power became realized. The elephants could gouge men

with their tusks while trampling others with their massive legs; however, it is believed that only one of the thirty-eight elephants survived the war.

Though Carthage was eventually defeated after the 17-year war, Hannibal's tactics have been taught in military schools ever since. His bold thinking consistently kept the mighty Roman Empire on its heels, reacting rather than asserting its own power. In the end, even his great enemy gave Hannibal his due, according to the Roman historian Livy: "there was no leader in whom the soldiers placed more confidence or under whom they showed more daring."

JAMES BECKWOURTH

1798–1866

-

Born a slave, James Beckwourth became a man for whom boundaries were truly meaningless.

While many African Americans helped pioneer the American frontier, few of them thoroughly documented their exploits. Accomplished mountain man James Beckwourth, however, had the foresight to write down his adventures as they happened.

Beckwourth was born into slavery, but by the time he became an adult he had been declared a free man. In need of work, he headed for the then-developing West. Fur trapping was a lucrative option at the time, so in 1824 he joined up with the third William Ashley expedition in the Rocky Mountains. Conditions were unforgiving, and the group was constantly staving off both Native American attacks and starvation. Still, Beckwourth felt he had found a calling, and he spent the next several years pursuing it.

After the Ashley expedition, Beckwourth began trapping with the Crow Indians of Wyoming. He fit in so well that he joined the tribe, though the degree to which he was a true Crow is uncertain. We do know that he learned their language and customs, and he claimed to have taken multiple Crow wives during his time with the Crow. But it was not to last; Beckwourth left the tribe behind in order to continue his nomadic life.

By the end of his life, Beckwourth had traveled all over. He fought with a Missouri volunteer military force and played a role in Florida's Seminole War under future president Zachary Taylor. By 1840, Beckwourth decided he had seen enough of Florida and resumed his life of travel. Eventually, he settled in Colorado, where he would take part in the Sand Creek Massacre of 1864: a brutal attack on a Native American village, which resulted in the senseless mutilation of dozens of women and children. As with many claims made by Beckwourth, the actual role he played in the massacre is disputed, though his very knowledge of it seems to indicate some level of involvement.

ROY CHAPMAN ANDREWS

1884–1960

-

In 1922, Roy Chapman Andrews was assigned to lead his first significant expedition to the Gobi Desert, an adventure that solidified him as a world-class explorer.

Roy Chapman Andrews always knew he wanted to be an explorer, and as he got older he realized that the best place to pursue this career would be at the American Museum of Natural History. So as soon as he graduated college, he traveled to New York and asked for a job, which is exactly what he got . . . as a janitor.

Andrews did not let his low rank and pay discourage him. He displayed vigor in all duties and consistently demonstrated his interest in the museum's subjects. Before long, the staff took notice of his abilities, and Andrews quickly rose through the ranks. In 1922, he was assigned to lead his first significant expedition to the Gobi Desert, an adventure that solidified him as a world-class explorer.

This trip to the Gobi yielded several significant discoveries: fragments of dinosaur bone and a number of complete dinosaur skeletons, as well as fossilized insects, findings that indicated the desert was rife with specimens. Once their study was complete, Andrews and his team resolved to return the following year to continue their work.

In 1923, they went back and promptly began digging. After

some time, a small skull was uncovered, which would later be identified as belonging to one of the earliest known mammals, a thrilling discovery at that time. As if that wasn't enough excitement, Andrews's team then discovered something that permanently altered the scientific discourse: fossilized dinosaur eggs. Yes, it was assumed that dinosaurs had laid eggs, but prior to this discovery there was no concrete evidence. Now the method of dinosaur reproduction was certain.

> **"I was born to be an explorer. There never was any decision to make. I couldn't be anything else and be happy, the desire to see new places, to discover new facts—the curiosity of life always has been a resistless driving force to me."**
> **—Roy Chapman Andrews**

Over time, Andrews conducted various other studies in the Gobi Desert, until his work became restricted by tensions in Mongolia and China. But his meteoric rise was not yet complete. In 1934, Andrews was named director of the American Museum of Natural History, a position he held until January 1, 1942, when he decided it was finally time to retire. He and his wife moved to California, where he spent his remaining years writing about his life of adventure.

THOMAS JEFFERSON

1743–1826

-

Halfway through his time abroad, Thomas Jefferson decided to expand his worldliness by traveling 1,200 miles through southern France and northern Italy.

Today, most people travel for one of two reasons: business or pleasure. In Thomas Jefferson's case, it was a bit of both. Before becoming the third president of the United States, Jefferson visited Europe on a number of occasions, and among his goals abroad was discovering and creating transatlantic trade channels in order to import his favorite indulgence: wine.

Jefferson lived in Paris from 1784 to 1789, a period he considered to be the most memorable of his life. Halfway through those five years, in 1787, he decided to expand his worldliness by traveling 1,200 miles through southern France and northern Italy. Exploring mostly by himself—as a private citizen, not a diplomat—Jefferson visited Champagne, Burgundy, Beaujolais, and Bordeaux, traveling by horse-drawn carriage and sampling vintage after vintage in an effort to better understand what makes a successful vineyard. In addition to consuming his share of whites and reds, he became well-versed in the various methods of optimizing soil and growing grapes. Overwhelmed by the rice produced by Italian agriculture, he smuggled a sack of it out of the country, an offense punishable by death. In Jefferson's opinion, it was a worthy risk.

On the road, Jefferson took an almost excessive pleasure in meeting locals. He would, in his words, "ferret" people out of their homes and discuss their lives in great detail before sampling their breads, snooping through their homes, and even laying on their beds; all of this simply to gather information.

By the time Jefferson had returned to Paris, he had effectively become a self-taught oenophile; he understood the winemaking process from planting and pruning to bottling and selling. Though these accomplishments are rightfully overshadowed by his many achievements as a founding father, Jefferson's knowledge of wine proved indispensable to America's future as a country of growers and drinkers.

EWART GROGAN

1874-1967

-

It wasn't Grogan's imperialist contributions that brought him fame—it was his storybook attempt to marry the beautiful Gertrude Watt, whose disapproving father rejected Grogan's overtures for her hand.

Everyone likes a love story. A dashing suitor, a beautiful damsel, a disapproving relative: it's a time-tested formula for capturing one's imagination. This is as true in real life as it is in fiction. Of course, life isn't a fairy tale, and Prince Charming usually has his share of skeletons in the closet. Such is the case for Englishman Ewart Grogan, national heartthrob and ruthless imperialist.

Grogan was only 19 when he enlisted in the Chartered Company, a division of fighters in the Second Matabele War in South Africa. The hardships, lack of food, and brutal violence he endured while fighting affected his psyche, and Grogan came away from the war more racist than ever, certain that Britain was Africa's savior. And few "saviors" were as well liked as Grogan. With his square jaw and handsome eyes, he was considered quite dashing. And, most importantly, he was in love with the beautiful Gertrude Watt.

Watt's disapproving stepfather rejected Grogan's overtures, and in an effort to gain the man's respect, Grogan got an idea: he vowed to travel the entire length of Africa, from Cape Town to Cairo. Should he succeed, he imagined, Watt's stepfather would agree to bless their marriage. It had never been done, and so Watt's stepfather agreed.

His participation in the invasion of South Africa finished, Grogan set off on his quest at the age of 24. By land and by water, he traveled for two years. By his account, he always treated the locals with respect, only resorting to violence in the name of self-defense. He claims that he was attacked by warriors in Rwanda and chased by cannibals in eastern Congo; of course, there is no concrete evidence to support this claim.

Though the journey was long, it seemed to go fairly smoothly. Grogan would grow quite ill at times and be forced to go without food for extended stretches, but ultimately he came away from the trip unscathed. He reached Cairo and returned to London, where he won Watt's hand and became celebrated throughout the nation.

This is usually where the storybook ends. But in reality, it's important to remember that Grogan was a violent racist, however much he loved his bride. After their marriage, the couple returned to Africa and Grogan continued his imperialist pursuits, famously pummeling three indigenous people to the brink of death on one occasion. Why? "Because I wanted to," he responded.

BRUCE CHATWIN

1940-1989

-

Among his many tales, Bruce Chatwin is perhaps best known for his journey in Patagonia.

Among storytellers, the fiction writer has one great advantage: omnipotence. They can mold, break down, and re-create their stories and characters until their message is properly—if not always clearly—conveyed. The nonfiction author faces a much more difficult task. Only with ironclad facts can they try and create a book that is more than the sum of its parts, something that not only informs but also inspires. British-born Bruce Chatwin accomplished this time and again by venturing into foreign lands, armed with the mind of a scholar and the soul of a poet.

Among his many tales, Chatwin is perhaps best known for his journey in Patagonia. As the story has it, this legendary journey was inspired by a childhood trip to visit his grandparents, during which he became infatuated by a strange fossil that his grandmother claimed to be a piece of brontosaurus from a cave in the Chilean region of Patagonia.

By 1974, Chatwin had already established himself as both a writer and an archaeologist, and he felt ready to make his first significant journey. He left his job at London's *Sunday Times Magazine* and made the trip to Patagonia. What followed was an emotional journey that changed him forever. Wanting to find his own "brontosaurus piece," some small totem that might serve as a physical manifestation of the fantastic unknown, Chatwin simply sat back and observed.

Detailing scenes as trivial as a boy in a sealskin hat or as historically significant as the final days of Butch Cassidy, Chatwin spoke with all manner of people and wrote down their stories, moving from one place to another in the land he had long imagined visiting. The result was a mosaic of seemingly unrelated tales, woven together with by a thin thread of nomadism.

Chatwin would continue traveling and writing until his death in 1989, but it was his first book, *In Patagonia*, that made him one of the world's leading voices on wanderlust. His life was itself an ode to exploration, and his beautiful prose captured the world's magnificence in ways few travel writers have before or since.

PAUL REVERE

1735-1818

-

Little did Paul Revere know that just 15 years after joining the revolutionaries he would make a journey that solidified his legacy as a hero of the American Revolution.

Boston was a hive of revolutionary activity during the 1760s. The economic situation was bleak, thanks to egregious British tax policies. This climate, however, led to the first whispers of rebellion among Bostonians, and even citizens of higher privilege took notice. Paul Revere, a well-off master silversmith, understood that if relations with England did not change, even he would be in danger of losing his livelihood. And so, like any other sensible colonist, he joined up with the revolutionaries. Little did Revere know that 15 years later he would make a journey that solidified his legacy as a hero of the American Revolution.

At first, Revere's political involvement was somewhat minimal. He primarily contributed to Samuel Adams's campaign for independence by acting as a courier. However, as tensions began to rise between England and the colonies, so too did the need for capable men, and Revere was called upon to participate in covert affairs. He was tasked with spying on enemy soldiers and reporting on their actions. This required a great deal of stealth, and Revere's initial successes brought him an increased confidence.

By 1773, Revere was a full-fledged patriot, steadfast in his dedication to the cause. This commitment was on full display in one of the revolution's early transformative moments: the Boston Tea Party. Three British ships intended to sell shipments of tea to the colonies at unfair prices, which was only allowed to happen because of the recently passed British Tea Act. As a direct response, on the night of December 16, Revere and the other men dressed up as Native Americans, boarded the ships, and threw all of the tea overboard. This act pushed the two parties closer to conflict.

Just two years later, the American Revolutionary War began, and in a way, it began with Revere. His job was quite simple: remain in Boston and keep an eye out for invading British troops. He had devised a plan to signal to his allies using lanterns placed in a bell tower: "one if by land, two if by sea," as he famously said. However, Revere soon learned that the British forces planned on marching inland toward the town of Lexington, where John Hancock and Samuel Adams were stationed with military supplies.

Revere took it upon himself to ride to Lexington and warn his fellow soldiers. He rode long into the night, arriving just past midnight. His entrance caused quite a commotion, and one guard told him to keep the noise down, to which he replied, "Noise! You'll have noise enough before long! The regulars are coming out!" Once Revere was finally able to convince Hancock that the news he carried was true, they got to work preparing for war.

Though Revere's contribution to the Revolutionary War

was significant, he did not become the folk hero he is today until 1861, when Henry Wadsworth Longfellow wrote his famous poem "Paul Revere's Ride." The story of his journey on horseback has been told and retold countless times, and, though the details are often inflated for the sake of the drama, the true story is plenty dramatic in its own right.

JOHN CHAPMAN

1774–1845

-

John Chapman was not some magical wanderer spreading delicious apples around America, as the story so frequently goes; rather, Chapman was a businessman, and his primary product was alcohol, not fruit.

The American apple: a crisp, juicy, sometimes sweet, sometimes tart, fruit. The garnish on a favorite teacher's desk; the finishing touch in a blue-collar lunch pail. But American apples were not always as delectable and pretty as they are today. Like most fruits, it required an intensive process of trial-and-error before its cultivation was perfected. Among the people who contributed to this process was none other than John Chapman, or as he is better known, Johnny Appleseed.

The legend of Chapman has been wildly embellished over the years, in part due to the fairy-tale-like portrayal his life has received in various movies over the years. The truth is,

Chapman was not some magical wanderer spreading delicious apples around America. He was a businessman, and his primary product was alcohol, not fruit.

American apples of the late 18th and early 19th centuries were much less edible than they are today. Tough and sour, they were more commonly used to make hard cider than, say, an apple pie. This was not done out of ignorance, but rather practicality. The process of growing tasty apples is quite involved, whereas cider apples are grown simply by planting a seed in soil. Most importantly, edible apples were not in such high demand as hard cider.

Chapman's story begins with a 1792 deal made by the Ohio Company of Associates. As a way to encourage settlers to develop the territory beyond Ohio's first permanent settlement, anyone who agreed to plant a minimum of 50 apple trees and 20 peach trees on their property would be granted 100 acres of land. Chapman realized that if he did all the heavy lifting by traveling across the countryside and planting vast apple orchards, he could claim the land from the government and sell it for a profit. So that's exactly what he did. He journeyed from Pennsylvania to Illinois, spreading apple seeds all along the way. His particular method of planting ensured that the produced apples would be perfect for crafting apple cider, which was the drink of choice on the frontier at the time, not only for its intoxicating effect but also because potable water was not always readily available. Wherever Chapman traveled, apple orchards would spring up in his wake, and happy settlers would soon be swimming in the hard stuff.

Though many of Chapman's trees were chopped down following his death in 1845, his methods were not forgotten. The Roman process of apple grafting produces edible fruits by combining different seed varieties; thanks to the extremely sour apples Chapman produced, the other end of the spectrum was established as well. And through a process of elimination, modern farmers were able to create an apple that landed pleasantly in the middle of the spectrum: the Red Delicious that we know and love today.

BY SEA (AND RIVER)

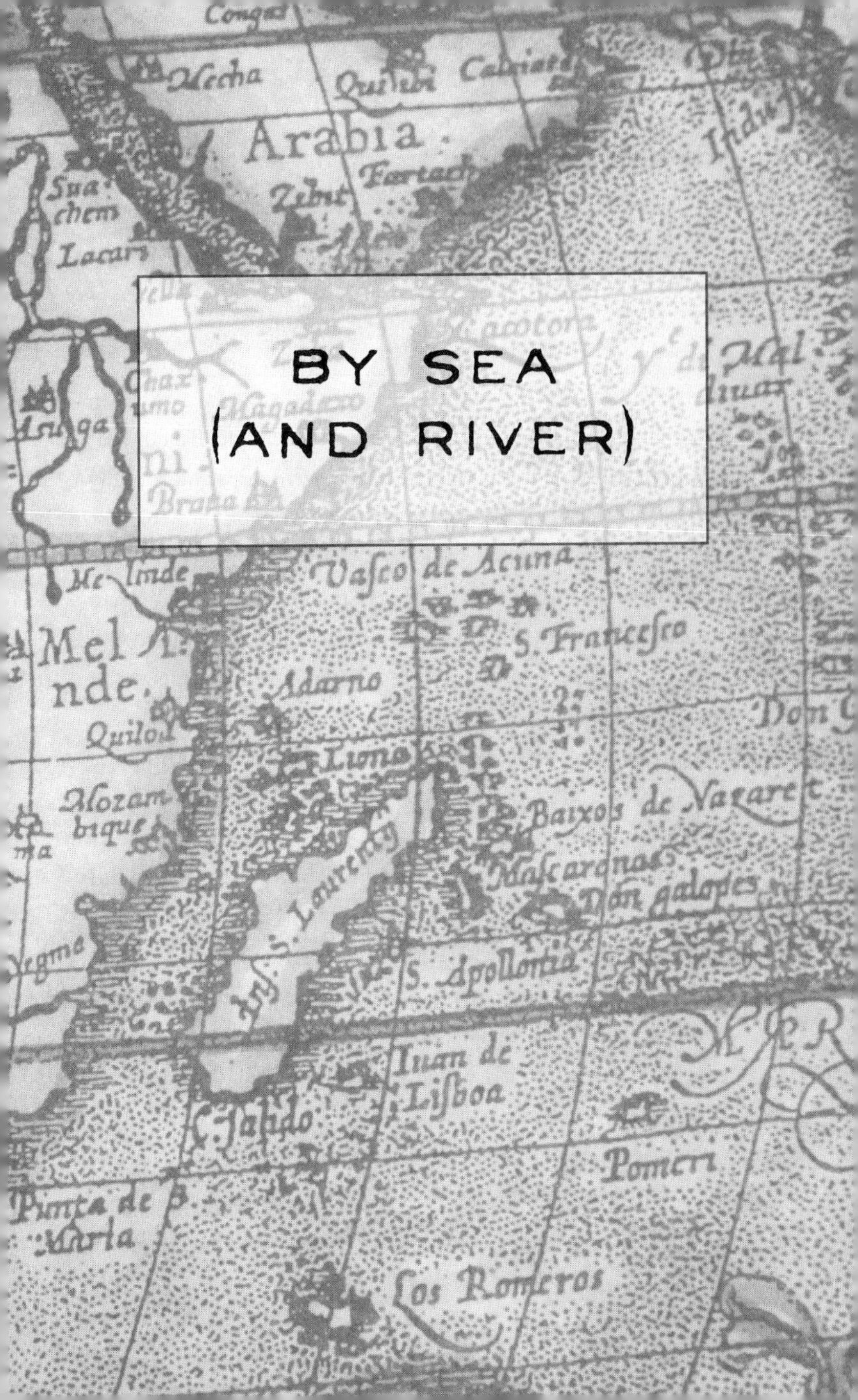

FERDINAND MAGELLAN

1480-1521

-

This Portuguese explorer led the crew that first circumnavigated the globe—but not without a little mutiny thrown in.

Ferdinand Magellan departed from Sanlúcar de Barrameda, Spain, in September 1519 as the head of five ships and roughly 265 men. The fleet, later known as the Armada de Molucca, had been commissioned by King Charles I, who'd appointed Magellan as the voyage's captain-general. The fleet set out to sail west around South America and establish a passage that could be used as a trade route to the Spice Islands, an archipelago in eastern Indonesia now known as the Maluku Islands.

Magellan was Portuguese, but after King Manuel I denied him the resources needed to make the trip, he traveled to Spain to petition King Charles. Spain and Portugal were historically rivals, and Magellan had a hard time gaining the trust and respect of his Spanish crewmembers. Upon making their first stop of the trip at the Canary Islands, Magellan received a letter from his father-in-law that warned of potential mutiny at the hands of Juan de Cartagena, one of Magellan's captains. A short time after departing the Canary Islands, Magellan realized his father-in-law might have been correct. Once Cartagena ceased obeying him entirely, Magellan sentenced him to the brig and the journey continued.

Magellan and his armada crossed the Atlantic and made

several stops along the east coast of South America as they continued to travel southward in search of a passage that would take them to the Spice Islands. The fleet eventually hit a terrible storm that forced Magellan to dock in South America on March 30, 1520, where he set up to wait out harsh conditions. This camp would come to be known as Port St. Julian.

As rations depleted in the camp and conditions grew worse, so too did the crew's morale. Despite the hardships that had already been endured, Magellan insisted on continuing the search for a passage through South America. Since the crewmembers already disliked Magellan for his nationality, and the mission appeared futile, it was not difficult for Juan de Cartagena to gain the support of a few sailors despite his confinement. With their help, Cartagena escaped his cell while the ships were still at port. He rallied three of Magellan's five ship captains to his cause, beginning his mutiny in earnest. But Magellan was ready for the insurrection.

Wary of potential collusion, Magellan had managed to intercept messages between the ship's captains. With advanced knowledge of the plan, Magellan was able to recapture two of the three ships, resulting in the third ship's surrender. As punishment for their betrayal, the mutineers were sentenced to hard labor, marooned, tortured, or executed.

With his men in line and the weather easing up, Magellan continued his mission. The smallest ship in the fleet was sent ahead to search for the mouth of a passage that would take them through South America, but it was shipwrecked during the search. The entire crew was rescued, but the ship could not be salvaged.

In October 1520, a passage was finally discovered. Unfortunately, it was around this time that the largest ship in the fleet, the *San Antonio*, decided to turn around and sail back to Spain, taking many men and supplies with it. Only three ships were left to continue the journey.

What Magellan and his men called the Estrecho de Todos los Santos, now known as the Strait of Magellan, took 38 days to navigate. And that was nothing compared to the trip they were about to endure.

On the other side of the Estrecho de Todos los Santos was what Magellan referred to as the Mar Pacifico (Pacific Ocean). Magellan, believing the world was smaller than it actually is, underestimated the amount of time it would take to cross this ocean and reach the Spice Islands. It ended up taking 98 days. Over the course of this journey many men died of disease or starvation.

Magellan and his crew reached the Philippines in March 1521. Magellan was eager to interact with the local populations of the island, and despite receiving no orders to do so, he took it upon himself to forcibly convert them to Christianity. Many of the island natives did not resist, but others were unwilling to accept this new religion and submit to the rule of Spain. Chief Datu Lapu-Lapu of Mactan resisted Magellan's orders, leading to violence between both groups. Greatly underestimating the abilities of Datu Lapu-Lapu and the Mactan fighters, Magellan only took 60 men into the battle. This proved to be a huge mistake: one that resulted in Magellan's death.

The rest of the crew remained on the ships, and saw no

reason to send reinforcements to aid their captain-general. Instead, they continued the mission. Despite Magellan's death, the Armada de Molucca was able to visit the Spice Islands and successfully return to Spain, making them the first men to completely circumnavigate the globe.

CHARLES DARWIN
1809-1882
-
This English naturalist developed the theory of evolution after exploring the Galápagos Islands, changing the study of biology forever.

The evolutionary process is a fundamental fact of life, something that seems so basic and obvious that it is hard to imagine a society that was not aware of it. Prior to July 1858, however, this was the case.

In hindsight, it seems that Charles Darwin was destined to theorize evolution. His grandfather Erasmus Darwin had published a book called *Zoonomia*, which hypothesized that different species could "transmute" into one another. This theory of transmutation served as a sort of jumping-off point for Darwin once he began his studies.

While at Cambridge, Darwin shifted his focus between various fields: medicine, religion, and biology. Eventually, his predilection for studying living things led one of his professors to recommend that Darwin join Captain Robert FitzRoy on his 1831 voyage to chart the coastline of South America aboard the HMS *Beagle*.

The purpose of the *Beagle*'s voyage was scientific in nature, although there was no specific goal in mind. The crew visited four different continents; Darwin took copious notes on local wildlife and geology. During his time on board, he had little to do besides think about everything he'd observed.

It was in 1835 that the *Beagle* reached the Galápagos Islands. Despite what many may think, Darwin did not experience a sudden aha moment while there; he simply wrote down everything he saw, just as he had before. However, the Galápagos does hold great significance in the development of Darwin's theory, for it was there that he closely studied various tortoises, mockingbirds, and, most famously, finches.

> "What are the boasted glories of the illimitable ocean. A tedious waste, a desert of water."
> —Charles Darwin

Darwin returned home with his head full of new ideas, albeit young ones. He did not quite know what he had observed, but he was skirting around the edges of a grand formulation. In examining the different breeds of finches, he was able to conclude that there was a correlation between beak shape and rate of survival. The finches that possessed beaks that better allowed them to access a particular food source thrived, while others died off. Darwin called this process "natural selection." Raised as a devout Christian, who once considered joining the clergy, Darwin struggled with this idea, as it conflicted with his entire worldview. For 20 years, he held off on releasing his theories to the public for fear of how the spiritual population might react.

It took the anxiety of not receiving credit for his discoveries for Darwin to make his ideas public. In 1858 he learned of a young man named Alfred Russel Wallace, who had arrived at the same conclusion that Darwin had 20 years earlier. Rather than lose his place in history, Darwin decided to risk public scrutiny. For the next year, Darwin and Wallace refined their theory and eventually presented it to the Linnean Society, Britain's leading natural history body. Following the presentation, Darwin wrote and published *On the Origin of Species*. And just like that, the theory of evolution crashed upon the world like a tidal wave.

IBN BATTUTA

1304–1369

-

A Moroccan scholar, he traveled through the majority of the Islamic world and became one of history's most prolific explorers.

Born in 1304 to a scholarly family, Battuta was immersed in education at a young age. As he grew older, his passion for education grew in tandem with his Muslim faith. Born in Tangier, a port city on Morocco's northernmost coast, Battuta grew restless after his schooling ended. The absence of an institute of higher learning, coupled with Battuta's desire to make the pilgrimage to Mecca, influenced his decision to leave in 1325 at age 21.

Battuta's pilgrimage to Mecca, or *hajj,* as it is known in Islam, made up an extremely small portion of his journey. To get to Mecca took about 16 months, and upon arriving he took part in all of the traditional ceremonies, a process that took about one month. Now a young man of 22, Battuta decided to keep traveling. He would not return to Tangier for at least 24 years.

Battuta's travels were full of adventure and romance. Records tell us that he married at least 10 times and fathered many children with his various wives. To condense his grand journey to just a few hundred words is a difficult task, but a few examples of his exploits paint a picture of how he lived during these years of wandering.

Following his time in Mecca, Battuta made his way toward Alexandria, Egypt. Here he held conferences with various holy men, all of whom prophesied that he was destined to travel to India, where he should remain for a long time. Battuta obliged these prophecies, and after a brief stay in Damascus, Syria, he made his way toward India via Afghanistan.

Battuta didn't make the journey alone. He traveled with a group of 22 men, who all proved to be necessary to Battuta's safe arrival. The first challenge: the Hindu Kush mountains. There were several routes the group could take in order to reach India, but eventually they settled on the Khawak Pass, a trail that reached an elevation of 13,000 feet. The group safely traversed the mountain range, but their test of endurance had barely begun.

While making their way to Delhi, India's capital territory, the group was confronted by 82 Hindu bandits. Battuta's group was outnumbered by about three to one, but they were able to kill 13 of the bandits and drive off the rest. They safely arrived in Delhi, where Sultan Tughluq appointed Battuta judge of the territory.

After eight years of political service, Battuta grew restless. His wanderlust took hold of him once more, and he found himself eager to discover yet more foreign lands. The sultan did not oppose his wishes; he allowed Battuta to travel to China as an ambassador, taking with him shiploads of Indian goods for the Yuan emperor. Here began another significant leg of Battuta's life of adventure.

The night before setting sail, Battuta had two ships prepared for the journey from Calcutta to China: one large ship carrying the Indian goods, one small ship for the men. In what can only be described as a lucky break, Battuta decided to attend Friday prayers by himself. That very night, a terrible storm blew in and caused the large ship to sink. In order to avoid the brunt of the bad weather, the small ship decided to set sail without Battuta, confident that he would be able to catch up.

In his attempt to reach the small ship, Battuta learned that it had been seized by a Sumatran ruler. Had he been aboard, his storied life likely would have come to an end. But Battuta did not let his entourage's absence discourage him from continuing on to China, as the allure of leisure enticed him like a siren song. He stopped at a group of islands called the Maldives, where he married four of his many wives. It is safe to say that while on these islands he lived a life of plenty.

Battuta's journeys would continue for many years and cover a number of territories before his death in 1369. He documented his travels in his journal, which would come to be known as *The Travels of Ibn Battuta*.

ERIK THORVALDSSON

950–CA. 1004

-

Known as "Erik the Red," this Viking likely founded the first Norse settlement in Greenland.

So many key discoveries have been motivated by a thirst for power or glory, the need to "plant one's flag." Rarer, and perhaps more interesting, are the discoveries borne not of vanity but necessity: natural disasters, bad blood, and persecution, to name a few examples. In the case of Erik "the Red" Thorvaldsson, it was a bit of all of these.

Thorvaldsson was born in Norway in AD 950, but he only lived there for 10 years before his father, Thorvald Asvaldsson, killed someone. His punishment was exile, so he traveled west with his son across the North Atlantic to the Nordic nation of Iceland. They settled into the volcanic, mountainous land, and lived together for about a decade. After his father's death, Thorvaldsson set out on his own.

It wasn't long before Erik married a wealthy Icelander named Thorhild. From her family they inherited a very large farm, where Thorvaldsson built a home. The couple soon had a son named Leif Erikson, who would go on to make quite a name for himself. After a few years of relative quiet on the farm, an unfortunate incident occurred—though it resulted in a very fortunate outcome.

In the year 982, a number of Thorvaldsson's servants somehow managed to cause a landslide. The deluge of dirt and debris ended up destroying a house belonging to a neighbor, who, in a fit of rage, killed the servants responsible for the landslide. Not one to stand idly by, Thorvaldsson killed the neighbor in retaliation. Suddenly, the entire family was forced to retreat to a small island off the northern coast of Iceland, known as Oxney.

At their new home, yet another disagreement led to violence between neighbors. A large altercation broke out and several people were killed. As a result, Thorvaldsson was once again banished, this time for three years.

Hearing of unsettled territory west of Iceland, Thorvaldsson and his family, along with a group of allies, decided to take a chance and made their way to a small island near the southwestern tip of the new land. Having arrived in the summer, Thorvaldsson found this southern tip to be surprisingly lush, filled with green meadows and vegetation. This inspired him to call the place Greenland, a name he hoped would attract settlers.

Thorvaldsson lived there for the duration of his exile. Once he was allowed to return to Iceland, Thorvaldsson made his way back and began to spread word of his new "green" home. His campaigning worked: eventually his colony on Greenland grew to a population of roughly 2,500.

JOHN CABOT

CA. 1450–CA. 1500

-

This Venetian navigator stumbled upon the North American coast while searching for a trade route to China.

In 1497, the European demand for Asian silks and spices was extremely high. Though trips were often made to bring these luxury items back for European royalty, there was only one known trade route, and it was popular. So popular, in fact, that middlemen would set up shop along the way, demanding money from the sailors and offering them safe passage in return. It was a short trip with a high price.

John Cabot knew there must be another way to Asia—one that was free of opportunistic gatekeepers. While examining Christopher Columbus's voyage just a few years earlier, Cabot came to believe that Columbus was onto something when he went west instead of east. Cabot decided he would travel in the same direction as Columbus, but would go farther north. All this "foolproof" plan needed was a powerful financial backer.

As it turned out, England's King Henry VII was equally interested in finding a different way to obtain Asian products. Cabot appealed to the kings, claiming that his experience sailing around the Mediterranean made him perfect for this voyage. Eventually, the two reached an agreement: Cabot would sail on behalf of the Crown and return to England with a ship full of goods and a new path to Asia. In May 1497, Cabot departed from England's west coast aboard the *Matthew* with a crew of 18 men.

The ship sailed for about a month before making landfall on June 24. Like Columbus, Cabot had no knowledge of exactly how far Asia was from England's west coast, and so he wrongly assumed that the territory off of which he anchored was on Asia's northeast coast. In reality, Cabot and his crew had reached North America, although the exact location is disputed. Some say he first landed in southern Labrador, while others claim it was the island of Newfoundland.

Regardless of the exact location, Cabot saw no inhabitants on the land and thus claimed it for England. He and his crew planted their flag, and as they explored the uninhabited terrain, began naming notable landmarks. Believing the voyage to be a complete success, Cabot returned to England in August, albeit without the silks and spices he had promised to acquire.

It did not take long to figure out that Cabot had not discovered a new route to Asia. In February 1498, Cabot set out on another attempt sanctioned by Henry VII. This time he would sail farther west, past the previously discovered land, until he reached Japan. This time, however, the trip was unsuccessful. The ship never returned, and the exact fate of its crew remains a mystery.

Though Cabot failed to achieve his primary goal, his landing on North America had significant long-term effects on world history: claiming this territory for Henry VII was crucial to England's international dominance in the 16th and 17th centuries.

THOR HEYERDAHL

1914–2002

-

This Norwegian adventurer sailed across the Pacific Ocean in a hand-built raft just to prove a point.

For most people, the name Thor evokes images of a hammer-wielding Nordic god, or at the very least a Viking king capable of waging war against any and all that challenge him. In the case of Thor Heyerdahl, neither is true. Nonetheless, Heyerdahl was a proud Norwegian whose accomplishments more than live up to the strength of his name.

Heyerdahl's academic interests revolved around zoology, botany, and geography, so it was only natural that he became a full-fledged adventurer and explorer. Most of his pursuits were for research purposes, but it was Heyerdahl's fearlessness and his masterful ability to tell a story that would make him famous.

During World War II, Heyerdahl became infatuated with the idea that Polynesian people descended from Peruvians. This notion went against popular opinion, which held that the inhabitants of the Polynesian islands were of South Asian descent. Heyerdahl cited similarities between the cultures of South America and Polynesia, and suggested that the first group of Polynesian settlers may have traveled from Peru in AD 500. Many were critical of this theory, claiming that the open-air sea vessels used by South America's pre-Incan civilizations could not possibly have made the treacherous journey across the Pacific.

In order to refute these claims, Heyerdahl decided to re-create this voyage.

With no nautical experience, Heyerdahl set out to build a raft similar to what the ancient people of Peru might have used. He recruited five friends to help with the daunting task, and together they built a 30-by-15-foot raft out of balsa wood and hemp rope. The only shelter available was a small bamboo cabin with a roof made of banana leaves. The spartan vessel was christened *Kon-Tiki*, after the Peruvian sun god. Many believed the mission to be foolish and extremely dangerous, but their concerns did nothing to give the crew pause.

On April 28, 1947, Heyerdahl, his crew of five men, and a Spanish-speaking parrot, departed Callao, Peru, aboard the *Kon-Tiki*. They used the sun and stars to navigate and they controlled the ship with a sail, paddles, and a difficult-to-control steering oar. At one point, a 30-foot whale shark circled the boat for nearly an hour. Well aware of how small their tiny vessel looked compared to the world's largest fish, the men became terrified, but the beast eventually lost interest, and they continued on.

After 4,300 miles, 101 days at sea, and countless fish dinners, the men reached their destination. Their arrival, however, was not entirely graceful. The *Kon-Tiki* smashed against a jagged reef and the men were forced to cling to floating debris as large waves hurled them onto the shore of Raroia (an atoll that is part of the Tuamotus chain in French Polynesia). Every passenger, save the parrot, survived.

Heyerdahl considered the adventure a resounding success: proof that it was possible the people of Peru had once made the very same voyage. However, while everyone is in awe of Heyerdahl's incredible voyage, many scholars continue to maintain that the first settlers of Polynesia came from Southeast Asia.

JACQUES PICCARD

1922-2008

-

This Swiss oceanographer reached the ocean's deepest point.

Oceans cover more than 70 percent of our planet's surface, concealing wonders that human eyes will likely never see. But that hasn't stopped people from trying to reach new heights— or depths, rather. Jacques Piccard is one such person.

Along with Lieutenant Don Walsh, Piccard set his sights on the Mariana Trench, which contains Challenger Deep, the lowest point on Earth, a place many believed unreachable. The pressure in this spot, conventional wisdom suggested, would simply be too immense for any human or vessel to survive. That is, until Piccard's father, Auguste, developed his bathyscaphe.

The bathyscaphe, meaning "deep vessel" in ancient Greek, was specifically designed to reach previously unfathomable depths. It took Auguste a few years to build his first model, and several more years before he built another. He called it *Trieste*, and reached an astounding depth of 10,168 feet in it.

Jacques took the *Trieste* to the U.S. Navy, and with their

help he was able to improve the vessel's capabilities. Eventually, Jacques felt confident that the *Trieste* could reach the deepest point on Earth. With the Navy's approval, and the assistance of co-captain Lt. Walsh, the descent began on January 23, 1960.

The two men had no idea what to expect on the bottom of the ocean, nor did the scientific community. Tensions were high as the *Trieste* plunged deeper and deeper below the surface. Both Piccard and Walsh knew that even the slightest breach would cause the ocean's pressure to crush them immediately. At 31,000 feet, a loud bang echoed through the darkness. Bewildered and terrified, the men prepared for the worst but quickly realized that all of the indicators and instruments appeared normal. A plexiglass window had cracked; the entrance tunnel flooded, but the men were safe behind a thick steel hatch.

The trip continued, and after five hours the *Trieste* touched down at 35,797 feet below the surface of the Pacific Ocean. Outside the window, little glowing life-forms floated. Unique fish and shrimp could be seen swimming amidst the murky silt that had been stirred up by the vessel's landing. Piccard and Walsh shook hands, congratulated each other, and remained in the Earth's bowels for 20 minutes or so before beginning their ascent.

Scientists were shocked to learn of life in the Mariana Trench, as most had believed that creatures wouldn't be able to survive the intense pressure. Sadly, though, the journey had little significant impact on the scientific community. No photos were taken, and not much could be seen out of the *Trieste*'s window. Both men believed that their mission would lead to countless manned expeditions to Challenger Deep, but researchers soon turned their focus to unmanned seacraft. To this day, Piccard and Walsh remain two of only three men to ever reach such depths. The other? Director James Cameron, who piloted his "vertical torpedo" sub to Challenger Deep in 2012.

JACQUES COUSTEAU

1910–1997

-

An innovator and explorer who developed
technology for underwater exploration.

There was a time when folks had little knowledge of the immense damage being done to our planet. Jacques Cousteau, through innovation and exploration, was one of the individuals who paved the way toward the environmentally conscious life we know today.

Cousteau trained as an aviator in the French Naval Academy. However, after a near-fatal accident left him unable to serve as a pilot, Cousteau spent a great deal of time swimming. He found that the movements helped strengthen his weakened muscles without demanding too much from his damaged physique. He also equated the feeling he got in the water to that of flying; the weightlessness allowed him to move any which way, just as an angel might. When a fellow soldier gifted a pair of goggles to Cousteau, everything clicked. He was able to glimpse what lay beneath the water's surface, and from that point on he applied all of his efforts to exploring any body of water he could.

In 1943, still early in his oceanographic career, Cousteau developed something that would enable him and all future divers to remain underwater for extended periods of time. It was called a self-contained underwater breathing apparatus, or scuba, as it is better known. This major step forward in marine exploration is typically considered Cousteau's most significant achievement, but he was far from hanging up his hat.

With the help of this new technology, as well as his large ship, the *Calypso*, Cousteau began familiarizing himself with all of Earth's oceans and seas. One of his most notable excursions saw him travel to the Grand-Congloué Shipwreck, located in the basin of Marseille. In their studies, Cousteau and his crew made an extremely important discovery regarding the Grand-Congloué: it was not one ship, but two. The first dated back to the 2nd century BCE, whereas the second

> **"From birth, man carries the weight of gravity on his shoulders. He is bolted to earth. But man has only to sink beneath the surface and he is free."**
> **—Jacques Cousteau**

ship was determined to have sunk a full century later. Using this information, experts were able to more effectively study artifacts found among the wreckage, such as wine amphorae and ancient dishes.

In addition to being a gifted explorer and innovator, Cousteau was a very charming and compelling man. These qualities led him to discover his true niche in the field of marine science: he would document his adventures and share them with the world in the hopes that people would come to realize how important marine life was. Fortunately for us, it worked.

For the remainder of his life, Cousteau created works of nonfiction that opened the eyes of people the world over. His efforts are considered essential, not just to oceanic conservation, but all environmental conservation.

JEANNE BARÉ

1740-1807

-

This Frenchwoman disguised herself as a man in order to accompany her husband on a journey around the world.

Jeanne Baré was born in France to an impoverished family, so a traditional education was not in the cards. Instead, her parents taught her how to identify plants that could be used for medicinal purposes. This was not an uncommon practice at the time; one did not need to be literate in order to be a botanist.

One day, the talented Baré met a young man, Philibert de Commerson, with a similar passion for plants. Commerson recognized Baré's unique talent and asked her to come on as his personal assistant and teacher. It was not long before the two became lovers.

Two years after their relationship began, the French government announced that it would be sending two ships around the world in order to claim new territories for France.

All members of the expedition were in place, save for one missing piece: the crew needed an expert botanist. Both Commerson and Baré wanted desperately to take part in the journey, but women were forbidden from traveling aboard French naval vessels. For Baré and Commerson, this seemingly major roadblock was no more than a minor bump.

Their plan was, in a word, absurd. Commerson would get himself hired as the ship's resident botanist. Then, on the day that the boat was set to depart, Baré would show up at the docks dressed convincingly as a man and plead to be hired as a helping hand of sorts. Commerson, already a member of the crew, would suggest that the "young man" serve as his assistant. The couple was convinced that this crazy scheme would succeed—and they were right. From that day forward, Jeanne Baré was known to the crew as Jean Baré, and she remained in disguise at all times.

Luckily, the couple was placed in the same cabin, so maintaining the ruse at night was not difficult. During the day, however, Baré needed to wear very tight chest bandages so as to make her figure appear more masculine. Still, it did not take Sherlock Holmes to realize that Baré was acting strangely. She was the only one who would not undress in front of the others, nor would she relieve herself in front of other crewmembers. Once the questions began, Baré's web of lies grew more complex.

She was able to convince the men that she had once been captured by Ottoman Turks, and been castrated while in captivity; the resulting embarrassment preventing "him" from undressing publicly. For quite some time, everyone bought the tall tale. After all, Baré was a hard worker, so nobody was looking for a reason to give "him" the boot. Unfortunately, the lies caught up to Baré before the journey's end.

Exactly how she was found out is a matter of debate. Some claim that a group of native Tahitians immediately smelled her femininity when the crew landed in Tahiti. They insisted that Baré was in fact a woman, and eventually she confessed. Others believe that her crewmates found her out; already suspicious, they waited until she was alone, tore off her clothes, and physically abused her. However unsavory it might have been, Baré and Commerson were banished from the voyage and left with French governor Pierre Poivre on the shores of Mauritius.

Perhaps nobody realized it at the time, including Baré herself, but in participating in the voyage she became the first woman to successfully circumnavigate the globe. Baré's achievements may not have been celebrated back then, but today she is lauded, both for her bravery and her contributions to the field of botany.

MARCO POLO

1254-1324

-

This famous Italian explored Asia and later recounted his tales in the widely read book The Travels of Marco Polo.

Though trading routes between Asia and Europe had been established for centuries, 13th-century Europeans knew little about Asia. Northeast Asia, then a part of the Mongol empire, was under the control of Kublai Khan, a significantly more diplomatic ruler than his warlord grandfather, Genghis Khan. Kublai was curious about the rest of the world, particularly the Christian faith. So when Marco Polo's father and uncle entered Kublai's court, he took the opportunity to learn about the culture of their homeland, Venice. Kublai dismissed the men and asked that they return with 100 Christian priests, so that they might enlighten him about the practices of the mysterious religion.

Though the two men did not make good on their promise to bring 100 priests to Kublai's court, they did make the return trip with young Marco Polo in tow. In 1271 the three men began their journey to present-day China, where Kublai resided. Traveling through the Middle East, Marco was surrounded by unfamiliar sights, smells, and sounds. He cherished these new experiences and, miraculously, committed many of the salient details to memory. However, all was not pleasant for the Polos.

While in present-day Afghanistan, Marco contracted a rather serious illness. The trio was forced to retreat to the mountains, where Marco would be able to recuperate. He recovered, but the incident added even more time to the already arduous trip. The crossing of the Gobi Desert was also quite taxing on the group. Never before had Marco experienced such terrain: challenging mountains, endless sand, and sweltering valleys. Despite these hardships, Marco continued to pay close attention to the fascinating details of unknown cultures, geography, and religions.

At last, in 1275, the Polos arrived at Kublai's summer palace in Xanadu. For a while, the three men remained in service to Kublai. He employed them for various pieces of business, like tax collecting or administration. But Kublai's health was declining, and the Polos feared that his successor might not treat them with the same kindness. They hastily sought a way out of Asia, and in 1292 Kublai granted them leave. In exchange, however, they were to escort a young princess to the Mongol ruler of Persia, whom she was set to marry.

Once in Persia the group learned that the Mongol ruler had died, and so the young princess married his son instead. Shortly thereafter, the Polos made their long journey home to Venice. The amazing tales of Marco's journey may have gone untold, if not for his own stroke of misfortune.

Years later, Marco was captured in battle by the Genoese army. While in prison, Marco met the Italian writer Rustichello de Pisa. Using his cache of memories, Marco recounted his adventures to Rustichello, telling him of the grand palaces, the paper money, the admiral postal service, and a slew of other innovations and systems he had encountered in Asia. Rustichello transcribed Marco's stories, and eventually they took the form of a book titled *The Description of the World* and, later, *The Travels of Marco Polo.*

The stories were read far and wide. Never before had such an expansive account of Asian culture been accessible to Europeans. However, as more people began to transcribe and possibly add false details and embellishments, fewer and fewer readers actually believed the tales in the book. Eventually, *The Travels of Marco Polo* took on an informal name: *Il Milione*, or *The Million Lies.*

Marco Polo stood behind his stories, however. And regardless of their truth, his exploits captured the imaginations of future travelers, inspiring them to pursue a broader understanding of the world and its many cultures.

FRANCISCO PIZARRO

CA. 1475–1541

-

This Spanish explorer was part of the first
European expedition to the Pacific Ocean.

Born a lowly pig farmer, Francisco Pizarro was certainly not expected to be a significant player in the Age of Exploration. But a teenage decision to join the Spanish army gained Pizarro the skills he needed to seek the life of excitement he had always dreamed about. And in 1502, he boarded a naval ship and sailed from Spain to Hispaniola (present-day Haiti and the Dominican Republic), the first chapter in what would be a life of adventure.

Pizarro remained stationed at the Spanish military outpost on Hispaniola for eight years before a new opportunity presented itself. In 1510, he and 300 settlers were tasked with forming a new colony on the South American coast. The large crew arrived in present-day Colombia and began establishing a colony they called San Sebastian. As development began, the mission's captain, Alonso de Ojeda, decided to briefly return to Hispaniola in order to gather more supplies for the colony. In his absence, Pizarro was left in charge. Unfortunately for him, things went very wrong very quickly. Settlers became terribly ill from tropical disease and began dying rapidly. As if that were not enough, several attacks from natives wounded or killed another large group of settlers. And lack of food was an equally threatening problem. Before long, 200 of the original 300 people had died from either sickness, starvation, or violence. The decision was made to abandon the failed colony, and Pizarro and the remaining survivors made their way to present-day Panama.

Upon arrival, Pizarro quickly became friends with an established conquistador named Vasco Núñez de Balboa. Balboa was forming plans to march across the uncharted Isthmus of Panama in the hopes of making significant discoveries. After the men got to know each other, Balboa decided to invite Pizarro to join him, and the team set off in 1513. They traveled westward and successfully made it across the narrow strip of land, where they ran into the "South Sea," now known as the Pacific Ocean. Pizarro, Balboa, and the rest of the crew were officially the first European men to lay eyes on the Pacific Ocean.

They returned to the growing colony, and Pizarro decided he would remain in Panama for some time. He was granted a large estate, as well as the position of mayor of Panama City. But Pizarro was not satisfied with this position, and soon began to dream of more. In 1526, alongside his friend Diego de Almagro, Pizarro sailed south from Panama in search of a land abundant with riches and resources. Upon discovering present-day Peru, they were granted permission from the king to claim the land for Spain.

Pizarro, Almagro, and a small army of men arrived just as civil war was raging within the Inca Empire. Two brothers were fighting for control of the land, so Pizarro, seeing an opportunity, exploited the weakness of both kings. When all was said and done, they had defeated the Inca Empire and gained control of Peru.

Like many explorers of the era, Pizarro and his allies brutally mistreated the natives they sought to conquer. They utilized subterfuge and extreme violence in most circumstances, even if they did not feel threatened. In what could be considered poetic justice, Pizarro and Almagro would end up turning on each other after their success. Almagro was killed first, but Pizarro was assassinated not long after.

MEL FISHER

1922-1998

-

One of the last modern-day treasure hunters,
he dedicated his life to finding one big haul,
resulting in tragedy for him and his family.

Children grow up on stories of buried treasure and sunken riches. X-marks-the-spot imagery conjures feelings of boundless potential; it allows us to dream that there really is a pot of gold at the end of the rainbow. With age, sadly, comes the knowledge that these stories are rarely based in reality. The majority of people who dream of pirate booty never actually come across it. But that wasn't the case for Mel Fisher.

Fisher dedicated his life to treasure hunting. One treasure, to be specific—the *Nuestra Señora de Atocha*, a ship that sank near the Florida Keys in 1622. Fisher began his search for the long-lost wreckage in 1969. Along the way there were a number of signs that pointed Fisher and his team in the right direction. In 1973, they found silver bars that matched the weight of those listed in the *Atocha*'s manifest, and in 1975 Fisher's son found bronze cannonballs that were believed to have been on the ship as well. When long periods of time would go by with no sign of the ship, Fisher would boost team morale by declaring, "Today's the day!" But for 16 years, that day never came.

They felt they were close, but their perseverance resulted in a family tragedy. The very same year that he discovered the cannonballs, Fisher lost his son and daughter-in-law, Dirk and Angel, when their boat capsized. The Fisher family was devastated, but the search continued, and in 1985 they discovered a substantial section of the *Atocha*'s wreckage. Fisher's lifelong goal was realized.

The haul included 40 tons of gold and silver, a necklace of valuable gems, a seven-pound gold chain, a 77.76-karat uncut hexagonal crystal, along with many other rare artifacts. The entire find was worth approximately $400 million. While that is a considerable score, a large section of the *Atocha* has yet to be discovered.

GIOVANNI BATTISTA BELZONI

1778-1823

-

This Italian engineer explored regions of Egypt in search of ancient artifacts, relying on his ingenuity and determination.

The tales of great explorers and archaeologists are typically romanticized so as to gloss over the boring details, but the fact is that these missions of discovery often require a high level of "boring" know-how. And some of the most interesting journeys do not belong to the explorers but rather the relics they uncover. Giovanni Belzoni's work epitomizes this notion; the great Italian utilized his background in hydraulic engineering to discover early Egyptian sites and transport artifacts of great value.

Belzoni grew up in Italy but relocated a number of times throughout his life. He had studied as an engineer, but as a young man felt that his expertise was not being put to proper use. That changed when he turned 40 and learned of a potential job opening in Egypt. Muhammad Ali, the Pasha, needed a hydraulic engineer to help advance Egypt's infrastructure. With some ideas in mind, Belzoni set off for the sandy country.

Belzoni had mocked up a design for a water pump powered by oxen, but the wind was taken out of his sails when Ali expressed little interest in the concept. Disheartened but not deterred, Belzoni remained and subsisted on a small amount of money that Ali granted him. Before long, his attention was drawn away from engineering after hearing of an ancient statue of Ramses II located in the city of Luxor. Belzoni made the trip down the Nile River and quickly became enthralled with the statue.

Belzoni hoped to remove the piece and have it transported to England, where he knew it would be safe from potential damage. There was just one problem: the statue was enormous. Standing nine feet tall and weighing over seven tons, it would be nearly impossible to move such a far distance. Adding to the difficulty was the fact that Belzoni had only wooden poles and some rope at his disposal. But he was an experienced engineer, and where some might have given up, Belzoni took on the seemingly unmanageable job.

After 17 days of dragging and shifting, Belzoni and the many men helping him finally got the statue to the Nile River. From there, a boat transported it to the British Museum in London, where it remains on display to this day. Though the statue was shipped to the museum without incident, Belzoni's ability to get the immensely cumbersome object to the shores of the Nile astounded his peers. One colleague said, "He handles masses of this kind with as much facility as others handle pebbles, and the Egyptians who see him a giant in figure, for he is over six feet and a half tall, believe him to be a sorcerer."

Belzoni continued his career in Egypt, exploring tombs and temples. It seems that the recovery of the now-famous statue of Ramses II (also known as the Young Memnon) gave him a taste for antiquities. Despite his many recoveries, the rescue of the statue remains his crowning achievement; especially because it was at risk of being blown up by the French consul if Belzoni had not stepped in.

ERNEST HEMINGWAY

1899–1961

-

This American writer revolutionized fiction, often drawing from his fantastic adventures abroad to create his many masterpieces.

Ernest Hemingway's "Iceberg Theory" revolutionized literature when he developed it in 1923. To this day, his minimalist style influences aspiring writers the world over. Though many young artists draw inspiration from Hemingway's work, few are able to emulate his lifestyle, either because they do not want to, or because they simply cannot keep up. Hemingway drank excessively, lived dangerously, and constantly sought out adventure. And even though he died by his own hands, his exploits consistently brought him to death's doorstep.

Hemingway's time in Paris with writers such as F. Scott Fitzgerald and Gertrude Stein is perhaps the most important era of his career. It was there among the so-called "Lost Generation" of expatriates that Hemingway first gained prominence as a writer. While in Paris, he also began to explore his adventurous side through hobbies like bullfighting and boxing.

Hemingway would frequently journey to East Africa to hunt big game or take his boat out to fish for 1,000-pound marlin. During World War II, he outfitted his 38-foot fishing boat *Pilar* with heavy artillery and firearms. Hemingway and like-minded friends would take *Pilar* off the coast of Cuba as if they were simply pals on a fishing trip; however, their true objective was to contribute to the Allied victory. The hope was that a Nazi submarine might spot the fishing boat and, thinking them harmless, surface, at which point Hemingway and his friends would attack. This never ended up occurring, but it's the thought that counts.

Later on in life, Hemingway survived two plane crashes while on safari in Africa. Such incidents added to the public's perception of Hemingway as an indestructible masculine figure, and all of his exploits, be they grounded or somewhat off-the-wall, served as the basis for much of his writing. For instance, there is a clear connection between his time spent fishing in Cuba and the plot of *The Old Man and the Sea*, his last great work. His vast collection of acclaimed short stories and novels, like *A Farewell to Arms* (a novel that would go on to be considered the definitive World War I story) often drew upon his experience with the military or his daring conquests, but he likely did not participate in these actions solely for source material. It seems that Ernest Hemingway had an insatiable desire to live life to its fullest, which for him meant doing things few are audacious enough to even contemplate. Small wonder that his work remains so influential.

CHRISTOPHER COLUMBUS

1451–1506

-

This Italian explorer is often credited with discovering America,
though the truth is much less impressive.

Christopher Columbus is, at least in America, one of the most prominent explorers of all time. For many years, he was falsely credited with having been the first European to discover the New World. And though this notion has been discredited, many people still think of him as a forefather of the United States. Columbus still has his own holiday, not to mention countless statues across the country, which always seem to depict him heroically. The truth, however, is that Columbus was a bad man, to say the least.

Like many sailors of his time, Columbus believed that a quicker route to Asia could be established if he were to journey west from Europe. In 1486, he took his plan of western voyage to Isabella of Castile and Ferdinand of Aragon, the monarchs of Spain. Isabella was somewhat intrigued by Columbus's ideas and decided to fund his expedition. He set sail in 1492 with his now-famous fleet of three ships: the *Niña*, the *Pinta*, and the *Santa Maria*.

After 36 days at sea, Columbus and his men docked in what is now the Bahamas, though he believed that he had successfully reached Asia. The indigenous people greeted Columbus and his men with curiosity, if not warmth. One of the first things

Columbus noticed was the enticing gold that the natives casually wore in various adornments. Columbus continued on to present-day Haiti and the Dominican Republic, where he gathered resources such as spices and gold to bring back to the Spanish monarchy, and built a settlement known as Villa de la Navidad. Leaving 39 of his sailors at the settlement, Columbus returned to Spain to present his findings.

Isabella and Ferdinand were pleased with Columbus's discoveries and encouraged a second voyage to the settlement he had established. Learning of the riches that may be waiting for them, Isabella made it known that she did not in any way condone enslavement of the native population. However, upon his return, Columbus discovered that the Villa de la Navidad had been destroyed, and the men he'd left behind killed. Isabella's wishes were ignored, and Columbus proceeded to enslave large numbers of the natives. He forced them to rebuild Villa de la Navidad, as well as search for gold in the surrounding areas.

The career of Columbus went significantly downhill from here. He left his brothers in charge of the settlement while he took to the seas in search of more land. While he was sailing, the relations between the colonizers and the natives grew increasingly hostile. Animosity was high and the gold yield was low. By the time Columbus returned to the settlement it was near the point of rebellion, and Columbus's men resented him for overestimating the amount of available gold. Columbus was subsequently arrested and sent back to Spain, where he was stripped of his titles and the wealth he had accumulated.

Columbus's voyages did help pave the way for European

exploration of the Americas, but his tyrannical actions far outweigh his mission's positive effects. Just as his holiday remains, his unsavory legacy can never truly be erased from our history books.

LYNNE COX

1957–PRESENT

-

This American woman who swam from Alaska to Russia during the Cold War.

Toward the end of the Cold War, an American prepared to swim across the Bering Strait. The only question? Whether Russia would tell her to turn around.

Lynne Cox has spent quite a bit of time in the water. She was the first woman to swim the Cook Strait in New Zealand, and the first person to swim the Straits of Magellan in Chile and around South Africa's Cape of Good Hope. She has twice held the record for fastest swim of the English Channel, and has even rescued and befriended a lost baby whale. But it is a 2.7-mile swim, child's play for Cox, that stands as her most memorable achievement.

Of course, this was not just any 2.7 miles. It was the Bering Strait: a stretch of the Pacific Ocean that connects the coast of Alaska to Russia—or as it was known in 1987, the Soviet Union.

The Cold War was still in a deep freeze, though it was slowly showing signs of thawing. Cox had first thought to swim between the feuding countries in 1976, but years of lobbying the Soviet government for permission had proven unsuccessful. By 1987, Cox had made up her mind: she was going to take the plunge regardless of how Moscow might react.

The night before the journey was scheduled to commence, the Americans and Soviets were engaging in something of a chicken fight. The Soviets moved two large ships into the Bering Strait; the Americans scrambled National Guard jet fighters to patrol. Things looked tense as Cox prepared for the journey. At last, with hours to go, Russian president Mikhail Gorbachev appeared on television to personally approve of Cox's mission.

One major hurdle had been removed, but it wasn't just the possibility of international interference that threatened Cox's swim: it was also the icy water. Cox knew that she had to keep moving at all times in order to avoid succumbing to the frigid ocean. About two hours after departing the Alaskan coast, Cox reached the Soviet Union's rocky shores. A delegation of Soviets greeted Cox, helped her onto shore, and sent her into a tent, where a Soviet doctor helped her recover from the near-hypothermia she had experienced.

The warm welcome Cox received from the Soviets symbolized something of an olive branch between the two countries. During the signing of the INF Missile Treaty at the White House, President Gorbachev stated, "Last summer it took one brave American by the name of Lynne Cox just two hours to swim from one of our countries to the other. We saw on television how sincere and friendly the meeting was between our people and the Americans when she stepped onto the Soviet shore. She proved by her courage how close to each other our peoples live."

ZHENG HE

1371-1433

-

A Chinese diplomat who expanded the nation's political influence.

The legacy of Zheng He may, at first glance, seem somewhat dull. He did not conquer any nations or discover new lands; he did not strike gold or become stranded on a deserted island; he simply traveled on behalf of China and the Yongle emperor. But through his seven voyages Zheng He was able to spread the Chinese political agenda throughout Asia, an act that had significant consequences.

Though he would later aid greatly in spreading Chinese politics, Zheng He's affiliation with China was forced upon him at an early age. He spent the first 10 years of his life under Mongolian rule in Yunnan, one of the last remaining Mongol holds in China. But in 1381, the growing Ming dynasty conquered Yunnan, taking it and its people under Chinese rule.

Zheng He was imprisoned, castrated, and forced to serve in the Chinese army as an orderly. With no other options, he did his best to set himself apart in hopes of one day achieving a rank that would improve his quality of life. By 1390, he had done just that, rising to the rank of junior officer and proving himself skilled in both combat and diplomatic affairs.

In 1405, Zheng He was appointed commander in chief of a political mission to various nations in the Indian Ocean. His goal was to ensure they fell in line and paid proper homage to the emperor. From 1405 to 1433, Zheng He sailed from place to place, succeeding in gaining allegiance at almost every stop. Only once was he met with backlash, in 1408, when the Chochin (present-day Kochi) king Alagonakkara refused to bend the knee. Zheng He commanded his forces deftly, defeated Alagonakkara in battle, and took him captive.

He visited many countries during his time as a diplomatic agent, including Egypt, Kenya, Arabia, and India. At one point he returned to China with representatives from 30 South Asian states, so that they could pay homage to the Yongle emperor. Though some historians believe that Zheng He's travels did nothing other than secure flattery for the throne, his journeys were still significant for their sheer scope, and likely helped pave the way for Chinese colonization of Southeast Asia. In any measurable way, Zheng He is one of the most prolific travelers in human history.

BARTOLOMEU DIAS

1450–1500

-

This explorer successfully established a route from Portugal to the Indian Ocean.

Trade between European and Asian nations was no simple task in the 15th century. An overland route had long been an option, but it was a difficult journey, and recent developments in the Ottoman Empire resulted in its temporary closure. Like most other European rulers, the king of Portugal, John II, wanted to create a passage between his nation and the nations of Asia. He chose Bartolomeu Dias to lead the mission.

Dias departed Lisbon with three ships in August 1487. Along with his crew, Dias was sent with six African slaves who had been captured and brought to Portugal. His orders were to drop these individuals along the coast of Africa with samples of rare metals and spices with the hope that natives would show them where to find more. In addition, they were to establish contact with Prester John, a figure of medieval Christian lore with whom John II had become infatuated. While it is doubtful Prester John ever existed, John II was convinced that he could be located.

By January 1488, Dias had dropped off the African messengers and reached South Africa. As he began navigating around the southern tip of the continent, strong storms blew them out to sea, but Dias used the wind to his advantage. Turning the ships 28° south, a gust carried them around the bottom of the continent. By February, they had successfully made it to the Indian Ocean, just off the coast of present-day Mossel Bay. Dias and his men sailed along the coast of Africa for a few more days until dwindling food supplies forced them to return home.

After almost 16,000 miles traveled and 15 months at sea, Dias and the surviving men returned to Lisbon. Technically, their journey was a resounding success: they had established a route from Portugal to the Indian Ocean and opened the door for future trade with Asian powers. Despite this, John II was not pleased. The king had sent two men on a journey across Africa to find Prester John and the Christian kingdom in Ethiopia. When Dias returned to Lisbon without having made contact, John II became furious. Despite the riches an established trade route to Asia could provide, it seems likely that discovering this mythological man was more important to the king, because Dias was never put in charge of a mission again.

OWEN CHASE

1797–1869

-

He survived a violent encounter with a whale and inspired Herman Melville to write Moby-Dick.

Moby-Dick, Herman Melville's novel about Captain Ahab's obsession with a white whale, is known far and wide. But few know the horrifying story that inspired the book. In August 1819, the *Essex* departed on a whaling voyage from the shores of Nantucket. Among the many men aboard was 21-year-old first mate Owen Chase.

In November 1820, the crew of the *Essex* found themselves about 1,000 miles from land. Chase noticed a large whale, approximately 85 feet long, looming in the water. Suddenly, the enormous being began swimming straight for the *Essex*, and smashed into the side of vessel. As the crew hurriedly tended to the damage, the behemoth circled back and attacked once more.

This time, the force of the blow was enough to sink the ship.

The 20 men boarded three 20-foot boats and sailed away from the wreckage. They decided to head south toward the Marquesas Islands, which were dauntingly far away. After two weeks at sea, having endured unbearable exposure to the sun and attacks from killer whales, they landed on a barren island. They remained for one week, but as supplies were dwindling, the men knew they had to push forward.

Three men remained on the island as Chase and the others returned to the sea. In January 1821, one of the men went insane and died. The crew cut him open, removed his organs, and ate his flesh. This became the procedure whenever one of the men perished. They would roast the meat deemed edible on a hot stone, and throw the remainder of the body into the ocean. Somewhere along the way, Chase lost sight of the other life rafts, and by February 18, 1821, only Chase and two other men remained.

By some miracle, the English ship *Indian* spotted the boat and rescued the men. One week later and 300 miles away, another *Essex* life raft (carrying just two men by then) was rescued by the American ship *Dauphin*. As they were pulled aboard, the two delirious sailors sucked at the bones of their cannibalized shipmates. Even more amazingly, the three men who opted to stay on the deserted island survived for four months until an Australian ship rescued them.

Ultimately, Chase was one of just five men who survived the nightmare that was the *Essex*'s last voyage. His firsthand account of the events, *Narrative of the Most Extraordinary and*

Distressing Shipwreck of the Whale-Ship Essex, served as the primary inspiration for *Moby-Dick*.

BLACKBEARD

CA. 1680–1718

-

Perhaps the most famous pirate of all time,
he tormented the American East Coast.

What child doesn't fantasize about the life of a pirate? Swashbuckling adventures on the high seas in search of treasure. A parrot on the shoulder. A hook for a hand. If only this sugarcoated version of pirate life were reality. The stories of peg-legged vigilantes are based in some measure of truth, but the horrendous details of their heyday are often left out. Edward Teach, or Blackbeard, as he is better known, was famous for the cruelty he and his crew exhibited in their hunt for booty.

Not all that much is known about Blackbeard's early life. It is believed he was born in Bristol, England, and that at some point he captured a French ship and converted it into a pirate ship that he christened *Queen Anne's Revenge*. He armed the ship with 40 guns and manned it with about 300 men, launching his career as a scourge of the high seas.

Blackbeard, named for his large, coarse facial hair, knew the power his beard commanded; during battle he put fuses in his beard and lit them, causing the smoke to curl around his head and make him appear even more fearsome. It got to where the mere sight of him could make an enemy surrender.

By May 1718, Blackbeard was in command of about five armed ships. He and his armada sailed up to the harbor of Charleston, South Carolina, where they looted any ship entering or leaving and gained such power that Blackbeard was able to order the governor to provide a chest filled with medication.

Following the Charleston campaign, Blackbeard disbanded his large pirate crew. In June of that year he convinced Governor Charles Eden of North Carolina to pardon him of all of his crimes, regardless of how heinous. For a little while he managed to live a nice, quiet life with his 14th wife, but the call of the sea proved too strong to resist, as he assembled a significantly smaller crew of marauders and resumed his life of crime.

Eventually, Governor Alex Spotswood of Virginia called upon the British naval force to put an end to Blackbeard's reign. They entered into the battle of Ocracoke Island in November 1718 and Blackbeard and his crew were defeated. According to legend, it took five bullets and 20 slashes of a sword to bring him down. Robert Maynard, lieutenant of the British fleet, ordered that Blackbeard's head be severed and hung from the bowsprit of his ship: a warning, yes, but a trophy as well.

LOUISE BOYD

1887-1972

-

After learning of the disappearance of legendary polar explorer Roald Amundsen, Louise Boyd decided to use her resources and expertise to join the search-and-rescue mission for Amundsen and his missing plane.

California native Louise Boyd did not see snow until she was well into her teens. But by the time she passed away at the age of 84, she'd seen more than her fair share. Born into great wealth, Boyd was able to pursue her passion for arctic exploration fervently and comfortably; in fact, she was even accompanied by a maid during one of several journeys to the far north. Yet that never stopped her from putting herself in harm's way.

Boyd took seven expeditions through Greenland and the Arctic, primarily to photograph the many land formations, glaciers, and plants found in the inhospitable climate. Boyd's first major expedition was in 1926, and was largely recreational in nature. She, along with a group of friends, set out on a chartered vessel named *Hobby* with the objective of hunting big game; Boyd bagged 11 polar bears herself. In addition to hunting, Boyd also enjoyed capturing photos and footage of the Arctic landscape, so much so that she decided to set sail on another adventure just two years later.

The 1928 journey began just as the first had. Boyd set out to hunt and photograph Arctic wildlife, but after learning of the disappearance of legendary polar explorer Roald Amundsen, Boyd adjusted the objective of her second journey, deciding to use her resources and expertise to join the search-and-rescue mission for Amundsen and his missing plane.

Though Boyd had lived a privileged life, she consistently maintained a firm sense of morality and empathy. Knowing that Amundsen and his many crewmembers were in mortal danger, she abandoned her trip in order to assist the rescue efforts. Aboard the ship *Hobby*, Boyd and her crew searched for over 10 weeks and 10,000 miles across the Arctic Ocean. Although it had become a rescue mission, Boyd still took the opportunity to film the journey as they traveled from Tromsø, Norway, to the Spitsbergen Archipelago, and then on into the Greenland Sea.

No trace of Amundsen or his team was ever found, but Boyd's selfless service did not go unrecognized. The Norwegian government awarded her the Order of St. Olaf, First Class. She was only the third woman in the world, and the first American, to receive the honor.

Boyd continued to photograph the Arctic for as long as she was able. During World War II, she even refrained from making her findings public, instead using her vast knowledge of northern geography to aid the U.S. Army in their secret missions.

AMERIGO VESPUCCI

CA. 1451–1512

-

Amerigo Vespucci discovered that lands he and Columbus believed
to be part of Asia were in fact a different continent altogether:
a place that had yet to be documented by modern geographers.

Few goals motivated early European explorers more than
establishing a reliable route to Asia. Asian exports like silk and
spices were in high demand, and the most ambitious explorers
vied for the opportunity to discover a new passage to the East.
Perhaps the most famous explorer to accept this undertaking
was Christopher Columbus, who sailed west with a substantial
fleet and landed in the present-day Bahamas. Believing he
had arrived in Asia, Columbus declared the voyage a success,
but fellow explorer Amerigo Vespucci would soon come to a
different conclusion.

Long before Vespucci became an explorer, he participated in
a variety of business ventures. It wasn't until a chance encounter
with Columbus in 1496 that he began to consider taking to the
seas. The two men could not have known how their legacies
would become intertwined from that moment on.

By 1499, many Europeans—including King Ferdinand and
Queen Isabella—had figured out that Columbus's "India" did
not possess the gold and spices for which the East was famous.
As a result, Spain's monarchy permitted Alonzo de Ojeda to
lead select explorers on an expedition that picked up where

Columbus had left off. One of these explorers was Vespucci.

Due to discrepancies across records of Vespucci's life, certain details have always been in question. For example, it is unclear what Vespucci's role was in Ojeda's expedition, or if Vespucci even had experience as an explorer prior to this outing. Some of his personal writings describe him coming upon present-day Venezuela in 1497, but since no official records support this claim, it is likely that his time with Ojeda was his first introduction to the New World.

Ojeda, Vespucci, and the rest of the crew departed Spain in May 1499 and began heading west. Once the men reached land, they split into two parties: Ojeda led an expedition of the present-day Venezuelan coast, while Vespucci's group ventured along the coast of present-day Brazil. After some time, the expedition regrouped and made its way to the island of Hispaniola, which they explored before returning to Spain in June 1500 with ships full of brazilwood and enslaved indigenous people.

Vespucci and his travel companions believed that the countries they'd explored were part of the Far East, just as Columbus had. But something about the foreign lands piqued Vespucci's interest. Unlike his peers, Vespucci was not overly concerned with monetary gains; instead he focused on furthering the fields of astronomy, geography, and anthropology, believing they would lead to great scientific and technological advancements. With the help of King Manuel I of Portugal, Vespucci began his return trip to present-day Brazil within a year of returning home.

Vespucci spent a large portion of his journey studying the rivers and skies of what we know today as Brazil and Argentina. He lived among the area's tribes for some time, diligently recording observations and noting their actions without interfering in any harmful way. Once his study was complete, Vespucci and his fleet returned to Portugal in July 1502, where he presented his findings. His most notable discovery? The lands he and Columbus believed to be part of Asia were in fact a different continent altogether, a place that had yet to be documented by modern geographers.

The claim staggered European scholars and laymen alike. Suddenly, society's worldview had to expand in order to include a frighteningly vast expanse of unknown territory. In 1507, the German mapmaker Martin Waldseemüller published a geography book with updated maps. He referred to the New World as America, in honor of Amerigo Vespucci.

DONALD CROWHURST

1932-1969

-

When the Sunday Times *announced that it would sponsor a nonstop yacht race around the world, Donald Crowhurst set off alone on the* Teignmouth Electron.

The final 243 days of Donald Crowhurst's life were a hurricane of adventure, deception, madness, mystery, and tragedy, and it all started when the *Sunday Times* announced that they would be sponsoring a nonstop yacht race around the world.

The year was 1968, and the people of England were obsessing over all things nautical. The previous year, Sir Francis Chichester had accomplished the monumental feat of sailing around the world alone. In order to cash in on the British sailing craze, the *Sunday Times* created the Golden Globe Race: a competition for any yachtsmen brave enough to enter, no experience required. The contestants were allowed to set off at any time before October 31, 1968, and would have to sail around the world via the five great capes. Due to the inconsistency in start times, two prizes were to be awarded: a trophy for the first person to complete the race, and £5,000 to the man with the best time.

Crowhurst, despite his amateur status, heard of the tournament and thought up a plan he believed to be foolproof. He would acquire a triple-hulled boat and install a balancing mechanism of his own design. Using this innovative vessel, he was confident that he would win the prize for fastest time. With October 31 quickly approaching, Crowhurst set sail aboard his makeshift boat, the *Teignmouth Electron*.

The *Electron* made dreadfully slow progress in the first few weeks, and if that weren't discouraging enough, the boat began to leak quite early on. Crowhurst knew that continuing along the designated route could result in death for him and his vessel, but to turn around would mean forfeiture and humiliation, so he chose neither. Instead he remained in one position, simply floating in the Atlantic while radioing back to the mainland in order to lie about how much distance he had covered.

Crowhurst's supposed progress astounded the people of Britain, and he was informed that the race for fastest time now came down to him and a man named Nigel Tetley.

With his ruse holding up, Crowhurst feared that he would not be able to sustain the lie should he "beat" Tetley. The contest's judges would review his journey meticulously in order to ensure that no rules were broken. Crowhurst decided to slowly travel back across the Atlantic and land in England safely after Tetley, so as not to arouse suspicion. What he did not count on was Tetley's ship sinking before winning the race. Now, as the only contender left, it seemed that Crowhurst had no choice but to win the race. As this news began sinking in, so too did Crowhurst's slow descent into madness.

He stopped sailing toward England altogether, writing prolifically in his journal as he floated alone on the Atlantic. His 25,000 words covered everything from time travel to death and divinity, plus his belief that he was the son of God. His entries indicated that he thought death would transform him into a "cosmic being," an assertion that makes it likely that Crowhurst took his own life on June 29, 1969. Though his boat and his journal were found 12 days later by a search party, his body has never been discovered, making the exact circumstances of his disappearance a mystery to this day.

NAPOLEON BONAPARTE

1769-1821

-

Napoleon had over 60 victories in battle, spanning the French Revolutionary Wars and the Napoleonic Wars, showed a tactical prowess that is still taught in military schools, and established an empire that spanned across much of Europe.

Attempting to succinctly summarize the equally famous and infamous political and military career of Napoleon Bonaparte is a futile task; his legacy is simply too great, and he is one of only a handful of historical figures best known by his given name. But of all of his many accomplishments, one stands out as being truly mind-blowing, even by his own lofty standards.

It was 1814, and Napoleon had already made enemies of many nations. Armies were closing in on all sides of France, and even the French citizens began to turn against their once-great emperor. Napoleon attempted to fight back, but by April 6 he realized his efforts were futile and he surrendered himself to the allied forces of Austria, Russia, Prussia, and Great Britain.

The question quickly arose: What should be done with the great Napoleon? A man of such prominence could not simply be imprisoned in some damp dungeon, but neither could he be left to live freely among the general population. The decision was made to exile Napoleon to the remote island of Elba. Here, it was thought that Napoleon could live happily while still unable to return to France and reclaim his position as emperor.

They would come to regret this severe underestimation of Napoleon's abilities.

Napoleon arrived at his tiny new kingdom on May 3, 1814. He was provided with two million francs per year, courtesy of the French government, and an armed guard of 400 men. With these resources, Napoleon quickly established himself as ruler of Elba's 12,000 inhabitants and took up residence in its palace. In classic Napoleonic fashion he immediately began making improvements to the island's infrastructure, developing roads, restructuring agricultural systems, improving defenses, and even designing a new flag. Before long, however, Napoleon grew bored with these small tasks. Dissatisfied with his position, and annoyed that France had stopped sending him funds, he began to consider other options.

Napoleon began quietly planning his return to Europe. He ordered that the ship *Inconstant* be prepared to look like an English vessel and be freighted with an abundance of supplies. By February 26, 1815, Napoleon was ready to make his departure. He announced his plans to the citizens of Elba and then took to the seas with about 1,150 people, including sailors, soldiers, civilians, and servants.

On March 1, Napoleon landed at Cannes, France. He and his men swiftly disembarked and began their march toward Paris. As they traveled, French citizenry caught wind of Napoleon's plan and began joining the cause. By March 20 he had arrived at Paris and somehow convinced enemy soldiers to rally around him. So began Napoleon's final 100 days as the emperor of France.

He retook the throne and quickly became a symbol of hope

for the French people. However, not everyone was convinced. The hype surrounding his improbable return to Europe quickly died away, and the European joint opposition moved to dethrone him once again. On June 18, Napoleon's forces were defeated at the Battle of Waterloo. Not wanting to make the same mistake twice, the British government made sure to exile Napoleon to a much more remote island: St. Helena, where Napoleon lived out the rest of his days, under the careful watch of English officers, of course.

MADISON WASHINGTON

UNKNOWN
-

Locked in chains and forced to work in the kitchen on the Creole, *Madison Washington organized a rebellion with 18 other slaves.*

By the autumn of 1841, Madison Washington had already gained his freedom. Previously enslaved in Virginia, he managed to escape captivity and cross the Canadian border with the help of abolitionist Robert Purvis. However, Washington's beloved wife still remained on the plantation.

Washington corresponded with a white man who agreed to secret his wife to a designated location where Washington could meet them and abscond back to Canada. Washington was wary of the plan, as he knew it was likely that one of the parties involved might betray him. Unfortunately, his suspicions were correct; someone, whose identity remains a mystery, alerted authorities. Washington was captured shortly after retrieving his wife and the two were separated. He was put back in chains and forced aboard the ship *Creole*, which was heading from Virginia to New Orleans.

Washington was assigned to work in the ship's kitchen, allowing him unique access to the other slaves on board. Taking advantage of this position, he was able to effectively organize a rebellion with 18 of the other slaves. After some days of planning, the slaves attacked on the night of November 7, 1841. They executed their plan perfectly, gaining control of all the ship's firearms, killing one sailor, and wounding the captain in the process.

The 135 captives were able to sail the *Creole* to Nassau in the Bahamas. The American consul of the island requested that the mutineers be held until proper arrangements could be made. However, the British government only agreed to put 19 of the men under arrest. The remainder were granted total freedom by Britain. Of the 19 imprisoned men, two died in captivity, and the rest were later released. These decisions created tension between the American and British governments.

Washington's actions led to a general unease among Atlantic slave owners, as they demonstrated that enslaved men and women were capable—and willing—to fight back against their oppressors.

FREDERICK DOUGLASS

CA. 1818–1895

-

He escaped captivity and became one of the
strongest voices in the abolition movement.

Few abolitionists played as big a role in ending slavery as Frederick Douglass. Born into slavery on the Eastern Shore of Maryland in 1818, Douglass lived there with his grandparents and aunt until he turned eight, at which time he was sent to live with a carpenter in Baltimore. It was there that he learned how to read, an ability that would prove invaluable in his future pursuits.

After several years with the carpenter, Douglass was sent to a farm owned by Edward Covey. Covey regularly beat and starved his slaves, and on January 1, 1838, Douglass began preparing for his escape. Unfortunately, his plot was discovered and he was thrown in jail, delaying his plans by several months. It wasn't until that September, while enslaved at a shipyard in Baltimore, that Douglass was able to gain his freedom in a remarkable series of events which would take him no longer than 24 hours.

Working on the waterfront had provided Douglass with a decent amount of nautical knowledge; using this knowledge, as well as a sailor's uniform, he was able to disguise himself as a free sailor and make his way to the Baltimore railroad station. In his pocket he carried a sailor's protection pass, which he had borrowed from an actual seaman; with any luck, the document would prove sufficient in lieu of "free papers."

Once close enough to the tracks, Douglass waited for the train to begin moving before discreetly hopping aboard and making his way to the segregated car, where he waited nervously for the conductor to inspect his protection pass. After brief consideration, the conductor accepted Douglass's story, collected his fare, and moved on.

The train sped along, eventually dropping Douglass off in Havre de Grace, Maryland, where the next leg of his journey began. He took a short ferry ride across the Susquehanna River before boarding yet another train, this one bound for Wilmington, Delaware. Upon his arrival, Douglass boarded a steamship that carried him to Philadelphia, the last of his pit stops before New York City.

He arrived in New York City less than 24 hours after making his nerve-racking escape in Baltimore. He stayed in the big city for several weeks before moving to New Bedford, Massachusetts. Once there, Douglass continued to educate himself by reading voraciously and familiarizing himself with the abolitionist movement. Before long, Douglass gained the confidence to become a vocal member of the movement, making his first speech at the Massachusetts Anti-Slavery Society's convention in Nantucket. This speech, the first of many where he denounced the horrors of slavery, catapulted Douglass to the forefront of the movement.

Douglass used his mastery of language to great effect. He made countless speeches, wrote three monumentally important books, and worked closely with Abraham Lincoln during the

Civil War. He even traveled to Europe, speaking in Ireland, Scotland, and England in order to fight for universal equality. Everything Douglass did served to combat prejudice and social injustice, and for that he remains one of America's most impressive historical figures.

LEIF ERIKSON

CA. 970–1020

-

Although Christopher Columbus is often credited as being the first European to set foot in North America, historians believe that Leif Erikson arrived in North America centuries before.

Christopher Columbus is often credited as being the first European to set foot in North America. However, most historians believe that the Norse explorer Leif Erikson reached North America centuries earlier.

The specifics of Erikson's journey are hotly contested by historians, since the primary actors did not keep detailed records of their voyage. The earliest sources of information are the traditional Norse sagas involving Erikson and his father, Erik the Red. Of course, these sagas hold no more credibility than a legend or folktale, so piecing together the truth is a difficult task.

Erikson, nicknamed "Leif the Lucky," is believed to have grown up in his father's settlement in Greenland. Once he reached an appropriate age, he sailed from Greenland to

Norway and, eventually, began to make his way back home. As *Eiríks saga (Saga of Erik the Red)* reports, it was on this return to Greenland that Erikson accidentally landed on North America. According to the story, he called the newly discovered land Vinland, in reference to the abundance of wild grapes he found.

The circumstances of Erikson's discovery are among several points of contention. Some scholars believe that he set out to discover this mysterious land, having heard tales of it from fellow voyagers. This information comes from the *Groenlendinga saga (Saga of the Greenlanders)*, which scholars generally consider more reliable than *Eiríks saga*.

There is also the matter of where exactly Erikson landed in North America. Various spots along the Northern Atlantic coast have been identified as the site of Vinland over the years. In the 1960s, a team of excavators on the northernmost tip of Newfoundland uncovered what they believed to be the remnants of the 11th-century base camp set up by Erikson and the Vikings, although some have suggested that this region does not fit the descriptions found in the original sagas.

Whether he stumbled upon it or sought it out, Erikson is almost unanimously considered to be the first European to explore part of North America. However, it seems he had no interest in claiming or colonizing the newfound landmass. Soon after discovering it he is believed to have returned to Greenland, where he spent the remainder of his life spreading Christianity.

PHILLIS WHEATLEY

1753–1784

-

For slaves, finding a publisher was nearly impossible, and for that very reason, Phillis Wheatley's accomplishments as a teenage poet and slave are nothing less than astonishing.

Born under a different name, Phillis Wheatley was kidnapped from her West African home at the age of seven and brought to America in 1761. There she was sold to the Wheatley family in Boston, who named her Phillis. Despite being slave owners, the Wheatleys treated Phillis with an uncommon level of respect. They quickly recognized how clever she was, and, with the help of their children Nathaniel and Mary, they taught her how to read and write. Her lessons included Bible studies, history, British literature, Latin and Greek classics, geography, and astronomy.

Before long Phillis discovered her love for the written word, specifically poetic expression. By age 13 she had written "On Messrs. Hussey and Coffin," a poem the Wheatleys helped get published in a Newport, Rhode Island, newspaper. Phillis continued to write poems over the next four years, and while it was hard to deny the quality of the work, most people still refused to support it because of her race. All of the Wheatleys were frustrated by this response, so they developed a plan: if the young poet's talent would not receive recognition in the States, perhaps it might fare better overseas.

It was decided that Phillis would accompany Nathaniel Wheatley on a voyage to London in May 1771. While she was there, she was able to share her poetry with the likes of the Earl of Dartmouth, Sir Brook Watson, and even Benjamin Franklin, who happened to be spending some time abroad. By the time Phillis was ready to travel back to America, her first collection of poems, *Poems on Various Subjects, Religious and Moral*, had been published in London. She was the first African American, and only the third woman in the United States, to get a book published.

Phillis returned to the Wheatley household and was emancipated by the family shortly thereafter. With her freedom, she continued to write poetry and antislavery prose. In the end, Phillis did receive acclaim in America, though not as much as she deserved, and she had the opportunity to meet George Washington after the two established a correspondence. Despite her immense talent, Phillis's life was never easy; she had to work as a servant even after being freed, and died alone and impoverished. It is believed she wrote over 140 poems in her lifetime, and hundreds of years later they are still celebrated by a country that once tried to silence her voice.

SIR ROBERT HART

1835-1911

-

Sir Robert Hart was not universally loved—especially in China, where he is still considered by some as an unwelcome British invader—but his unique approach to foreign affairs did receive recognition from both sides.

During the 19th century, Western culture gradually began to exert influence in China. As the Eastern power slowly began to lose its cultural independence, ancient traditions gave way to some of the West's modern innovations, such as railways, factories, and a new postal service. At the center of these changes stood the British statesman Robert Hart.

Hart's role in China's redevelopment began when he was a customs officer in the 1850s. Although he could easily have abused his position, he took his duties very seriously and always strived to set a good example for his subordinates. It was very important to Hart that Chinese citizens had a positive opinion of foreigners, an effort that would prove futile under his administration.

As a result of Hart's principled conduct, the Chinese citizens with whom he worked generally appreciated him. However, the foreign influence he represented was not nearly as well received. And in the summer of 1900, China's frustration with the West came to a head. The Boxer Rebellion broke out as a result of the Chinese desire to purge their country of Western colonialism and Christian missionary activity.

Hart lost all of his property, his home, and his offices in the uprising, but his attitude toward China did not change. He remained entirely sympathetic to their viewpoints and even took a stronger stance against Western encroachment. In his diary, he wrote that the Boxer Rebellion was not a senseless surge of violence, but the result of boiling tension and a longstanding desire "to destroy Christian converts and stamp out Christianity and to free China from a foreign cult, and on the whole not to hurt or kill but to terrify foreigners, frighten them out of the country and thus free China from the intrusion of aliens—and this is the object which will be kept in view, worked up to and in all probability accomplished during the new century."

Despite his lack of authority, Hart decided to remain in China into his old age, just in case his assistance was required. He was not universally loved—especially in China, where he is still considered by some as an unwelcome British invader—but his wholly unique approach to foreign affairs did receive recognition from both sides. For his service to England, he received a knighthood; for his work in China, a peerage.

OCTAVIE COUDREAU

1867-1938

-

*After her first expedition ended in disaster, Octavie Coudreau
found herself alone and with unfinished business;
amazingly, she decided to carry the torch all the same.*

Some explorers work alone, called by a solitary wanderlust that leaves no room for relationships that might produce emotional baggage. But for others, an adventure is best done with friends and loved ones; a shared experience that is only improved by a partner. Octavie and Henri Coudreau were one such couple whose shared love of exploring helped bring them together. Unfortunately, after their first expedition ended in disaster, Octavie found herself alone, and with unfinished business. Amazingly, she decided to carry the torch all the same.

When Henri and Octavie were married, he had been working for the Brazilian government, charting rivers and identifying potential sites for the harvesting of natural resources. After their wedding, Henri was tasked with exploring the Trombetas River in northern Brazil. The couple decided to carry out the mission together and set off in 1899.

Already weak from his years in the Amazon, Henri developed malaria early on in their honeymoon voyage and died in Octavie's arms before the end of their first year together. She would have been forgiven for turning around right then and there, but she decided to press on and finish her late husband's work.

After bringing his remains home to his birthplace in Angoulême, France, Octavie resumed her husband's research and continued it over the next seven years. Not only did these efforts allow her to help complete Henri's book, but she was eventually named an official explorer for the French government.

JACQUES CARTIER
1491–1557
-

Cartier's objective, like that of most European explorers, was to find a Western route to Asia and search for valuable resources.

In 1534, North America was on the minds of many Europeans, thanks to the likes of Amerigo Vespucci and others. In the eyes of eager explorers, the newly recognized land was a limitless trove of riches and resources just waiting to be snatched up, with no regard for the indigenous populations. France's big player in the game was a skilled navigator named Jacques Cartier.

Cartier's objective, like that of most European explorers, was to find a Western route to Asia and search for valuable resources. However, it was also stressed that he should devote some time to exploring these new "northern lands." His first expedition traveled to Newfoundland and the Gulf of St. Lawrence, which he explored with his crew. Returning to France with two Native American captives, he met with King Francis and was promptly sent back to the region to continue exploring.

Cartier returned the following year and, using his two prisoners as guides, sailed up the St. Lawrence River. They made it as far north as present-day Quebec before establishing camp on September 7. Eventually, they left this camp to sail even farther down the river, reaching Hochelaga (present-day Montréal) on October 2. It was here that Cartier heard the tale of the fabled city that would inspire his third expedition: the Iroquois who inhabited Hochelaga told him of a land to the west that was home to untapped riches. Cartier, eager to claim them for himself, sailed back to the mouth of the St. Charles River, where he and his crew spent the winter. The Iroquois, friendly toward the French explorers at first, turned hostile as winter dragged on. Between this and the harsh elements, 25 men passed away during the course of the winter, forcing Cartier to return to France—with several more Native American prisoners in tow.

Upon arriving in France, Cartier told King Francis of the untapped riches that he had heard about. The king approved a third voyage, but it would not be until 1541 that the journey got underway. Unfortunately, the sojourn was rather uneventful, turning up little else than a few pieces of quartz, which Cartier mistook for diamonds. While this bid came up empty, it should not diminish Cartier's most significant achievement: his exploration of North America, which allowed France to lay claim to much of the land in the future. He is also credited with giving the country its name, after the Huron-Iroquois word *kanata*, meaning "village." O Canada!

ADA BLACKJACK

1898-1983

-

*Having lived in Alaska for 23 years, Ada Blackjack set off for
Wrangel Island in order to claim the territory for Great Britain.*

It was not wanderlust that prompted Ada Blackjack to
participate in the Wrangel Island Expedition of 1921: it was
necessity. She was the single parent of a young, chronically ill
son, and she needed money to take care of him. Blackjack also
thought that she might find a new husband on this journey,
someone who could be a father to her boy. Instead, all she
found was hardship.

The purpose of the expedition was to explore Wrangel Island,
off the northwest coast of Alaska, and claim the territory for
Great Britain. Blackjack had lived in Alaska for 23 years. Though
she was not particularly skilled in the ways of backcountry
survival, she seized the opportunity for work and signed on as
an aid. On September 9, 1921, she and four explorers set off for
the island with just six months' worth of supplies.

At first, the group was relatively comfortable. They raised
the British flag on Wrangel Island and established their camp.
However, the lack of wildlife on the island concerned them. The
original plan was to supplement their rations by hunting game
as they waited for a supply ship to arrive in the summer of 1922.
But much to their dismay, the relief ship never came.

As the months dragged on, food and supplies grew scarce.

They managed to kill a few walruses, but the meat was tough and somewhat unenjoyable, despite Blackjack seasoning it with what little she could forage. Their plight came to a head in January 1923. One of the men, Lorne Knight, had contracted scurvy. The other three men decided they would depart the island while Blackjack attempted to nurse Knight back to health. Though they promised to return, the men disappeared at sea.

Blackjack managed to keep Knight alive for about six more months, keeping him as comfortable as possible by tending to his sores with warm oatmeal. Perhaps delirious, perhaps just a miserable person, Knight constantly criticized Blackjack, blaming her for his condition and never expressing gratitude. In a heartbreaking portion of her diary, Blackjack wrote, "He never stop and think how much its hard for women to take four mans place, to wood work and to hund for something to eat for him and do waiting to his bed and take the shiad out for him." Before long, though, Blackjack was left on her own, as Knight died in June. In one final act of selflessness, Blackjack built a structure around the body, so as to protect it from wild animals.

Alone, cold, and hungry, she was left to fight for her life. The fear of polar bears never subsided, and Blackjack always slept with a gun nearby; she even went so far as to build a platform on top of the shelter that she could use to stand atop and spot bears in the distance. For two months, Blackjack survived on seals she shot herself. She used their skins to make new shoes, and sustained herself on their meat. Finally, on August 19, 1923, a rescue boat arrived. Upon returning to Alaska, she was heralded as an international hero, even though she was paid even less than she was initially promised. Still, the journey provided what she sought from it, and Blackjack managed to get treatment for her son.

Perhaps that is enough to soften the burden of what followed: the initially warm welcome Blackjack received upon her return quickly cooled, as she was vilified and portrayed as a careless, selfish person whose neglect led to Knight's death.

CHARLES LIGHTOLLER

1874-1952

-

A survivor of the Titanic, *Charles Lightoller set sail towards Dunkirk, France, during World War II with one objective: save as many Allied soldiers as possible.*

One would think that survivors of the *Titanic* would be apprehensive about ship travel following such a harrowing experience. But Charles Lightoller didn't just go on to sail again: he became part of a story that rivaled his experience on that legendary ship.

Lightoller served as the second officer on the *Titanic*'s first and only voyage. He was responsible for directing many women and children to lifeboats as the ocean liner sunk. By the time the survivors were rescued, Lightoller was the highest-ranking crewmember to survive.

Fast-forward 28 years: World War II was in full swing, and

Axis forces had surrounded Allied troops in Dunkirk, France. The soldiers fled to the beach, where there were naval vessels offshore, but not nearly enough to carry all of them to safety. As a last resort, Allied forces called upon small, private boats to transport desperate troops from the shores of Dunkirk to England.

Charles Lightoller, 66 years old and living in England, answered the call. He boarded his small ship, *Sundowner*, along with his son Roger and a young deckhand named Gerald Ashcroft. Showing courage beyond comprehension, the three brave men assisted in the rescue of an estimated 130 soldiers, ferrying them to safety on a boat licensed to carry 21 people. That heavy load was plenty of danger for a civilian to take on; the enemy gunfire that Lightoller was able to evade on the return trip proves that he had one of his country's coolest heads in times of strife.

HERNÁN CORTÉS

1485–1547

-

Although it is true that Hernán Cortés was a natural leader, he was a killer more than anything else.

Born in Medellín, Spain, Hernán Cortés initially had dreams of studying law. However, after a brief stint in law school he realized that he was not destined for the courtroom. Instead, he sailed to Santo Domingo in 1504, and moved on to Cuba in 1511 to aid in its conquest, beginning what would be a long life of organized slaughter.

Cortés's initial role in Cuba was as a soldier in the army of Diego Velázquez. But before long, Cortés set his sights on Mexico to the west, where there were said to be vast riches. Velázquez did not approve of the proposed mission to Mexico, but Cortés did not care; in 1518, he took about 500 men, 16 horses, and 11 ships and made his way to the country.

In March 1519, Cortés and his fleet landed in Tabasco, Mexico. They spent a short time there, just enough to allow Cortés to mingle with the local Indians, from whom he learned that the Aztecs were in control of vast parts of the country, and that Montezuma II ruled from the capital city of Tenochtitlan (present-day Mexico City).

Shortly thereafter, Cortés took his army back to the sea and sailed to a hospitable but unsettled spot on the southeastern coast, where he founded the city of Veracruz and began preparations for an assault on Mexico's interior. Cortés quickly began to discipline his troops, molding them into a responsive army under his command. In a successful attempt to emphasize his commitment to conquering Mexico, Cortés sank all 11 of his ships, making inland travel the only option.

As Cortés and his army marched, they gained allegiance from various Indian populations, in particular members of the nation of Tlaxcala, many of whom were fed up with Aztec rule and wished, like Cortés, to see them defeated. Little by little, the army swelled, and by the time they reached Tenochtitlan on

November 8, 1519, an extra 1,000 soldiers were serving under Cortés.

Initially, Cortés was received warmly. It has been speculated that this was because his arrival coincided with an Aztec prophecy describing a white-skinned god from the east; however, others think that he was simply greeted with what was considered the hospitality typical of Mexico at the time. Regardless of initial pleasantries, things turned sour quite quickly. Cortés took Montezuma captive, gaining him a tentative hold on the city. However, in 1520, the still-vindictive Velázquez sent an army to capture Cortés. Upon hearing word of this, Cortés left the city with a large group of soldiers, leaving just 80 Spaniards and a few hundred Tlascala to maintain control.

Cortés managed to defeat the army of Velázquez quite quickly, but upon returning to Tenochtitlan he discovered that the Aztecs had revolted against the small group he had left behind. He rallied his soldiers and fled the city with an Aztec army in pursuit. After six days of alternating between retreat and battle, Cortés finally managed to defeat the pursuing Aztecs. After taking some time to reorganize his forces, Cortés once again marched on Tenochtitlan in December 1520 and captured it in August of the following year.

THEODORE ROOSEVELT

1858-1919

-

Although most reflect on his time as the president of the United States, Theodore Roosevelt's time as an explorer is far overlooked.

Theodore Roosevelt's presidency is generally viewed in a positive light, as most historians see him as a capable man who led his country into the 20th century. His legacy as head of state has been analyzed and recounted many times. His time as an explorer, however, does not get nearly as much attention.

Roosevelt's frail build and sickly nature as a young boy didn't exactly predict a robust future. Through a strict regimen of weightlifting and aerobic training, though, Roosevelt was able to condition his body, maintaining his health and stamina throughout his days as a Rough Rider and two terms as president. He was an avid boxer and a passionate hunter, a hobby that would push him toward an expedition in South America.

By 1913, Roosevelt had completed two terms as president, run for a third term, started a new political party, and survived an assassination attempt. But he was far from ready to rest on his laurels. Learning of the adventures to be had in the jungles of South America, Roosevelt petitioned the American Museum of Natural History to sponsor an expedition. The former president assured the museum that he would return with a significant amount of new animal specimens for their collection.

Along with two American naturalists, Roosevelt arrived

in Brazil with the expectation of a much-needed vacation with some scientific exploration thrown in. But after meeting with his guide, Brazilian explorer Colonel Candido Rondon, Roosevelt's plans changed. Rondon told him of a mysterious waterway that had not yet been charted by foreigners: the River of Doubt. Roosevelt could not resist the temptation of conquering an uncharted river, and so despite protests from the head of the American Museum of Natural History, he accepted the challenge.

The team of Roosevelt, Rondon, the scientists, a group of porters, and Roosevelt's son Kermit (who had been living in Brazil) began a two-month trek to the River of Doubt in late 1913. It was 1914 by the time the group reached the river, and the situation was already bleak. A lack of supplies and the devastating effects of tropical illness forced many members of the crew to drop out. By the time they set off on the river, only three Americans remained: the Roosevelts and the naturalist George Cherrie. The remaining crewmembers were South American explorers or porters.

From the outset, it was clear that this river was not for the faint of heart. Alligators snapped at the boats as they moved downstream and swarms of mosquitoes made even the calm stretches of water a nightmare.

Native tribes also made it apparent that outsiders were not welcome in their territory by overtly hunting Roosevelt and his team. When Rondon's dog was found dead, its body shot with multiple arrows, tensions neared their boiling point. And then ... nothing. By some miracle, the tribes stopped their antagonism.

It is not known whether Roosevelt's party simply traveled beyond the tribes' jurisdiction or just became less interesting to them, but the men were allowed to pass unharmed. For a brief time, they enjoyed some optimism.

Still, the high morale did not last. No matter how many external threats the team was able to ward off, the spectre of disease and starvation hovered at all times. Roosevelt himself suffered from high fevers, and on numerous occasions asked to be left in the jungle to die. By the time the men miraculously reached their destination on April 26, the former president had lost a quarter of his body weight.

Their success was so unlikely that many critics refused to believe that Roosevelt and Rondon had actually done it. It wasn't until another group of explorers completed the journey in 1926 and confirmed most of their geographic findings that the men received the credit they were due. By then, the waterway had already been renamed the Roosevelt River, and the former president considered his journey on the River of Doubt to be one of the greatest adventures of his exciting life.

ESTEVANICO

1500–1539

-

Though his very presence in America was against his will,
Estevanico ended up receiving much respect
and admiration in the new world.

Like many Africans in the 16th century, Estevanico was transported to America against his will. He was sold to a man named Andrés de Dorantes de Carranza at a young age, and together they joined a 1527 expedition to Florida. The goal was to wrest control of the territory from its native population. Joined by an estimated 300 men, Estevanico and Dorantes de Carranza endured difficult conditions and a Native American attack outside of present-day Tallahassee. As a result, they were forced to flee.

As they sailed up and down the coast, only 80 men remained, and their bad luck was far from over. When they traveled west, they were pummelled by storms, resulting in the death of many more men. By the time their ships wrecked on a small island off the coast of Texas, only 15 men remained, 13 of whom, including Estevanico and Dorantes de Carranza, attempted to head to Mexico through Texas.

Before long, however, the dwindling party, now consisting of just four men, was taken captive by Native Americans. After several years of attempted escapes, Estevanico and the other three men managed to gain their freedom.

As a means of survival, the men took on the identities of medicine men, imparting wisdom to the natives they came across. Estevanico in particular was lauded for his ability to pick up new languages, and his commitment to the role of healer—which included a "medicine rattle," a gourd decorated in beads and feathers—was commendable. Utilizing these skills, the small group made it to Sinaloa, Mexico, in 1536, where they were excitedly welcomed by Antonio de Mendoza, the viceroy of what was then New Spain.

It was decided that Estevanico, acting as guide, would accompany a priest named Fray Marcos de Niza to New Mexico. He complied, but tragedy struck before he could occupy his new role. Arriving ahead of the priest's party, Estevanico was quickly killed by Zuni warriors.

ABUBAKARI II

CA. 1400

-

Ruler of what was arguably the wealthiest empire on Earth, Abubakari II gave it all up to pursue his true passion: exploration.

The story of Abubakari II is at once both ancient and familiar. Ruler of Mali, arguably the wealthiest empire on earth at the time, he gave it all up to pursue his passion: exploration. Specifically, he believed that the Atlantic Ocean had another "bank" besides the African west coast with which he was so familiar. He came to this notion by studying the Nile River, a large body of water in its own right. If the Nile could have two banks, it was only reasonable that all bodies of water followed the same rule, no matter their size. In 1311, Abubakari gave control of Mali to his brother and set sail on the Atlantic Ocean with a fleet of 2,000 ships.

These many ships were loaded with both men and women, as well as plenty of food, water, and livestock. But little is certain about what happened once the expedition was underway. Though historians disagree, most evidence suggests the fleet landed in Brazil. Those in favor of the theory point to comments made by Christopher Columbus, who described black traders living on the American continents, as well as spears he found that likely contained West African gold.

The truth only gets murkier from there. It is believed that Griots, a group of West African historians whose tradition spans for centuries, possess concrete information regarding Abubakari II—information they refuse to share. As a group, they view Abubakari's renunciation of the throne as something worthy of condemnation and scorn, not praise. Therefore they view any and all of his accomplishments as acts of treason.

Still, Abubakari II's decision had a profound historical impact. Not only was he among the earliest explorers to attempt a transatlantic voyage, he was also one of the most visible figures to attempt such a passage. While the details of his quest continue to evade researchers, Abubakari II remains one of Africa's most famous explorers.

JUAN GARRIDO

CA. 1480-CA. 1550

-

Juan Garrido—or "Handsome John" in English—never tried to make history, but his impact on the world stands up against any other explorer's.

When measuring the achievements of history's most famous travelers, it helps to have the benefit of hindsight. Able to see the big picture, we're usually able to pinpoint the exact moment history was "made," so to speak. In some cases, those pivotal moments were complete accidents—in others, the result of a deliberate choice. But if there's any through line, it's that most of these adventurers were driven by a desire to make history. Columbus may not have made it to India, but his motivation was still gold and glory. Then there's Juan Garrido. Garrido—or "Handsome John" in English—never tried to make history, but his impact on the world stands toe to toe with any other explorer's.

Around 1495, Garrido traveled to Portugal as a slave, where he was forced to convert to Christianity. Following his conversion, he was allowed to accompany a Spanish man to Santo Domingo. Though records conflict, it is assumed that Garrido was either acting as the man's servant or his protégé: constrained, maybe, but technically free by 16th-century standards. He participated in Spain's 1508 invasions of Puerto Rico and Cuba, a role that would bring him in contact with the notorious Hernán Cortés in advance of his conquest of Mexico. Garrido fought in those battles as well, distinguishing himself as a soldier while committing his share of atrocities against the native people.

By rising from slave to celebrated free man, Garrido had already made his own sort of history. But his true impact was yet to come. After the Mexican conquest, he was awarded a plot of land situated on a lake bed near Tenochtitlan: the newly conquered Aztec capital. Hoping to create a sustainable life for himself, he did something that had never before been done on the continent: he planted wheat. The harvest that came later marked the first known instance of wheat farming in the Americas, and it was far from the last.

Garrido did not set out to change the world. All he did was cultivate a small field in order to feed hungry Spanish soldiers. What he never could have known was that wheat would go on to cover more of the planet's surface than any other crop, fundamentally changing the agriculture and diets of the New World.

MIKE FINK

1770-1823

-

Of the Mississippi River brawlers of the early 19th century, none were as feared as Mike Fink, "King of the Keelboaters."

The Mississippi River of the early 19th century was abuzz with activity. Keelboats would sail up and down the river, ferrying cargo and passengers between towns. The men who ran these vessels were hard-living, physically impressive individuals who relied on their strength to keep their boats moving against the current. A confrontational attitude often accompanied that brawn, and a majority of these men preferred to solve their problems with drunken brawls. Of these brawlers, Mike Fink, "King of the Keelboaters," was the most notorious.

Fink was born in Pittsburgh, and from an early age it was clear that he was a talented marksman. He put his skills to use as a scout during the Indian wars around the Fort Pitt region. However, once the fighting ended in 1790, Fink found that he had nothing to do. He had grown fond of the danger that accompanied the life of a soldier and felt averse to settling down as a farmer. So he decided to head west and earn his living on the Ohio and Mississippi Rivers.

Before long, Fink became well known: for his navigational abilities, yes, but also for his quirks. He was fond of practical jokes, and would frequently play them on unsuspecting victims.

If the victim of the joke did not appear amused, Fink would take it as an insult and proceed to threaten or attack them. Fink, standing at a burly six-foot-three, was unbeatable when it came to fisticuffs, and word of the hot-tempered, heavy-drinking man's abilities spread quickly.

Even newspapers began to report on stories of Fink's exploits. They described him as "half horse, half alligator" and stated that he could "outrun, out-hop, out-jump, throw down, drag out, and lick any man in the country." It was said that he had ridden on the back of a moose and had killed a wolf with his bare hands. These obvious exaggerations were typical of the time, skewing the history of many a frontiersman for the sake of a good story. This resulted in Fink becoming a folk hero in the vein of Daniel Boone and Davy Crockett.

As the practice of keelboating died off, Fink was forced to pursue other opportunities, and little is known of his later life. It is said that he continued west, drifted into obscurity, and left his confrontational ways largely behind. Not to say that he gave them up entirely. The most widely accepted cause of his death, though still unconfirmed, has him being beaten to death in a brawl. If the legends are true, he wouldn't have wanted to go out any other way.

MATTHEW WEBB

1848-1883

-

Prior to Matthew Webb's successful attempt in 1875,
swimming across the English Channel had never been done.

Separating southern England from northern France, the English Channel is approximately 150 miles across at its widest point. Most people would shudder at the thought of trying to swim across such an expanse. How could one possibly swim such a distance without succumbing to sheer exhaustion, poor conditions, or the terrifying creatures that live below the surface? Why would one even try? Of course, a fair number of people have done it. But prior to Matthew Webb's successful attempt in 1875, it had never been done.

It started in 1873, when Webb heard news of a failed attempt to swim across the channel. He became inspired and decided it was his destiny to complete the feat. Webb was so dedicated to his pursuit that he quit his job as a sea captain and began training full-time. By 1875, he felt ready to make his first attempt.

On August 12, Webb dove into the channel and began his swim. However, his progress was cut short when an unforeseen storm began brewing. Dejected, Webb was forced to give up, but he did not stay discouraged long. He immediately began prepping for a second attempt, and just 12 days later, Webb tried again.

He dove in from the end of England's Dover Pier, covered from head to toe in porpoise oil. Accompanied by three boats, Webb progressed slowly. With the currents working against him, he zigzagged in a way that added to the total distance. The swim demanded astounding endurance, and at one point, Webb was even stung by a jellyfish. But he refused to quit. After 22 hours, he arrived on the other side of the English Channel, having swam approximately 40 miles.

Webb's accomplishment made him an international celebrity. Unfortunately, his initial success spurred him on to other endeavors, one of which resulted in his death: he perished just eight years later in an attempt to swim across the Whirlpool Rapids of Niagara Falls.

LORD BYRON

1788-1824

-

Lord Byron's many great works did not serve as his proudest achievements; rather, Byron would point to the day he swam across the Hellespont as the proudest of his life.

Romanticism was one of the largest artistic movements of the 1700s, highly visible in music, literature, and art. The poetry of the time was full of florid language and evocative imagery, and the methods employed by romantic poets are still used to this day. Of these masters of language, none are more famous than George Gordon, or, as he is better known, Lord Byron. Surprisingly, though, Byron's many great works did not serve as his proudest achievements. He gave that distinction to the day he swam across the Hellespont.

Byron always loved to swim. His club foot, a malady he had dealt with since birth, made even the simplest movements difficult. So he adopted swimming as a hobby, feeling that he was freer in water than he could ever be on land. It was only after becoming inspired by an ancient tale that Byron decided to attempt this crossing.

The Hellespont is a narrow stretch of water separating Europe from Asia. Its significance comes from ancient Greek mythology, where it appears in many stories. Unsurprisingly, Byron took interest in one of the most romantic tales featuring the waterway: A young man named Leander who would swim across the strait every night to visit his lover, Hero, on the European side. Traveling in darkness, he found his way with the aid of a lamp that Hero had lit in a high tower. Byron, by then an exceptional swimmer, decided to make the journey himself, both as an homage to the story and to prove that it was possible.

He decided he would make his attempt on May 3, 1810. The point at which Byron chose to cross was only one mile wide, but rapid currents made the crossing extremely difficult. By the time Byron reached the opposite shore he had swam about four miles. Completing this now-famous swim inspired Lord Byron to write his first successful work, "Childe Harold's Pilgrimage," a poem that details the travels of a young man not unlike Byron; born into wealth but tired of his lavish lifestyle, he seeks his purpose by traveling. Even if it is not his most famous historical contribution, Byron's swim across the Hellespont arguably marks the turning point in his artistic career.

BY ANY MEANS NECESSARY

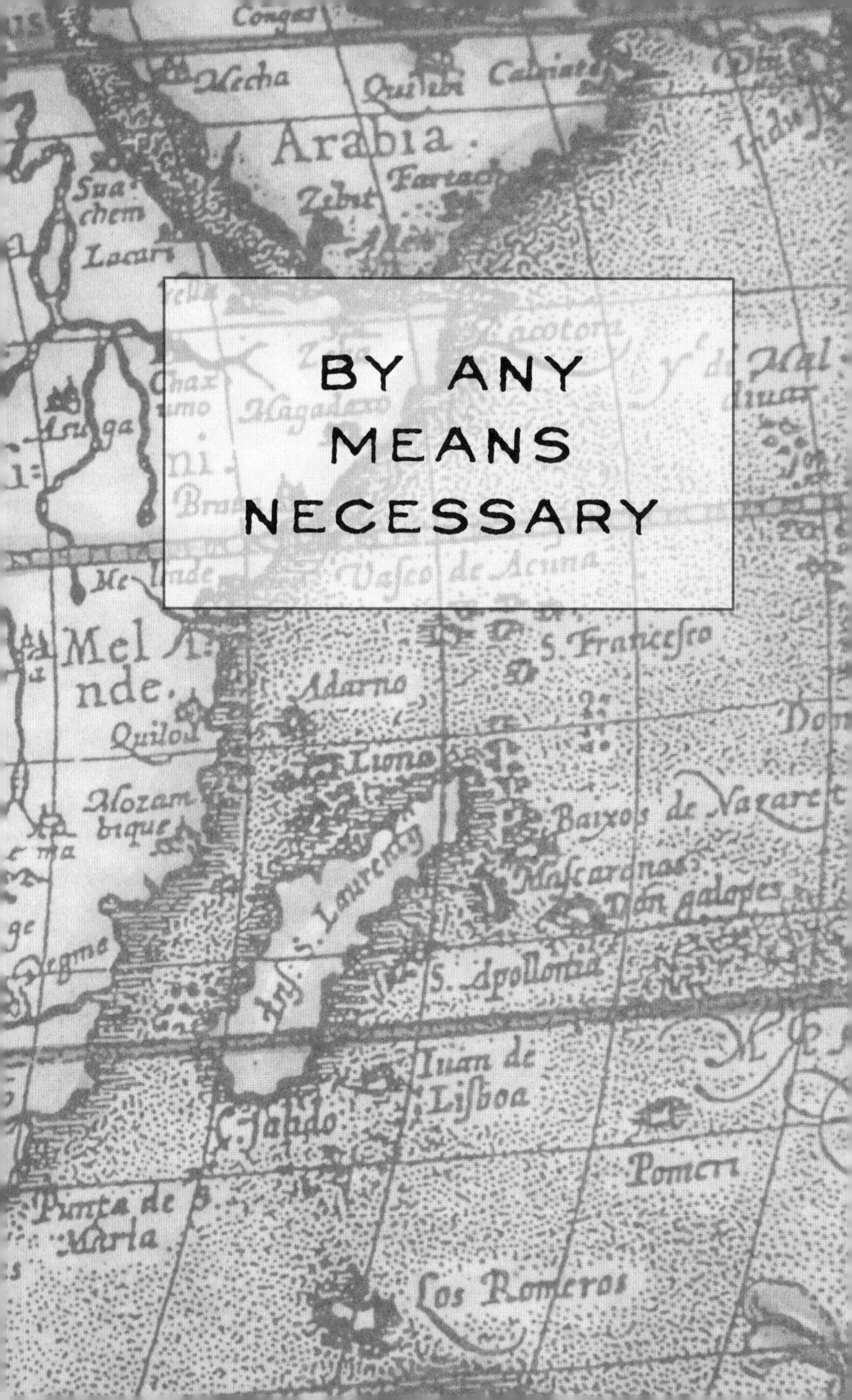

NELLIE BLY

1864-1922

-

*Forget 80 days: this American journalist
needed only 72 to travel around the world.*

In 1873, *Around the World in 80 Days* became something of
an instant classic upon publication. The author, Jules Verne,
had already released two acclaimed adventure novels, and so it
was not difficult to find a substantial readership for his third.
Among those readers was investigative journalist Elizabeth
Cochran Seaman, better known by her pen name, Nellie Bly.

Bly's first brush with national recognition was in 1887,
when, on assignment for Joseph Pulitzer's newspaper the *New
York World*, she spent 10 days undercover in the Women's
Lunatic Asylum on Blackwell's Island. The candid exposé was a
rousing success that shed light on the deplorable conditions of
the asylum. The coverage fostered harsh criticism of New York
City's Department of Public Charities and Corrections, which,
as a result, made drastic improvements to its facilities.

By 1889, Bly had proven herself a capable journalist, and
she was ready to take on her most ambitious assignment yet.
She approached her editor with the idea of attempting to beat
the record set by Phileas Fogg, the protagonist of *Around the
World in 80 Days*. Bly believed she could make the trip in
less time, but the staff at the *New York World* needed some
convincing. Business manager George Turner was not opposed

to the concept, but he thought a man should go instead of Bly. Among his reasons was the belief that a woman would require a chaperone, and that she would not be able to make the trip without an inconvenient number of cumbersome trunks.

Bly, in her typical headstrong fashion, said, "Very well. Start the man and I'll start the same day for some other newspaper and beat him." The *New York World* could not argue with Bly's passion, and so they agreed to support her journey. On November 14, 1889, with £200 worth of English gold, a small bag containing essentials, and little else besides the clothes on her back, Bly departed from Hoboken, New Jersey, on the *Augusta Victoria*.

> **"I said I could and I would. And I did."**
> **—Nellie Bly**

Her planned itinerary was as follows: London, Calais, Brindisi, Port Said, Ismailia, Suez, Aden, Colombo, Penang, Singapore, Hong Kong, Yokohama, San Francisco, then finally back home. The journey was followed closely by readers, who excitedly submitted estimations of her travel time to the *New York World*. By the end of her adventure, the paper had received over 500,000 guesses.

Bly traveled by horse, rickshaw, sampan, burro, steamship, bicycle, and train. Along the way, she made many pit stops at destinations that piqued her interest. She visited a Hindu temple in Singapore and a leper colony in China, and she even purchased a monkey. On her way to Japan, Bly got caught in a storm that threatened to halt her travels. Frustrated but undeterred, she exclaimed, "I'd rather go back to New York dead than not a winner."

Fortunately, it did not come to that. She ended up making it to San Francisco without major incident, and from there her travels were uninterrupted. She made the final leg of the journey amidst celebration and greetings from fans who had been following her trip. She arrived in New Jersey via private railroad car 72 days, 6 hours, 11 minutes, and 14 seconds after beginning her mission. At the age of 25, Nellie Bly had successfully become the protagonist of her own adventure story.

DAME FREYA MADELINE STARK

1893–1993

-

A British-Italian explorer and writer who bravely traveled to regions of the Middle East where few Westerners dared go.

Writer Lawrence Durrell once called Dame Freya Stark "one of the most remarkable women of our age," and it is hard to disagree with that assessment. She was born into an artistic Parisian household; her father, Robert, was a sculptor and her mother, Flora, was a painter and pianist. With parents like hers, Stark was destined to develop a keen artistic sense, but it was her blending of art and her experiences traveling that would make her legendary.

Her experience with other cultures began at a young age, when she taught herself Arabic, Turkish, French, German, and Italian. Stark was a brilliant learner, and her knowledge of these languages would prove to be invaluable to her future adventures. Though she was primarily an autodidact, Stark did receive some formal schooling in London before abandoning her studies to serve as a nurse in World War I. Following her service, she returned to London in order to improve her Arabic at the School of Oriental and African Studies. It was there that Stark developed a strong desire to visit the Middle East, though it wasn't until 1927 that she achieved her goal.

Approaching her mid-30s and dissatisfied with life in London, Stark made a seminal journey to Lebanon. From there she traveled to Damascus, familiarizing herself with local customs and refining her Arabic along the way. At the time, these trips were typically not made by women traveling alone—or any women, really—since so much of the Middle East was considered unsafe. But Stark's time there only inspired her further, and after returning to London for a short time, she traveled to the Middle East once more in 1930 to explore Persia (present-day Iran).

> "To awaken quite alone in a strange town, is one of the pleasantest sensations in the world."
> —Dame Freya Madeline Stark

Stark had a specific goal in mind: she wanted to travel the Valleys of the Assassins, a region no other European had ever explored. Accompanied by a local guide and a pack mule, she set off for the valley with the intention of conducting geographical and archaeological studies. Along the way, Stark contracted malaria, dengue fever, and dysentery, but she carried on. Upon completing her studies, Stark returned to Baghdad and then

London, where she was lauded for her achievements and began writing the first of what would be many books: *The Valleys of the Assassins and Other Persian Tales*.

The book was met with considerable success and allowed Stark to launch what became an extremely prolific career. She continued to explore and write until her death in 1993, at the impressive age of 100.

ISABELLA BIRD

1831–1904

-

This English explorer found love in an unlikely place.

From an early age, Isabella Bird was curious, outspoken, and adventurous. Unfortunately, her desire to explore was quelled by a number of ailments, including a tumor that was removed from her spine at age 18. She recovered slowly, but as soon as she was healthy she set out on her first adventure: a trip accompanying her second cousins from England, where she was raised, to the United States. The events of this trip would be used as material for her first book, *An Englishwoman in America*, published in 1856.

After getting her first taste of travel, Bird became insatiable. She journeyed back to Britain, explored Australia, and climbed mountains in Hawaii. But it's the time she spent in the Rocky Mountains that stands as her most definitive accomplishment.

Bird moved to Colorado, at the time the youngest state in the U.S., with the intention of exploring the Rocky Mountains. In 1873, the night before her journey was to begin, she received disconcerting news: her guide was a man with a penchant for self-destructive behavior, despite his proper upbringing and artistic soul. His name was Jim Nugent, or "Mountain Jim."

Mountain Jim had lived as an outlaw since completing university. His uncontrollable anger and affinity for alcohol and swearing made it difficult for him to live a civilized life. It seemed to Bird that having him in her company would make for an unpleasant, and possibly unsafe, journey.

And then the unexpected happened: Bird brought out the very best in Mountain Jim. During the weeks the pair spent traversing the Rocky Mountains they became deeply involved with each other. Bird described Mountain Jim, a man with just one eye and a love for writing poetry, as "a man any woman might love but no sane woman would marry."

In Bird's presence, Mountain Jim swore off all that made him who he was before they met. He gave up drinking, fighting, and swearing, and he tried his hardest to make himself into someone worthy of Bird.

Upon reaching the end of her planned journey, however, Bird painfully bid her "dear desperado" farewell. He assured her that the influence she had over him would not be lost, and they promised to reunite in whatever life there was after death.

Bird left feeling confident that Mountain Jim would live up to his assurance. They exchanged letters regularly for a time. Not even a year had passed, however, when Bird received the horrible news of Mountain Jim's death: he had been overcome with rage at a perceived slight from a man named Evans, and was shot and killed on the spot.

EVELYN WAUGH

1903-1966

-

This British journalist and author spent considerable time in Africa, penning acclaimed works of fiction and nonfiction.

For many artists, travel often serves as a means of inspiration. Whether it's a painter hiking up a mountain to view a landscape or a writer journeying to Africa to gain a broader understanding of the world, the simple act of going somewhere new has led to some of history's greatest works of art. British novelist Evelyn Waugh put this tactic into practice when he departed his home for the Ethiopian Empire in 1930. During his stay in what was then Abyssinia, Waugh played the role of both artist and reporter. He approached the material not with the unbiased eye of a traditional journalist, but with the critical, satirical eye he had developed over the years.

Those closest to Waugh have suggested that he became far more cynical following his separation from his adulterous wife in 1929. This newfound bitterness quickly made its way into his work: his second novel, *Vile Bodies*, which was published just a few months after his divorce, was described by biographer

Martin Stannard as "a manifesto of disillusionment." Perhaps it was just a coincidence, but nine months later, in October 1930, Waugh was ready to get out of England. So he agreed to travel to Abyssinia to write an article, and he brought his cynicism right along with him.

Waugh's assignment was to cover the coronation of Emperor Haile Selassie for several British newspapers. But the state of affairs in Abyssinia led him to broaden his scope. Waugh viewed the juxtaposition between the splendor of the political class and the barbarism of the surrounding areas as both comical and deplorable. The grand festivities of the inauguration, he believed, only served as a facade intended to convince the world that Selassie had earned the position rather than obtained it through villainous means.

Waugh's intentions were benevolent at first; his initial goal was to shed light on a part of the world that was little known to readers in the UK. But the ethics of his coverage should be called into question: for at what point does drawing upon the real-life suffering of people go from reporting to exploiting?

Waugh continued to travel after leaving Abyssinia, journeying to East Africa, South America, and even the Arctic, collecting stories along the way that inspired him to write a number of books (including his well-known novel *A Handful of Dust*). It seems his time in the Ethiopian Empire sparked an interest in experiencing and commenting on other cultures, and he even returned to Abyssinia six years after his initial visit to report on the second Italian-Abyssinian war. He applauded the efforts of the Italians, viewing their actions as necessary to tame an otherwise out-of-control population.

AIMÉE CROCKER

1864–1941

–

Eccentric, proud, and brave,
she explored the Far East as few ever had.

Aimée Crocker was the heiress of a large railroad empire, a booming industry in California circa 1864. From an early age she had a taste for the exotic, specifically anything related to Eastern cultures. By the time she was 10, Crocker demanded that a "Chinese bed" be placed in her room. This infatuation did not pass with her childhood. As soon as she was old enough to travel, Crocker took off.

The stories of her many travels are well documented in her book *And I'd Do It Again*. Crocker's first foray into the world of exploration came in the 1890s during a trip to the kingdom of Hawaii, long before it became a state. While there, she claims that King Kalākaua became quite enamored with her, giving her the unofficial title of Princess Palaikalani, which translates to "Bliss of Heaven." According to Crocker, the king even gifted one of his many islands to her. But the lavish treatment could only keep Crocker in place for so long, and after some time she was ready to make the trip she had always dreamed of: a journey to the Far East.

Crocker made it successfully to China, but it wasn't long before she found herself a captive of a feudal Chinese warlord— or as she called him, "a wild man of Borneo." This warlord made Crocker watch a person be executed slowly by means of 1,000 gashes. The warlord then informed her, "I am the master of all that is beautiful in this house. I may keep those things, give them away, or break them if it pleases me." For most people, a predicament this extreme would be enough to paralyze them with fear, but Crocker seemed to salivate at the high stakes.

She made her escape under the cover of night, but not before an assassin narrowly missed her with his blade, which cut through her gown but not her skin. The adventures only got more extravagant from there, and they all shared a common denominator: men. Crocker was not shy about her desire for male company. She had five husbands in her lifetime, among countless other flings. There was an ugly hypnotist in Honolulu, a Spaniard in a sombrero fitted with jewels, a handsome Englishman named Huntingdon Meer, and Baron Takamini, who she considered the perfect specimen. And one cannot forget the old man who entranced her into a lustful euphoria by playing a stringed instrument, or the 60-pound boa constrictor whose muscular build she found erotic.

> "I do not believe there is a woman alive or ever has been who can stand whimpering on the part of a full-grown man."
> —Aimée Crocker

Whether all of Crocker's accounts are entirely accurate is up for debate. After all, there is not much to go on besides her writing. And while these tales may be exaggerated or skewed for the purpose of a good yarn, the fact remains that Crocker lived daringly and unapologetically. Her notions of sexuality and female empowerment were extremely progressive for her time, and, true or not, her storytelling ability is nothing short of admirable.

JAN MORRIS

1926–PRESENT

–

A prolific English travel writer who underwent
gender reassignment surgery in 1964.

Jan Morris has taken countless journeys throughout her life, penning over 15 books that detail her travels everywhere from Africa to Spain to China. But perhaps more significant than any of her physical journeys was the path she walked on the inside. Morris was born male, but from an early age she understood that she had been born into the wrong body, and began pursuing gender reassignment in 1964. Her inward odyssey, along with the physical travels it required, constitute a remarkable life, a never-ending quest which Morris described as, "an outer expression of my inner journey."

By the time Morris was ready to undergo gender reassignment surgery, she had already traveled extensively. Her work as a journalist took her to the top of Mount Everest with Edmund Hillary and Tenzing Norgay, and to the Negev desert, where she witnessed fighting between British and Egyptian forces. But despite her impressive resume, it was her journey to Morocco for gender reassignment that would be the most trying. Morris had long been married to the love of her life: Elizabeth Tuckniss. Together, they had five children. Though their love for each other was apparent, Morris's gender reassignment would force them apart, for reasons that were beyond their control.

Due to the archaic societal attitude toward gender reassignment at the time, few places in the world allowed the procedure. However, there was a reputable clinic in Casablanca, Morocco, that offered to complete the surgery for Morris. There was just one catch: if Morris were to receive the surgery, she would have to divorce Tuckniss upon her return to Britain, since same-sex marriage was against the law at the time. Every member of the family understood how important this procedure was to Morris, and so she traveled to Morocco, completed the surgery, and divorced Tuckniss.

Thankfully, though, the story has a happy ending. Morris and Tuckniss continued to live together despite their legal separation. On May 14, 2008, the couple legally married again and remain together to this day.

Following the successful procedure, Morris continued to travel and write extensively. And she now had something else to be passionate about: the rights of transgender people. Since her reassignment, she has been a pioneer for the transgender community and marginalized people in general: a hero for anybody who isn't sure how to take that first step down a path that continually beckons for them.

> "[T]he best travel writers are not really writing about travel at all. They are recording the effects of places or movements upon their own particular temperaments—recording the experience rather than the event, as they might make literary use of a love affair, an enigma or a tragedy."
> —**Jan Morris**

GERTRUDE BELL

1868–1926

–

A polarizing female trailblazer who aided
British efforts in the Middle East.

From an early age, Gertrude Bell exhibited qualities of an independent, freethinking individual. Her penchant for mountaineering and archaeology indicated that she would not be content living the life of a typical 19th-century woman.

After graduating from Oxford University in 1892, Bell took a trip to Tehran. This trip sparked a lifelong interest in the Middle East, and later in the decade she took extended trips to Syria and Palestine. She recorded her experiences on these trips, and gained a wide readership in Britain after publishing them.

Once World War I started, Bell began her career with the Arab Bureau, a British intelligence division stationed in Cairo. Amongst her cohorts was T. E. Lawrence, or as he is better known, Lawrence of Arabia. Bell worked closely with Lawrence as they attempted to establish relations with Arab tribes in an attempt to gain alliances in the region. Once Baghdad came under British rule in 1917, Bell refocused her efforts on the establishment of a stable government in the Iraqi state. With Bell's help, Faisal I was positioned as monarch of Iraq. Bell's expertise also contributed to the 1921 Conference in Cairo, where, as the only woman present, she assisted Winston Churchill and others in determining Iraq's borders.

Following the conference, Bell remained in Baghdad and continued her work, this time calling upon her archaeological experience to establish a museum where Mesopotamian antiquities could be studied and displayed. Her hard work resulted in the National Museum of Iraq, and her early writings continue to be studied and referenced to this day.

Bell lived a rather extraordinary life, but despite all of her achievements she was firmly against the suffrage movement in Britain. She believed that she was an outlier, that most contemporary women lacked the experience needed to contribute to political discourse. Of course, the suffrage movement ended up succeeding without her support, and countless women have gone on to prove Bell wrong.

IDA PFEIFFER

1797-1858

-

For women in the early 1800s, gender norms were nearly impossible to ignore. But Ida Pfeiffer managed to shrug off society's expectations and achieve her dream of traveling the world.

With her father's encouragement, Ida Pfeiffer, born Reyer, grew up with a healthy appreciation of traditionally male activities like sports, adventure, and travel. But after her father passed away just before her 10th birthday, that all changed. Her mother went to great lengths to discourage her interests while encouraging typical early 19th-century feminine behavior. Indeed, Ida's mother succeeded in changing her daughter's habits, save for one: her wanderlust. No matter what, Ida always showed interest in seeing the world, and she blamed her inability to do so on the restrictions of her gender.

She wasn't wrong. Her mother, upon learning of a budding romance with a past tutor, insisted that Ida marry an older widower named Dr. Pfeiffer. The doctor was 24 years older than Ida, but in order to appease her mother she accepted his hand in marriage in 1820. Ida's inability to make her own choices was a direct result of a woman's expected place in society back then. Rather than explore the world, as she wanted to, Ida had to obey her mother and take the last name of a suitable husband. And so she became Ida Pfeiffer.

> "In exactly the same manner as the artist feels an invincible desire to paint, and the poet to give free course to his thoughts, so was I hurried away with an unconquerable wish to see the world."
> —Ida Pfeiffer

Their marriage lasted 18 years, until Dr. Pfeiffer's death in 1838. Ida respected her husband greatly, and so it seems that there was no resentment between the two of them. But following his death and the maturation of her children, Ida's suppressed wanderlust began to bubble up once more. She traveled from her homeland of Austria to Istanbul, and from there to Palestine, Egypt, and Italy. Ida wrote a book about her travels, and its success allowed her to keep following her dreams.

Ida would go on to travel around the world—not once, but

twice. Along the way she visited countries like India, Greece, China, Brazil, Chile, and Australia. In 1857, Ida decided she wanted to visit Madagascar. She succeeded in fulfilling this desire, though it ultimately resulted in her death.

About a year following her return from Madagascar, Ida passed away. The cause is believed to have been illness she had contracted while abroad. Though Ida's story may not be the most compelling or captivating, its importance cannot be overstated. Despite society's attempt to force her into a role she didn't want to play, Ida was still able to accomplish her unlikely goals. In doing so, she helped pave the way for future generations of female explorers.

ISABELLE EBERHARDT

1877-1904

-

This Swiss woman traveled from continent to continent in a life of carefree adventure. All she had to do was disguise herself as a man.

Toothless, liberated, and possibly dressed as a man, Isabelle Eberhardt died at the age of 27 while attempting to save the life of her husband, who had been caught in a flash flood. Amazingly, her premature death was the least surprising aspect of her life: Eberhardt herself may have been shocked she lasted as long as she did.

Born in Switzerland, Eberhardt always exhibited interest in living elsewhere, particularly Algeria. From the time she was little, Eberhardt often dressed up like a boy, per her father's suggestion. Perhaps it originally served as a method of advancing her social position, but it seemed that she cross-dressed even when the situation did not call for it. Before long she was more comfortable dressing as a man than a woman.

> **"Now more than ever do I realize that I will never be content with a sedentary life, that I will always be haunted by thoughts of a sun-drenched elsewhere."**
> **—Isabelle Eberhardt**

Eberhardt was fluent in Arabic by the time she was 16 and converted to Islam when she was 20. Her parents both died in the 1890s, and by that time Eberhardt had already made up her mind to leave Europe. All she had to do was save up the necessary funds.

In order to make money for her move to Algeria, Eberhardt went to France and passed herself off as a man to get a job as a dockhand in Marseilles. Before long she had saved enough for the ferry passage across the Mediterranean. Upon arriving in the coastal city of Bône (present-day Annaba), Eberhardt lived almost exclusively as her alter ego: a young man named Si Mahmoud Essaadi.

Many were shocked by Eberhardt's lifestyle. She drank heavily, smoked powerful hashish, behaved promiscuously, and voluntarily lived with the locals in the poorest part of town. Through devout worship and study she eventually earned the title of Sufi: an Islamic mystic. Despite her spiritual nature, Eberhardt never abandoned her adventurous lifestyle. She joined up with the Qadiriyya Sufi sect, a secretive institution dedicated to opposing French colonialism in Africa. Their protests often turned violent and, in 1901, an assassination attempt was made on Eberhardt's life. It is believed that the attempt came from the French government as a response to her rebellious nature. Following this attack, the French government determined that she was too provocative a presence, and thus banned her from all of France's North African colonies. But Eberhardt had a workaround.

For some time, she had romantic interest in an Algerian sergeant named Slimane Ehnni. In him, Eberhardt saw not only a potential lover, but an opportunity: if she were to marry Ehnni, she would have to be permitted in the land where he served. So the two wed. Following their union, Eberhardt had complete access to all levels of North African society.

But just because she benefited from the arrangement is no reason to call Eberhardt's love for Ehnni into question. After all, it was him she was trying to save when she drowned in the small town of Aïn Séfra in 1904. Eberhardt's lifestyle certainly took its toll, but it seems she would not have wanted it any other way.

T. E. LAWRENCE

1888-1935

-

Also known as Lawrence of Arabia, this British soldier fought alongside Arab forces during their war with the Turkish.

In tales of war, individual efforts often get lost in the greater story. That's no surprise; with so many active participants, it would be impossible to immortalize each person's contribution. But every now and again someone's impact is so dramatic that they earn themselves a place in history. T. E. Lawrence's involvement in the Arab Revolt against the German-allied Turks is such a story; his work made him a legend, and earned him the moniker we still use today—Lawrence of Arabia.

When World War I began, the British-born Lawrence was eager to serve his country. His knowledge of Arab affairs set him apart from the other soldiers and earned him a spot in the intelligence operations, specifically those pertaining to the Turkish Army. Lawrence spent 1914 in Cairo, where he gained information from Turkish prisoners and drew maps of their territories. By mid-1915, though, Lawrence was eager to get out of the back room and onto the battlefield.

Receiving permission from his commander, Lawrence joined an Arab force southwest of Medina. According to his autobiography *Seven Pillars of Wisdom*, he served as the brains behind many of the attacks carried out by this branch of the Arab uprising. His tactics largely utilized guerrilla warfare, focusing on bridges and railways that were essential to the Turkish strategy. By eliminating these means of travel, as well as ambushing Turkish forces, Lawrence and the Arabs restricted enemy combatants to areas where they were essentially useless.

Lawrence's ability to communicate and gain the respect of the Arab people as a foreigner was commendable, but before long the war had taken its toll on him. According to his own accounts, he was captured by opposing forces in Daraa while behind enemy lines. As a prisoner he was abused both physically and sexually. These events would emotionally scar Lawrence, and though he participated in Arab actions following his release, he would never fully recover from his imprisonment.

> "All men dream: but not equally. Those who dream by night in the dusty recesses of their minds wake in the day to find that it was vanity: but the dreamers of the day are dangerous men, for they may act their dreams with open eyes, to make it possible. This I did."
> —T. E. Lawrence

Traumatized from the hardships he had endured, Lawrence returned home in October 1918. Despite his many contributions to the Arab uprising, he felt dejected that they were unable to attain nationhood. For this reason, not only did Lawrence refuse the medals and honors the British government tried to bestow on him, he even politely rejected King George V's attempt to knight him.

LADY HESTER STANHOPE

1776-1839

-

*Born in England, she explored the Middle East in
an effort to help those who could not help themselves.*

In 1810, long before Gertrude Bell and T. E. Lawrence traveled
to the Middle East, Lady Hester Stanhope journeyed to the
region and unintentionally paved the way for future explorers.
She was only able to do so, however, after denouncing her
family's high society and permanently rejecting England, her
home country.

Shortly after departing, Stanhope ended up in
Constantinople, the capital of the Ottoman Empire. It was
here that she found the confidence she would embody for the
rest of her journeys. Muslim culture dictated that women did
not have the same rights as men, yet Stanhope never abided by
these restrictions. She refused to bow as the sultan passed before
her, even though all the men and women nearby genuflected
as he made his way to the mosque. Yet the sultan never sought
persecution for her apparent show of disrespect. Perhaps he took
it as a sign of her fortitude, for he allowed her to travel freely
throughout his dominion, and in turn she showed support for
his cause and leadership.

Stanhope left Constantinople to pursue further knowledge
and adventure, and eventually found herself in Damascus.
Though it was generally closed off to Europeans, Stanhope

had adopted the garb of Arab gentlemen and more or less renounced her European heritage, so she faced no issue while in the city. Before long, though, the plague had made its way across the land. Stanhope fell ill despite retreating to a secluded location. Weakened and unsure how to proceed, she ventured back to Lebanon, where she was invited to settle down in the mountainous village of Djoun.

After Stanhope recuperated, she did everything she could to assist the refugees of the battles raging below. There were domestic issues, such as local warlords vying for the position of power left in the wake of the sultan. There was the Battle of Navarino, which saw an entire Turkish armada destroyed by Russian, French, and British forces. And there was the Egyptian invasion of Lebanon and Syria in the 1830s. Through all of this, Stanhope aided those who sought a safe haven high up in the Lebanese mountains where she lived.

Lady Hester Stanhope's generosity earned her heavy praise from those she assisted. At one point she was even believed to be a holy prophet. This was not the case, but the truth is even more inspiring: she was simply a brave woman who took an interest in the Middle East's downtrodden folks. She may have been the first European to substantially contribute to Arab causes, but thanks to her efforts she was certainly not the last.

HEINRICH SCHLIEMANN

1822–1890

-

This German was determined to discover the historic site of Troy,
but may have been a bit overeager.

Homer's epic poems are foundational texts in Western civilization. German-born Heinrich Schliemann recognized the importance of Homer's tales, and his passion for them fueled a burning desire to uncover the ancient city of Troy.

Troy had long been considered primarily mythological, but to Schliemann, Homer's accounts of the ancient city seemed far too realistic to be fabricated. By the time he was middle-aged, Schliemann had made a considerable amount of money as a merchant—enough to fund this personal mission, which began in 1868. He surmised that Troy must have been east of Greece and that it likely occupied an important geographical position, based on the wealth that Homer detailed. Other than that, though, he was in the dark.

While researching and exploring, Schliemann heard through the grapevine that a mound had been discovered in Turkey. Large mounds often indicate the ruins of a city, and Schliemann had likely come across many of them in his quest. He traveled to the expanse of land located near the village of Hissarlik and began digging. Before long, he had uncovered ancient pieces of gold jewelry as well as the remains of fortified walls that appeared similar to those described by Homer in *The Iliad*.

Schliemann was convinced he had found Troy, and he hastily announced his discovery to the world in the 1874 book *Troy and Its Remains*. This proclamation was heard far and wide, and before long excavations were taking place all over Turkey.

However, not everybody was convinced by Schliemann's claims. Certainly, he had uncovered relics of the past, but many of his contemporaries found the evidence to be inconclusive. The ancient artifacts discovered on the site came from a wide range of eras, and the city's remaining foundation offered insufficient proof as well. One of the biggest tells was that the remains showed no signs of fire damage, which was supposedly the cause of Troy's destruction.

Schliemann brought a level of charisma to the field of archaeology that it previously lacked. Without a doubt, his showmanship helped to raise awareness of the history lost in Asia Minor. But this very showmanship also led to questionable professionalism. In his excitement and enthusiasm, Schliemann hurriedly dug into many sites he believed might have been Troy, and his verve produced a carelessness that damaged many ancient sites. Though he made many important discoveries, Schliemann's greatest contribution to his field was the promotion of it.

MARY KINGSLEY

1862–1900

–

Herself an Englishwoman, she condemned British
colonialism after spending time in West Africa.

In the 19th century, many English citizens had stereotypical notions of what life in African society was like. Words like *savage* and *uncivilized* were used quite often, and these attitudes contributed to the indifference many felt toward British colonization. Initially, Mary Kingsley embodied this ignorance. She set out for West Africa with little else but an exotic vacation in mind. But what she found there led her to campaign for the rights of African people and cultures for the rest of her life.

In 1893, Kingsley made her first trip to Sierra Leone. She spent a lot of her time collecting specimens and touring the western coast. Her interest had been piqued, and a year later she returned to West Africa with more ambitious exploration in mind. Kingsley ventured into the country's interior, often employing members of West African tribes as guides. She rode the rapids of big rivers and is believed to have been the first woman to climb Mount Cameroon.

Throughout her travels, dangers consistently threatened to bring her journey to a premature end. Disease, predators, and hostile natives were a constant presence during the year Kingsley spent in Africa. Mosquitoes and sandflies carried fatal illnesses such as malaria and leishmaniasis. But Kingsley was never shaken. On one occasion, she was traveling down a river when a large crocodile lunged into her canoe. Calmly, Kingsley disposed of the imposing beast with a firm smack on the snout. Another instance found her hiding behind a rock formation as a large leopard rested just a few yards away; peeking over the rocks every few moments, Kingsley waited for about 20 minutes (which felt more like a lifetime, she recalled) before the big cat moved on.

Upon returning from her arduous travels, Kingsley was determined to share her experiences with the people of England. Now firmly against colonialism, Kingsley knew that she would not find an abundance of support for beliefs that challenged popular thinking of the time, beliefs held by a woman, no less. But despite these impediments, Kingsley was intent on accomplishing her goal.

Through a series of lectures and a number of books, she spread her message about the intricacies of African culture and wildlife. She aimed to undermine the misinformed, offensive ideas Europeans held about the African people and their religions. Kingsley had observed that these people were not savages, but rather members of unique and complex societies. She believed that European interference was entirely unnecessary and that Africa would be better off left to its own devices.

The courage that Kingsley displayed in traveling to a part of the world that most deemed too dangerous is impressive in its own right. But what really sets her apart was the resolve she showed in condemning Britain's colonial administration.

TIMOTHY LEARY

1920–1996

-

A college professor who helped introduce
psychedelic drugs as a form of treatment.

As any traveler will tell you, the simple act of going from Point A to Point B can often shake something loose in the mind, helping one see the world through fresh eyes. But what if you could accomplish that same feeling without physically traveling anywhere? What if you could sit on your couch or lie in your bed and, by ingesting a substance, bring yourself somewhere new? Timothy Leary, famed psychotropic advocate, certainly believed it was possible; through responsible use of these substances, he argued, human experience could be improved and consciousness could be expanded.

Leary's first experience with psychedelics came while he was teaching at Harvard. He traveled to Cuernavaca, Mexico, with the intention of consuming psilocybin mushrooms after he heard about them from a colleague. Leary's experience in Mexico would profoundly alter his life, and from that point on he became committed to studying mind-altering substances.

He returned to the university in 1960 and almost immediately began the Harvard Psilocybin Project: a college-funded program that analyzed the effects of psilocybin on human subjects. Word spread relatively quickly, and soon Leary had gained the attention of the Beat Generation poet Allen Ginsberg. Together, Leary and

Ginsberg began publicly championing the legalization and use of psychedelic substances.

Before long, Leary made the jump from magic mushrooms to LSD. So strong was his belief that people should experiment with these drugs that he allowed students to dip into his own supply. The college administration found out, and Leary was discharged from Harvard in 1963. His career was far from over, though, as he would go on to become a prominent figure in the counterculture.

Now free to behave in any manner he chose, Leary began making the rounds within the hippest scenes. He tripped with William Burroughs and Jack Kerouac, sang with John Lennon, ate dinner with Roman Polanski, and even shared a jail cell with Charles Manson. Though the scientific community did not validate his findings, his life was no less rich for it. Perhaps the clearest sign that Leary was someone worth knowing was Richard Nixon's claim that he was "the most dangerous man in America."

Leary continued to write books and experiment with drugs until his death. As a man who had experienced much of what the world had to offer, it seemed as if he looked forward to whatever waited for him on the other side. He urged those around him to not make his death a sad occasion. For Leary, death was just another trip. So it only seems fitting that in April 1997 his ashes were sent into space on a Spanish satellite.

WILLIAM MONTGOMERY MCGOVERN

1897–1964

-

*This real-life Indiana Jones may not have found the lost ark,
but his exploits were no less daring.*

The dashing, adventurous professor is an archetype everyone knows by now, thanks to Harrison Ford's performance in *Raiders of the Lost Ark*. But as iconic as Ford's whip-bearing, fast-talking Indiana Jones might be, he hardly measures up to the real thing. Because when William Montgomery McGovern traveled the world to conduct his research, he had several adventures worthy of the silver screen.

McGovern's most famous story involved sneaking into the forbidden city of Lhasa, Tibet. It was the 1920s and the area was closed off to foreigners. McGovern, a U.S. citizen, could not simply stroll up and conduct his research there. So he disguised himself as a working-class Tibetan man, even going as far as to squeeze lemon juice in his eyes to darken their bright shade of blue.

Upon successfully reaching the city, McGovern revealed his true identity to officials, who took no issue with his being there. But not everyone agreed. After some local monks caught wind of his presence, they formed a mob and began pelting his lodging with rocks. Cunning as ever, McGovern reapplied his disguise, sneaked out the back of the house, and joined the mob in hurling stones. He managed to escape Lhasa unscathed.

McGovern went on to live an incredible life, serving as an adviser in World War II, learning 17 languages, and exploring the Amazon and South American ruins. His travels in South America involved a violent encounter with a 28-foot anaconda, which ended with McGovern standing over the great snake's corpse, smoking gun still in hand. He lived for days on nothing but plump, furry caterpillars and tough monkey meat. During another notable trip to the Amazon basin, McGovern adopted the customs of a local tribe and drank a hallucinogenic concoction intended to banish evil spirits.

It may seem impossible for a man so lively to hold down a steady job, but McGovern taught political science at Northwestern University for many years. Still a legend there, his stories echo through the halls as generations of professors and students pursue their own personal adventures.

HARRIET CHALMERS ADAMS

1875-1937

-

Harriet Chalmers Adams's passion for exploration led her deep into jungles and high onto mountaintops, where she captured all the world's wonders with her camera.

Harriet Chalmers Adams, born Harriet Chalmers, was lucky enough to recognize her passion at the young age of eight. Born in Stockton, California, there was no shortage of wilderness for young Adams to take in, and as soon as she was old enough her father took her horseback riding in the Sierra Nevada mountains, an experience that introduced her to a way of life that would come to define her.

Understanding that she wanted a life full of adventure, Adams began prepping herself early on in her education. Her homeschooling allowed her to modify the curriculum in a way which would benefit her the most, and she wisely chose to focus on foreign languages. By the time her schooling was complete, she had become fluent in Spanish and quite competent in Portuguese, German, French, and Italian.

In 1899, Adams married Franklin Pierce Adams, a man with a similar lust for adventure. Together, they took their first major trip in 1904, traveling all around South America for three years. During their trip, they crossed the Andes by horseback, explored ancient Incan temples, canoed down the Amazon River, visited indigenous villages, played with llamas, and visited every single country on the continent, covering more than 40,000 miles. Adams had experienced the adventure she had always dreamed of, and it exceeded her expectations.

When the couple returned to the United States, Adams visited the offices of the National Geographic Society to pitch a number of stories she had been developing throughout her travels. The editors were floored by everything she brought to the table: strong writing, color photography, filmed footage of significant moments, and her overwhelming charisma. Quickly, Adams became the publication's most important female contributor, and was sent all over the world to report on exotic locations and have daring adventures.

Adams retraced Columbus's steps in the West Indies, and Magellan's journey from Spain to the Philippines. She traveled throughout Western Europe and North Africa, and by 1913 had earned a place in Britain's Royal Geographical Society as one of history's most important adventurers. But even with all that, Adams was not ready to hang up her hat.

As World War I broke out, Adams recognized the importance of documenting the horrors, not from a distance, but up close and personal. Adams, commissioned by *Harper's Magazine*, ended up being one of only a handful of female reporters to cover the war. Before returning home, she spent three months in the notorious French trenches, making her one of the few women to experience the front lines.

EDITH DURHAM

1863-1944

-

Known as the "Queen of the Highlanders," Edith Durham brought international attention to the struggles of Albania.

Though she would eventually come to be known to Albanians as the "Queen of the Highlanders," it was not until Edith Durham explored a handful of other Balkan countries that she found herself heavily involved in the politics of the developing nation.

Durham began her relationship with the Balkan Peninsula in 1900, when she and a friend set off on a vacation down the Adriatic Sea toward the town of Kotor in Montenegro. The country's beauty led her back the following year, and then on to the neighboring country of Serbia the year after. She began familiarizing herself with the Serbian language in order to have a firm grasp on the culture before beginning her first book, *Through the Lands of the Serb*.

Her early fondness for Serbia and Montenegro was cooled by the nations' expansionist strategies, which led her to shift allegiances further south to Albania and its wild populations. She traveled extensively in the region under the protection of an ancient Albanian custom, "sworn virgins," which dictated that a woman should not be harmed if she wore men's clothing. Despite the relative safety this provided, her travels were rarely comfortable. Durham would ride or walk very long distances at a time, often alone, taking shelter wherever it was available. On one particularly arduous journey, she traveled all day in torrential rain. Finally, she came upon a harem and was offered a bed for the night. The exhausted Durham gratefully accepted, only to find out that the bed was located in a barn full of onions.

In the end, Durham gained the respect of the Albanian highland people and published *High Albania*, a book detailing the Balkan country and its quest for independence. As a result of her unwavering passion and bravery, Durham was able to bring international attention to the country's struggles.

ALEXANDRINE TINNÉ

1835-1869

-

*Despite her tragic death, Alexandrine Tinné is
celebrated today as one of the earliest women explorers
to conduct ethnographic research in Africa.*

Like many passionate young explorers of her day, Alexandrine
"Alexine" Tinné was intelligent, curious, and fearless.
Unfortunately, that passion would lead to her violent demise,
and her story now exists as a sort of cautionary tale for budding
adventurers looking to travel the world.

In 1855, the young Dutch woman visited Africa for the
first time, stopping in the Egyptian cities of Cairo, Luxor, and
Karnak. From then on, Alexine focused the majority of her
attention on the Nile River. In 1861, she set out for the regions
surrounding the White Nile, accompanied by her mother
and aunt.

The three women traveled far up the Nile River with a small
party of other explorers, and made it as far as Uganda when
Alexine's illness forced them to stop. The following year they
made another attempt, only to be struck down by illness once
again. Alexine lost her mother, her aunt, and her dog on that
expedition. These tragedies severely impacted her disposition,
and for a while Alexine stopped exploring altogether and settled
down in Cairo, where she worked on a book and took small
trips to different places on the Mediterranean Sea. Eventually,

Alexine became deeply interested in a particular group of North African natives: the Tuaregs. It was in 1869, during her second attempt to reach the Tuareg regions of the Libyan Desert, that she successfully established contact with the tribes.

Her trip across the Sahara was trying, and Alexine had pushed on through illness and fatigue in order to reach the Tuaregs. Along the way, she collected scores of ethnographic data: work that luckily found its way into several museums after her death. Sadly, during what should have been a moment of triumph, Alexine's life was ended by a mysterious attack by Tuareg tribesman on August 1, 1869. She was struck down by a sword to the neck and left to die.

Strangely, no motive for the slaying was ever confirmed. Some historians believe that the Tuaregs sought out gold, though the explorers did not have any. Others believe the attack resulted from strife within the Tuaregs, and that Alexine was simply in the wrong place at the wrong time. Despite her tragic death, she is celebrated today as one of the earliest women explorers to conduct ethnographic research in Africa.

MARIANNE NORTH

1830–1890

-

*Marianne North's prolific career not only brought joy
to those who viewed her colorful oil paintings, it also made
a significant scientific contribution.*

Marianne North traveled far and wide in order to observe new and interesting species of plants, but her motivation was not scientific. Gifted with an innate ability to paint, she loved to capture the intimate details of flowers.

North didn't discover her talents until middle age, and it wasn't until the death of her father in 1869 that she decided to travel far from her family home in London in order to illustrate the world's tropical plants. Though she would go on to experience some of the earth's most exotic locations, her first adventure was to somewhere quite unremarkable: Boston, Massachusetts.

Despite its general plainness, North was still overwhelmed with the sheer number of new plants that existed in that American city. She saw white orchids, ferns, and scarlet lobelia dancing around the gardens. North was enraptured, and she was quickly motivated to plan another trip, this time to a destination worthy of awe: Jamaica. She rented a small home on the island nation and spent her days painting the many species of flora: orchids, passionflowers, and palms—not to mention the bananas. From that point, North decided she would never stop traveling or painting.

Her travels lasted for 14 years, and took her to many countries: Japan, Canada, Brazil, Australia, New Zealand, Sri Lanka, and India, just to name a few. Though she traveled alone, her trips were rarely treacherous, but British citizens remained enraptured by her adventuring, closely following her whereabouts and waiting to see what she'd painted.

Before long North had a massive portfolio of flower paintings, all depicted as they appeared in nature. After her first public showing, North offered to build a gallery for Kew Gardens in which she could display her work, and the UK institution happily accepted. In 1882, 833 of North's original paintings were hung in a dedicated space, arranged by geographical locales. North's prolific career not only brought joy to those who viewed her colorful oil paintings, but they also made a significant contribution to science, as quite a few of the flowers she depicted had not yet been discovered by botanists.

KIRA SALAK

1971-PRESENT

-

Since her first expedition to Mozambique, Kira Salak has traversed Papua New Guinea, cycled 700 miles across Alaska, and has became the first person to kayak solo down West Africa's Niger River.

Kira Salak has long been devoted to a low-tech, solo traveling style, which largely stems from her admiration for explorers of the past. Not to say that Salak does not utilize technology at all, but her methods are stripped down. And while traveling alone has made her a target for predators of all kinds, she has found that surviving these experiences is deeply empowering.

At the young age of 20, Salak found herself in Mozambique during the country's civil war. Without her own means of transportation, she hitched a ride in a truck that was headed down a particularly dangerous road known as the "Bone Yard Stretch." The truck broke down, and Salak was quickly accosted by a group of government troops. She ran as fast as she could, lungs burning, not daring to look back until she made it across the border to Zimbabwe. Salak barely escaped with her life.

Despite this traumatic introduction to the world of exploration, it seems that Salak's desire for adventure only increased. On one of her more trying journeys, Salak kayaked nearly 600 miles along Mali's Niger River, paddling up from Old Ségou to Timbuktu. Her trip started with what some may have perceived as an ominous warning: a great thunderstorm, consisting of deafening thunder, violent rain, and lightning that seemed to strike every surface all at once. But it was July 2002, storm season in Mali, so Salak was unfazed by this turn in the weather. She set off the next day, seeming to follow the storm as it moved north.

Unsurprisingly, the weather on the river was no more forgiving than it was on shore. Before long, large waves were crashing into Salak's small inflatable kayak, and she felt a muscle in her right arm tear as she fought against the current with all of her might. Finally, the storm subsided, the river calmed, and she began to progress at a steady rate. When it was time to rest for the night, she'd stop at a village along the river and take shelter with a friendly local; if none could be found, she would build a makeshift camp.

Continuing up the river, paddling meekly past packs of hippos and quickly away from villagers who seemed to want nothing more than to capsize her, Salak finally reached Timbuktu, making her the first person to kayak along the whole stretch alone. When she reached the city, she was disgusted by the apparent enslavement of the Bella tribal people, despite the Malian government's denial of it. The conditions for these people were miserable, and Salak felt compelled to assist in the best way she could: she purchased two of the Bella slaves and immediately granted them freedom.

> **"To Whom It May Concern— Only four words of advice: It can be done."**
> **—Kira Salak**

To this day, Salak continues to insert herself in situations that most would shy away from. Since her journey up the Niger River, she has visited some of the earth's most inhospitable destinations and cycled 700 miles across Alaska. She has not once been deterred by the men who tell her she should not travel alone; the only voices she hears are those of the women she inspires.

FRIDTJOF NANSEN

1861–1930

-

Fridtjof Nansen is considered a pioneer of polar exploration, even if he has slipped through the cracks of history.

Fridtjof Nansen put himself in peril countless times in the name of scientific exploration, a daring that started when Nansen's mother introduced him to skiing at a very young age. He proved masterful at the sport, and ended up utilizing his skills throughout his life as an explorer and scientist.

A zoologist who studied at the University of Oslo, one of Nansen's most lauded adventures took place in March 1895. About two years earlier, he'd departed the coast of Siberia aboard the ship *Fram*. Outfitted to withstand thick Arctic ice, the ship was also full of scientific equipment meant to gather data on ocean currents, weather, and marine biology. Nansen's hope was to use the water's natural currents to drift to the North Pole, a controversial idea that many established seamen denounced as too dangerous among the massive blocks of ice. But *Fram* was strong enough to withstand "the embraces of ice," as Nansen put it. Unfortunately, the ice wasn't Nansen's real problem. About 18 months into the expedition, he grew impatient with inconsistent currents and slow going, and hatched a plan of his own: Nansen and his shipmate Hjalmar Johansen would leave the *Fram* behind and trek to the North Pole by themselves.

Relying partly on his skiing prowess, Nansen dashed over snow and ice with 28 dogs, three sleds, and two kayaks. The pair made decent time, covering roughly nine nautical miles per day, but as they traveled conditions worsened. The skiing surface became increasingly more uneven, which slowed them down greatly. Having packed enough rations for only 30 days, the decision was made to turn back after 23 days of travel. However, they came extremely close to the pole—the farthest north ever recorded at the time—before turning south to intersect with the ship's planned course. By August 21, 1896, the men reached Norway. That same day, the ship broke free of the ice and entered open water, and Nansen and Johansen were reunited with the vessel.

Nansen would go on to conduct multiple scientific studies, always publishing his findings and teaching those who were interested. And while he has slipped through the cracks of history, he is still considered a pioneer of polar exploration. Part of the reason his Arctic achievements may not receive their due are the other sizable achievements in Nansen's life: after becoming quite interested in international politics, Nansen helped the Norwegian government with the repatriation of

450,000 Norwegian prisoners of war in 1920, an act for which he was awarded the 1922 Nobel Peace Prize.

SIR JOHN MANDEVILLE

1300–1371

-

In Travels, *Mandeville comes into contact with such mutants as dog-headed cannibals, humans with ears long enough to reach their knees, and a race of people with no noses or mouths, to name a few.*

There's a particular strangeness to Sir John Mandeville's fame, and not just because of the mutants and beasts he claimed to have met during his travels. Mandeville's influence is especially bizarre because it's assumed he never existed at all.

Mandeville became a public figure due to the release of his travel memoir, *The Travels of Sir John Mandeville*, circa 1360. The book focuses primarily on Mandeville's travels throughout the East, drawing upon real-life accounts from explorers such as Vincent of Beauvais and Odoric of Pordenone in order to create a realistic description of the kingdom of

"Of Paradise I cannot speak properly, for I have not been there; and that I regret."
—Sir John Mandeville

the Great Khan. Realistic, that is, until the creatures enter the story. In *Travels*, Mandeville comes into contact with dog-headed cannibals, humans with ears long enough to reach their knees, a race of people with no noses or mouths, and men whose heads grow beneath their shoulders.

It is widely accepted that Mandeville never existed, at least not under that name. Outside of his "memoir," no historical records or gravesites suggest the author was a real person. But the fictional Mandeville is still noteworthy for his ability to amaze and inspire countless future explorers, including Christopher Columbus. And while Mandeville's memoir is unreliable, not all of it is fantasy, implying that the author may have had real experiences in far-flung lands. However, it's just as likely that the author simply read about the places he discussed. To this day, no one can say for certain who wrote the book or why, making its popularity and influence all the more astonishing.

STRABO

CA. 64 BCE–CA. AD 25

-

Throughout his life, Strabo journeyed to Egypt,
Ethiopia, Asia Minor, and beyond.

Ancient maps bear little resemblance to the atlases we know today. There were plenty of uncharted territories that were often marked by strange, mythical monsters, as if to say, "Go forth at your own peril." Little by little, though, brave souls did go forth in order to gain an accurate understanding of their world's geography and selflessly share it with the masses. Greco-Roman historian and *Geographica* author Strabo of Amasia was one such brave soul. Utilizing both historical sources and personal experience, he created one of the largest works of ancient geography known to man.

Above all, Strabo valued precision in his maps. He condemned several previous geographers for their apparent disregard for accuracy and vowed that he would improve upon their efforts. In order to do so, he selected a handful of sources he deemed respectable and used their contents to inform his own work. The work of men such as Polybius and Poseidonius, who knew both geography and ethnography extensively, aided Strabo in his decision to project the entire sphere of Earth onto a flat surface. This particular method was balked at by mathematicians, but Strabo was not concerned with mathematics, only the contents of the world.

In addition to the few sources he respected, Strabo also tapped into his own memories in order to create his maps. Although he barely mentions his personal experiences in his work, his journeys to Egypt, Ethiopia, and Asia Minor, as well as his voyage up the Nile River, clearly impacted his work. Sections of his book that detail expanses of land between Tuscany and Armenia, for example, rely on Strabo's firsthand experience in the regions, though details of his actual travels are virtually absent from the text.

It is not known when exactly Strabo wrote *Geographica*, his famous 17-volume text, but today it is considered perhaps the ancient world's most comprehensive geographical text, covering the territory of the Greek and Roman Empires and much of their history as well.

CHRISTOPHER MCCANDLESS

1968-1992

-

Setting off into the Alaskan frontier never to return,
Christopher McCandless inspired multitudes of
unsatisfied people to reject the ordinary, no matter the cost.

To many, Christopher McCandless is a hero. He embodied a love of freedom that appeals to anybody who struggles with the banalities of everyday life, and rejected the comforts he knew for something unpredictable: a life outside of society's boundaries. To others, he is representative of the very things that make such a lifestyle problematic—a cautionary tale for those who wish to keep the Beat Generation alive years after it rightfully came to an end.

Unlike many adventurers, McCandless did not have a specific goal in mind when he set out on the open road. In 1990, following his graduation from college, he decided to leave civilization. He donated the majority of his money, abandoned his car, and simply began traveling the world. By 1992, McCandless found himself on the Alaskan frontier. He had nothing but a rifle, a camera, some books, a diary, and a bag of rice. Eventually, after the rice ran out and attempts at hunting proved unsuccessful, McCandless took shelter in an abandoned bus near Denali. There he remained, penning entries in his journal until he died of starvation.

Following his death, McCandless's story gained significant

attention, even more so with the release of *Into the Wild*, a biography written by Jon Krakauer. The book, which was lauded upon release and now appears widely on advanced high school English curriculums, paints a rosy picture of McCandless's rejection of society. In a way, it glorifies the fundamental foolishness of his endeavor. After all, McCandless was seeking enlightenment, not death. Had he had the basic foresight to bring a map on his quest, which would have enabled him to discover a nearby river crossing, his story may not have ended in tragedy. Some people, however, draw inspiration from McCandless; they seem him as someone who felt unsatisfied with society and took action.

McCandless's story is, in a word, polarizing, and his accomplishment is difficult to put into words. His success was not of a material nature; he did not discover new lands or save lives. Nor was it necessary, in a universal sense; many saw his death as the ultimate foolishness, easily avoided and never worth it from the start. But McCandless was just doing what he felt he had to do, and he was able to forge relationships along the way—at one point, an elderly man even offered to adopt him— that very few others do.

Acknowledgments

This book is possible because of the many people whose stories I had the privilege to tell, and the many brilliant people who have told those stories before me. Between the books, newspapers, and essays I've read, there was never any shortage of inspiration or help.

In addition to the incredible source material I scoured, I also drew inspiration from a number of people in my life. To my publisher John Whalen, and editors Patrick Scafidi and Buzz Poole, three people who have contributed directly to this book's conception and completion, I say thank you for staying the course with me. To my brother Jake, I say thank you for doing everything with me. And to my parents, I say thank you for the world.

Danny

AFRICA.
Agi:
iymba.
Berdoa
Albaili
Targa
Digir
Borno
Cano
Guan-
guara
Benin
Cago
Alma
Melegete
Nubi
Nu
Ambia
Ab
Gaga
con:
Antonio
C. Bonæ Spei
Tristan
de
NW
W
SW
S
SE
E
NE

WORKS CITED

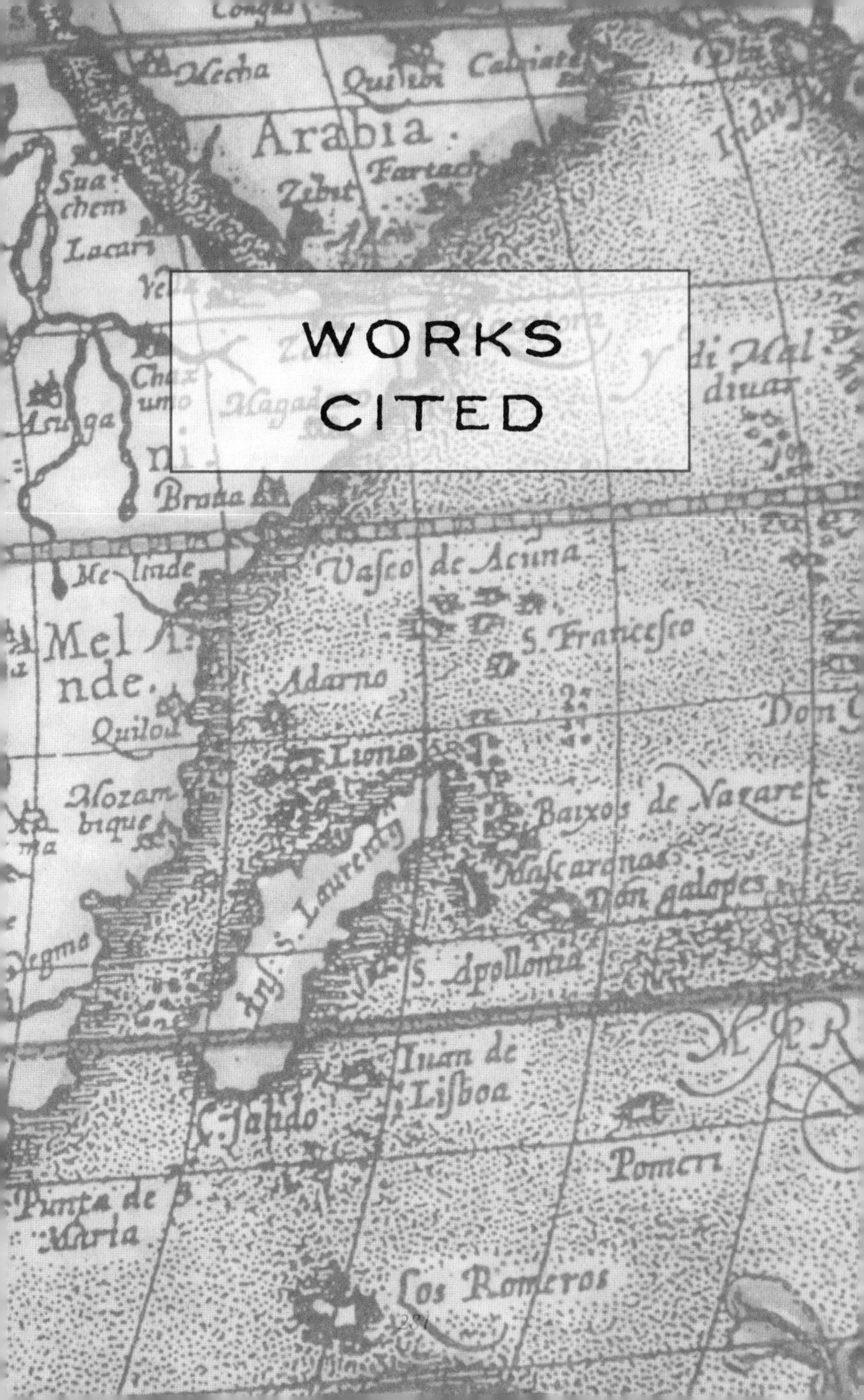

Mecha
Arabia.
Zebet
Lacari
Mel
nde.
Quiloa
Mozambique
Brava
Vasco de Acuna
S. Francesco
Adarno
Baixos de Nazaret
Mascarenas
S. Apollonia
Iuan de
Lisboa
Pomeri
Los Romeros
Punta de
Maria

Works Cited

Wilbur and Orville Wright
"1903—The First Flight." National Parks Service. Web. Accessed 20 Apr. 2018.

"The Wright Brothers: The Invention of the Aerial Age." Smithsonian Air and Space Museum. Web. Accessed 20 Apr. 2018.

Wright, Wilbur. "Some Aeronautical Experiments. Mr. Wilbur Wright, Dayton, Ohio." *Wright: Aeronautical Experiments*. Presented to the Western Society of Engineers, 18 Sept. 1901. Web. Accessed 20 Apr. 2018.

Amelia Earhart
"Amelia Earhart." Ameliaearhart.com. Web. Accessed 20 Apr. 2018.

"Amelia Earhart." History.com. 2009. Web. Accessed 20 Apr. 2018.

Charles Lindbergh
Berg, A. Scott. *Lindbergh*. Simon & Schuster, 2013. Print.

Duffy, James P. *Lindbergh vs. Roosevelt: The Rivalry That Divided America*. MJF Books, 2012. Print.

Robinson, Roger E. "Historic Missourians: Charles Lindbergh (1902–1974)." *The State Historical Society of Missouri*. Web. Accessed 20 Apr. 2018.

Neil Armstrong
"Neil Armstrong." History.com. 2010. Web. Accessed 20 Apr. 2018.

Dunbar, Brian. "Biography of Neil Armstrong." *NASA*. 10 Mar. 2015. Web. Accessed 20 Apr. 2018.

Pyle, Rod. "Apollo 11's Scariest Moments: Perils of the 1st Manned Moon Landing." Space.com. Web. Accessed 20 Apr. 2018.

Wilford, John Noble. "Neil Armstrong, First Man on Moon, Dies at 82." *New York Times*. 25 Aug. 2012. Web. Accessed 20 Apr. 2018.

Yuri Gagarin
Jaggard, Victoria. "What Yuri Gagarin Saw on First Space Flight." *National Geographic*. 13 Apr. 2011. Web. Accessed 20 Apr. 2018.

Pruitt, Sarah. "What Really Happened to Yuri Gagarin, the First Man in Space?" History.com. 12 Apr. 2016. Web. Accessed 20 Apr. 2018.

Valentina Tereshkova
"First Woman in Space." History.com. Web. Accessed 20 Apr. 2018.

"Valentina Tereshkova." *Encyclopædia Britannica*. 07 Sept. 2017. Web. Accessed 20 Apr. 2018.

Dejevsky, Mary. "The First Woman in Space: 'People Shouldn't Waste Money on Wars.'" *The Guardian*. 29 Mar. 2017. Web. Accessed 20 Apr. 2018.

Jim Lovell

Cortright, Edgar M. *Apollo Expeditions to the Moon*. Scientific and Technical Information Office, National Aeronautics and Space Administration, 1975. Print.

Howell, Elizabeth. "Apollo 13: Facts About NASA's Near-Disaster." *Space.com*. 09 Oct. 2017. Web. Accessed 20 Apr. 2018.

Juliane Koepcke

Koepcke, Juliane. "Juliane Koepcke: How I Survived a Plane Crash." *BBC News*. 24 Mar. 2012. Web. Accessed 20 Apr. 2018.

Macdonald, Katherine. "The Girl Who Fell from the Sky." *Reader's Digest*. 01 July 2013. Web. Accessed 20 Apr. 2018.

Pleitgen, Frederik. "Survivor Still Haunted by 1971 Air Crash." *CNN*. 02 July 2009. Web. Accessed 20 Apr. 2018.

Bessie Coleman

"Bessie Coleman." *PBS*. Web. Accessed 20 Apr. 2018.

Kline, Alex. "Celebrating Women's History Month with a Little Inspiration." *Florida Courier*. 14 Mar. 2014. Web. Accessed 20 Apr. 2018.

Neta Snook

"Amelia Earhart to her former flight instructor, Neta Snook, 1929." Gilderlehrman.org. Web.

"Neta Snook." Ameshistory.com. Web.

Ken Kesey & the Merry Pranksters

"Signboard, Pass the Acid Test." National Museum of American History. Web. Accessed 21 Apr. 2018.

Andersen, Kurt, and Gibney, Alex. "Ken Kesey's Magic Trip and Extreme Tango." *WNYC*. 12 Aug. 2011.

Kerr, Euan. "The Harsh Reality Behind the Merry Pranksters 'Magic Trip.'" *Minnesota Public Radio News*, 02 Sept. 2011. Web. Accessed 21 Apr. 2018.

Kesey, Ken. *One Flew Over the Cuckoo's Nest*. New American Library, 1989. Print.

Lehmann-Haupt, Christopher. "Ken Kesey, Author of 'Cuckoo's Nest,' Who Defined the Psychedelic Era, Dies at 66." *New York Times*. 10 Nov. 2001. Web. Accessed 21 Apr. 2018.

Stone, Robert. *Prime Green: Remembering the Sixties*. Harper Collins, 2008. Print.

Annie Londonderry

Berkenwald, Leah. "Annie Londonderry and the Bicycle as a Vehicle of Social Liberation." *Jewish Women's Archive*. 23 June 2011. Web. Accessed 21 Apr. 2018.

Zheutlin, Peter. *Around the World on Two Wheels: Annie Londonderry's Extraordinary Ride*. Citadel, 2008. Print.

Annemarie Schwarzenbach

Leybold-Johnson, Isobel. "Swiss Writer's Life Was Stranger Than Fiction." Swissinfo.Ch. 23 May 2008. Web. Accessed 21 Apr. 2018.

Lorey de Lacharrière, Barbara. "Annemarie Schwarzenbach: A Life." Swissinstitute.net. 1989. Web. Accessed 21 Apr. 2018.

Schwarzenbach, Annemarie. *All the Roads Are Open: The Afghan Journey*. Seagull Books, 2011. Print.

Paul Theroux

Salzman, Mark. "He Hated Sightseeing." *New York Times*. 19 June 1988. Web. Accessed 21 Apr. 2018.

Theroux, Paul. *The Tao of Travel: Enlightenments from Lives on the Road*. Mariner Books, 2012. Print.

Theroux, Paul. *Riding the Iron Rooster: By Train through China*. Houghton Mifflin, 2006. Print.

Thomas Stevens

Docevski, Boban. "Thomas Stevens: The man who cycled the world on a penny-farthing bicycle." *The Vintage News*. 27 May 2017. Web. Accessed 21 Apr. 2018.

Kennedy, Tristan. "The 5 Most Incredible Journeys You've Never Heard Of." Mpora.com. Web. Accessed 21 Apr. 2018.

Stevens, Thomas. *Around The World on a Bicycle: From Teheran to Yokohama*. Forgotten Books, 2016. Print.

Sir Edmund Hillary

"Sir Edmund Hillary." *Encyclopædia Britannica*, Encyclopædia Britannica, Inc., 03 Aug. 2017. Web. Accessed 21 Apr. 2018.

Kuchler, Bonnie Louise. *That's Life: "Wild" Wit & Wisdom*. Willow Creek Press, 2003. Print.

McFadden, Robert D. "Edmund Hillary, First on Everest, Dies at 88." *New York Times*. 09 Jan. 2008. Web. Accessed 21 Apr. 2018.

Yuri Trush

"The True Story of a Man-Eating Tiger's 'Vengeance.'" *NPR*. 14 Sept. 2010. Web. Accessed 21 Apr. 2018.

Vaillant, John. *The Tiger: A True Story of Vengeance and Survival*. Alfred A. Knopf, 2011. Print.

Sir Ernest Henry Shackleton

"Antarctic Explorers: Ernest Shackleton." South-Pole.com. Web. Accessed 21 Apr. 2018.

"Ernest Shackleton." Biography.com. 03 Feb. 2016. Web. Accessed 21 Apr. 2018.

"History—Ernest Shackleton." BBC.com. Web. Accessed 21 Apr. 2018.

Butler, George, director. *The Endurance: Shackleton's Legendary Antarctic Expedition*. Discovery Channel, 2000.

Hussey, L. D. A. *South with Shackleton*. Purnell, 1949. Print.

Joe Simpson

Reed, Susan, and Healy, Laura Sanderson. "Left for Dead on a Peruvian Peak, Joe Simpson Survives to Write Movingly About the Climbers' Code." *People*. Web. Accessed 21 Apr. 2018.

Simpson, Joe. "Joe Simpson: My Journey Back Into the Void." *The Telegraph*. 22 Oct. 2007. Web. Accessed 21 Apr. 2018.

Simpson, Joe, and Colwell, Tony. *Touching the Void*. BookBaby, 2012. Print.

Xuanzang

Keyes, W. Noel. *Bioethical and Evolutionary Approaches to Medicine and the Law*. American Bar Association, 2007. Print.

Lee, Der Huey. "Xuanzang (Hsüan-Tsang) (602–664)." *Internet Encyclopedia of Philosophy*. Web. Accessed 22 Apr. 2018.

Alison Hargreaves

"Tom Ballard Conquers the Alps 20 Years After His Mother's Death on K2." *The Telegraph*. 26 Feb. 2016. Web. Accessed 22 Apr. 2018.

Boggan, Steve. "K2: The Final Hours." *The Independent*. 19 Aug. 1995. Web. Accessed 22 Apr. 2018.

Child, Greg. "The Last Ascent of Alison Hargreaves." *Outside*. Nov. 1995. Web. Accessed 22 Apr. 2018.

Glauber, Bill. "Woman Who Lived to Climb Is Mountain's Latest Victim." *Baltimore Sun*. 19 Aug. 1995. Web. Accessed 22 Apr. 2018.

Venables, Stephen. "Obituary: Alison Hargreaves." *The Independent*. 20 Aug. 1995. Web. Accessed 22 Apr. 2018.

Sacagawea

"Sacagawea." Biography.com. 27 Apr. 2017. Web. Accessed 22 Apr. 2018.

"Sacagawea." *PBS*. Web. Accessed 22 Apr. 2018.

Marks, Lara. "Lewis and Clark Speak." 16 Dec. 1998. Web. Accessed 22 Apr. 2018.

Swaminarayan

"Bhagwan Swaminarayan's Life: Biography—Early Days, Leaving Home." Swaminarayan.org. 1999. Web. Accessed 22 Apr. 2018.

"Brief Biography of Bhagwan Shree Swaminarayan." *ISSO LA News*. 2010. Web. Accessed 22 Apr. 2018.

Kincaid, C. A. *The Outlaws of Kathiawar, and Other Studies*. Times Press, 1905. Print.

The Upanishads: Translations from the Sanskrit. Amereon House, 2011. Print.

Fanny Bullock Workman

Pauly, Thomas H. "Vita: Fanny Bullock Workman." *Harvard Magazine*. 03 Mar. 2014. Web. Accessed 22 Apr. 2018.

Woolf, Jo. "Fanny Bullock Workman—A Woman of Substance." *Royal Scottish Geographical Society*. 18 Nov. 2016. Web. Accessed 22 Apr. 2018.

Genghis Khan
"Genghis Khan." History.com. 2009. Web. Accessed 22 Apr. 2018.

Bawden, Charles R. "Genghis Khan." *Encyclopædia Britannica*. 15 Nov. 2017. Web. Accessed 22 Apr. 2018.

Edwards, Mike. "Genghis Khan." *National Geographic*. December 1996. Web. Accessed 22 Apr. 2018.

Juvaini, Ata-Malik, et al. *Genghis Khan: The History of the World Conqueror*. Manchester University Press, 1997. Print.

Robert Falcon Scott
"Explorer Robert Falcon Scott: The British Antarctic Expedition 1910." Scottslastexpedition.org. Web. Accessed 22 Apr. 2018.

"Scott of the Antarctic." *BBC*. Web. Accessed 22 Apr. 2018.

"Scott of the Antarctic Could Have Been Saved If His Orders Had Been Followed, Say Scientists." *The Telegraph*. 30 Dec. 2012. Web. Accessed 22 Apr. 2018.

Scott, Robert Falcon. *Scott's Last Expedition: The Journals of Captain R. F. Scott*. Dodd, Mead, 1913. Print.

Meriwether Lewis & William Clark
"Lewis and Clark." History.com. 2009. Web. Accessed 22 Apr. 2018.

Gass, Patrick. *Journal of the Lewis and Clark Expedition, Reprinted From the Edition of 1811*. McClurg, 1904. Print.

Perry, Douglas. "Lewis & Clark Expedition." Archives.gov. Web. Accessed 22 Apr. 2018.

Osa & Martin Johnson
"Women's History Month: A Filmmaker and a Microfossil Expert." Amnh.org. Web. Accessed 22 Apr. 2018.

Horak, Laura. "Osa Johnson." *Women Film Pioneers Project*. Columbia University: Center for Digital Research and Scholarship. 27 Sept. 2013. Web. Accessed 22 Apr. 2018.

Robert O'Hara Burke
"Robert O'Hara Burke." *Encyclopædia Britannica*. 16 Mar. 2017. Web. Accessed 22 Apr. 2018.

Fitzpatrick, Kathleen. "Robert O'Hara Burke." *Australian Dictionary of Biography*. Web. Accessed 22 Apr. 2018.

Burke, Robert O'Hara. "Robert O'Hara Burke's Notebook." Burkeandwills.net.au/Journals. Web. Accessed 22 Apr. 2018.

Robert Peary
"Robert Peary." Bowdoin.edu. Web. Accessed 22 Apr. 2018.

Smith, Dinitia. "An Eskimo Boy and Injustice in Old New York; a Campaigning Writer Indicts an Explorer and a Museum." *New York Times*. 14 Mar. 2000. Web. Accessed 22 Apr. 2018.

Alexander the Great
"Alexander the Great." History.com. 2009. Web. Accessed 22 Apr. 2018.

"Alexander the Great: Alexander of Macedon Biography." Historyofmacedonia.org. Web. Accessed 22 Apr. 2018.

Walbank, Frank W. "Alexander the Great." *Encyclopædia Britannica*. 16 Feb. 2017. Web. Accessed 22 Apr. 2018.

Rufus, Quintus Curtius, and Froesch, Hartmut. *Historiae Alexandri Magni*. Reclam, 2015. Print.

Balto
"Sled Dogs: An Alaskan Epic." *PBS*. 22 Oct. 2014. Web. Accessed 23 Apr. 2018.

Shamleh, Abdelhadi Abu. "The Real Story of Amblin's Balto." Akc.org. 13 Feb. 2014. Web. Accessed 23 Apr. 2018.

"Nome, Alaska." Nomealaska.org. Web. Accessed 23 Apr. 2018.

Erik Weihenmayer
"Erik Weihenmayer." Nobarriersusa.org. Web. Accessed 23 Apr. 2018.

Angley, Natalie. "'All of Us in a Way Are Climbing Blind.'" *CNN*. 11 May 2016. Web. Accessed 23 Apr. 2018.

Norris, Chris. "Who Is Erik Weihenmayer? A Blind Man's Ambitious Adventure." *Men's Journal*. 04 Dec. 2017. Web. Accessed 23 Apr. 2018.

Wang, Christine. "This Man Scaled Mt. Everest Against All Odds." *CNBC*. 04 Apr. 2016. Web. Accessed 23 Apr. 2018.

Weihenmayer, Erik. *Touch the Top of the World*. Coronet, 2002. Print.

Yuichiro Miura
Henderson, Barney. "Meet Yuichiro Miura, the Man Planning to Conquer Everest at 90." *The Telegraph*. 01 Jan, 2016. Web. Accessed 23 Apr. 2018.

Joan of Arc
"Joan of Arc." History.com. 2009. Web. Accessed 23 Apr. 2018.

Vale, Malcolm G.A., and Lanhers, Yvonne. "Saint Joan of Arc." *Encyclopædia Britannica*. 01 Feb. 2016. Web. Accessed 23 Apr. 2018.

Williamson, Allen. "Biography of Joan of Arc." Joanofarc.org. Web. Accessed 23 Apr. 2018.

Hugh Glass
Landry, Clay. "Fact vs. Fiction: The True Story of Hugh Glass." Hughglass.org. Web. Accessed 23 Apr. 2018.

Peterson, Nancy M. "Hugh Glass: The Truth Behind the Revenant Legend." *Wild West*. 19 Oct. 2016. HistoryNet.com. Web. Accessed 23 Apr. 2018.

The Revenant. Dir. Alejandro G. Iñárritu. 20th Century Fox, 2015. Film.

Tikkanen, Amy. "Hugh Glass." *Encyclopædia Britannica*. 24 Nov. 2017. Web. Accessed 23 Apr. 2018.

Aleister Crowley
"Aleister Crowley." *Encyclopædia Britannica*. 13 Oct. 2017. Web. Accessed 23 Apr. 2018.

Flood, Alison. "Unseen Aleister Crowley Writings Reveal 'Short-Story Writer of the Highest Order.'" *The Guardian*. 15 Oct. 2015. Web. Accessed 23 Apr. 2018.

Jones, Josh. "Aleister Crowley: The Wickedest Man in the World Documents the Life of the Bizarre Occultist, Poet & Mountaineer." Openculture.com. 20 Mar. 2014. Web. Accessed 23 Apr. 2018.

Harriet Tubman
"Africans in America: Harriet Tubman." *PBS*. Web. Accessed 23 Apr. 2018.

"Harriet Tubman." History.com. 2009. Web. Accessed 23 Apr. 2018.

"Timeline of the Life of Harriet Tubman." Harriet-tubman.org. Web. Accessed 23 Apr. 2018.

Biggs, Mary. *Women's Words: The Columbia Book of Quotations by Women*. Columbia University Press, 1996. Print.

David Crockett
"Davy Crockett." History.com. 2010. Web. Accessed 23 Apr. 2018.

Lofaro, Michael. "David Crockett (1786–1836)." Sonsofdewittcolony .org. Web. Accessed 23 Apr. 2018.

Shackford, James Atkins, et al. *David Crockett: The Man and the Legend*. Bison Books, 1994. Print.

Witold Pilecki
"Auschwitz." Ushmm.org. Web. Accessed 23 Apr. 2018.

"Meet the Man Who Sneaked Into Auschwitz." *NPR*. 18 Sept. 2010. Web. Accessed 23 Apr. 2018.

De Sola, David. "The Man Who Volunteered for Auschwitz." *The Atlantic*. 05 Oct. 2012. Web. Accessed 23 Apr. 2018.

Pilecki, Witold, and Garlinski, Jarek. *The Auschwitz Volunteer: Beyond Bravery*. Aquila Polonica, 2014. Print.

Snyder, Timothy. "'Were We All People?'" *New York Times*. 23 June 2012. Web. Accessed 23 Apr. 2018.

Annie Smith Peck
"Annie Smith Peck Quotes." Brainyquote.com. Web. Accessed 23 Apr. 2018.

Potter, Russell A. "Annie Smith Peck: Scholar and Mountaineer." Ric.edu. Web. Accessed 23 Apr. 2018.

Sutton, Brook. "Annie Smith Peck." *Adventure Journal*. April 2014. Web. Accessed 23 Apr. 2018.

Wroth, Katharine, and Quinby, Kate. *The Zen of Mountains and Climbing: Wit, Wisdom, and Inspiration*. Mountaineers Books/Skipstone, 2009. Print.

Apsley Cherry-Garrard
Cherry-Garrard, Apsley. *The Worst Journey in the World*. Empire Books, 2011. Print.

Martin, Jynne. "Tough Commute This Morning? Your 'Journey' Could Have Been Worse." *NPR*. 03 Jan. 2014. Web. Accessed 23 Apr. 2018.

McKie, Robin. "How a Heroic Hunt for Penguin Eggs became 'The Worst Journey in the World.'" *The Observer*. 14 Jan. 2012. Web. Accessed 23 Apr. 2018.

Moore, Lucy. "Cherry by Sara Wheeler." *The Observer*. 04 Nov. 2001. Web. Accessed 23 Apr. 2018.

Roald Amundsen
"Amundsen Reaches South Pole." History.com. Web. Accessed 23 Apr. 2018.

"Roald Amundsen." *Encyclopædia Britannica*. 10 May 2017. Web. Accessed 23 Apr. 2018.

"Roald Amundsen." Famous-explorers.org. 2013. Web. Accessed 23 Apr. 2018.

Amundsen, Roald. *South Pole: An Account of the Norwegian Antarctic Expedition in 'The Fram,' 1910–1912*. Cambridge University Press, 2014. Print.

Herodotus
"Herodotus." *Encyclopædia Britannica*. 04 Jan. 2017. Web. Accessed 23 Apr. 2018.

"Herodotus." History.com. 2010. Web. Accessed 23 Apr. 2018.

Herodotus, and Hornblower, Simon. *Histories*. Cambridge University Press, 2013. Print.

Mark, Joshua J. "Herodotus." Ancient.eu. 02 Sept. 2009. Web. Accessed 23 Apr. 2018.

Percy Fawcett
Andrews, Evan. "The Enduring Mystery Behind Percy Fawcett's Disappearance." History.com. 29 May 2015. Web. Accessed 23 Apr. 2018.

Grann, David. "The Lost City of Z." *New Yorker*. 29 Aug. 2017. Web. Accessed 23 Apr. 2018.

Fawcett, Percy Harrison, and Fawcett, Brian. *Exploration Fawcett*. The Overlook Press, 2010. Print.

Pickup, Oliver. "The Lost City of Z: What Happened to Percy Fawcett?" *The Telegraph*. 10 Mar. 2017. Web. Accessed 23 Apr. 2018.

Sitting Bull
"New Perspectives on the West: Sitting Bull." *PBS*. 2001. Web. Accessed 23 Apr. 2018.

"Sitting Bull." *Encyclopædia Britannica*. 21 Apr. 2017.

"Sitting Bull." History.com. 2009. Web. Accessed 23 Apr. 2018.

Sitting Bull, and Diedrich, Mark. *Sitting Bull: The Collected Speeches*. Coyote Books, 1998. Print.

Wilfred Thesiger
"Sir Wilfred Thesiger." *The Telegraph*. 26 Aug. 2003. Web. Accessed 23 Apr. 2018.

Lewis, Paul. "Wilfred Thesiger, 93, Dies; Explored Arabia." *New York Times*. 26 Aug. 2003. Web. Accessed 23 Apr. 2018.

Thesiger, Wilfred. *Arabian Sands*. Motivate Publishing, 2010. Print.

Alex Honnold

MacKinnon, J. B. "Alex Honnold's Perfect Climb." *New Yorker*. 19 June 2017. Web. Accessed 23 Apr. 2018.

Synnott, Mark. "Exclusive: Climber Completes the Most Dangerous Rope-Free Ascent Ever." *National Geographic*. 23 June 2017. Web. Accessed 23 Apr. 2018.

Annie Oakley

"Annie Oakley Shot a Cigarette Out of the Kaiser's Mouth, Had She Hit Him, She Could Have Prevented WWI." *The Vintage News*. 21 June 2017. Web. Accessed 24 Apr. 2018.

Edwards, Bess. "The Life and Career of Annie Oakley." Annieoakleyfoundation.org. Web. Accessed 24 Apr. 2018.

Righthand, Jess. "How Annie Oakley, 'Princess of the West,' Preserved Her Ladylike Reputation." Smithsonian .com. 11 Aug. 2010. Web. Accessed 24 Apr. 2018.

Sorg, Eric. "Annie Oakley." *Wild West*. February 2001. HistoryNet. com. Web. Accessed 24 Apr. 2018.

Daniel Boone

"Daniel Boone." History.com. 2010. Web. Accessed 24 Apr. 2018.

Filson, John. *Discovery, Settlement, and Present State of Kentucke; and an Essay Towards the Topography and Natural History of that Important Country*. Forgotten Books, 2015. Print.

Frick, Lisa. "Historic Missourians: Daniel Boone." Shsmo.org. Web. Accessed 24 Apr. 2018.

Nicholson, Jamie, and Drager, Marvin. "Kentucky Derby." *Encyclopædia Britannica*. 10 Nov. 2017. Web. Accessed 24 Apr. 2018.

George Mallory

"George Mallory." *Encyclopædia Britannica*. 14 Oct. 2014. Web. Accessed 24 Apr. 2018.

Mallory, George, and Peter Gillman. *Climbing Everest: The Complete Writings of George Leigh Mallory*. Gibson Square, 2012. Print.

Squires, Nick. "Mallory and Irvine's Everest Death Explained." *The Telegraph*. 04 Aug. 2010. Web. Accessed 24 Apr. 2018.

Wild Bill Hickok

"Wild Bill Hickok Is Murdered." History.com. Web. Accessed 24 Apr. 2018.

Certo, Joseph J. Di. "Wild Bill Hickok." *Encyclopædia Britannica*. 05 June 2015. Web. Accessed 24 Apr. 2018.

Holcombe, Return I. *History of Greene County, Missouri*. Western Historical Co., 1883. Print.

Alexandra David-Néel

Dapsance, Marion. "Who Was Alexandra David-Neel? A Brief Story of a Buddhist Anarchist." Buddhistdoor.net. 30 Sept. 2016. Web. Accessed 24 Apr. 2018.

David-Néel, Alexandra. *My Journey to Lhasa: The Personal Journey of the Only White Woman Who Succeeded in Entering the Forbidden City*. Important Books, 2013. Print.

Ross, Ailsa. "The Prima Donna Who Snuck Into Tibet in 1912 to Meet the Dalai Lama." *Atlas Obscura*. 21 June 2016. Web. Accessed 24 Apr. 2018.

Wetering, Janwillem Van De. "Astral Bodies and Tantric Sex." *New York Times*. 09 Jan. 1988. Web. Accessed 24 Apr. 2018.

Ella Maillart
Anderson, Sarah. "Ella Maillart." *The Independent*. 09 Apr. 1997. Web. Accessed 24 Apr. 2018.

Thomas Jr., Robert McG. "Ella Maillart, a Swiss Writer and Adventurer, Is Dead at 94." *New York Times*. 30 Mar. 1997. Web. Accessed 24 Apr. 2018.

Carl Akeley
"Carl E. Akeley." *Encyclopædia Britannica*. 27 Dec. 2017. Web. Accessed 24 Apr. 2018.

Conry, Tara. "Secrets of the American Museum of Natural History." Amby. com. 07 July 2016. Web. Accessed 24 Apr. 2018.

Aron Ralston
Hannaford, Alex. "127 Hours: Aron Ralston's Story of Survival." *The Telegraph*. 06 Jan. 2011. Web. Accessed 24 Apr. 2018.

Ralston, Aron. *127 Hours Between a Rock and a Hard Place*. W. Ross MacDonald School Resource Services Library, 2015. Print.

George Donner
"Donner Party." History.com. 2010. Web. Accessed 24 Apr. 2018.

Stewart, George R. *Ordeal by Hunger*. Washington Square Press, 1971. Print.

Worrall, Simon. "Beyond Cannibalism: The True Story of the Donner Party." *National Geographic*. 02 July 2017. Web. Accessed 24 Apr. 2018.

Miyamoto Musashi
"Rōnin." *Encyclopædia Britannica*. 12 Oct. 2015. Web. Accessed 24 Apr. 2018.

"Who Is Musashi Miyamoto?" Musashi-miyamoto.com. Web. Accessed 24 Apr. 2018.

Evangelista, Nick Forrest. "Miyamoto Musashi." *Encyclopædia Britannica*. 30 Nov. 2016. Web. Accessed 24 Apr. 2018.

Miyamoto, Musashi. *Go Rin No Sho*. Főnix Alapítvány, 1994. Print.

Hannibal Barca
"Hannibal." *History.com*. 2009. Web. Accessed 24 Apr. 2018.

Ball, Philip. "The Truth About Hannibal's Route Across the Alps." *The Observer*. 03 Apr. 2016.

Livy, et al. *The War with Hannibal*. Folio Society, 2011. Print.

Wilford, John Noble. "The Mystery of Hannibal's Elephants." *New York Times*. 17 Sept. 1984. Web. Accessed 24 Apr. 2018.

James Beckwourth
"James Beckwourth Is Born." History.com. Web. Accessed 24 Apr. 2018.

"James P. Beckwourth, Explorer Born." Aaregistry.org. Web. Accessed 24 Apr. 2018.

Beckwourth, James Pierson, and Bonner, T. D. *The Life and Adventures of James P. Beckwourth, Mountaineer, Scout, Pioneer, and Chief of the Crow Nation of Indians*. Kessinger Publishing, 2005. Print.

Roy Chapman Andrews
Andrews, Roy Chapman. *This Business of Exploring*. G.P. Putnams Sons, 1935. Print.

Boettcher, Kaitlyn. "Roy Chapman Andrews: A Real Life Indiana Jones." Mentalfloss.com. 25 Mar. 2013. Web. Accessed 24 Apr. 2018.

Thomas Jefferson
Goss, Betty. "Journey Through France and Italy (1787)." Monticello.org. 05 May 2009. Web. Accessed 24 Apr. 2018.

Goss, Betty. "Paris." Monticello.org. Nov. 2008. Web. Accessed 24 Apr. 2018.

Jefferson, Thomas, and Ford, Paul Leicester. "Letter to John Page (15 July 1763)." *The Works of Thomas Jefferson*. Silver Street Media, 2009. Print.

Stone, George. "10 Badass Travelers Throughout History." *National Geographic*. 20 Apr. 2017. Web. Accessed 24 Apr. 2018.

Ewart Grogan
"A Man Who Did Derring-Do." *The Telegraph*. 31 Mar. 2001. Web. Accessed 24 Apr. 2018.

Braun, David Maxwell. "For Love and Glory, Crossing the Heart of Africa." Blog.nationalgeographic.org. 21 Nov. 2011. Web. Accessed 24 Apr. 2018.

Grogan, Ewart S. *From the Cape to Cairo: The First Traverse of Africa from South to North*. Forgotten Books, 2016. Print.

Bruce Chatwin
Chatwin, Bruce. *In Patagonia*. Vintage Classics, 2017. Print.

Chatwin, Bruce. *The Songlines*. Penguin Books, 2012. Print.

Clapp, Susannah. "'Dazzling and Worrying': My Memories of Bruce Chatwin and *In Patagonia*." *The Observer*. 24 Sept. 2017. Web. Accessed 24 Apr. 2018.

Yanagihara, Hanya. "Bruce Chatwin: One of the Last Great Explorers." *New York Times*. 07 Sept. 2017. Web. Accessed 24 Apr. 2018.

Macfarlane, Robert. "Book of a Lifetime: In Patagonia, by Bruce Chatwin." *The Independent*. 22 June 2012. Web. Accessed 24 Apr. 2018.

Paul Revere
"Boston Tea Party." History.com. 2009. Web. Accessed 24 Apr. 2018.

"Paul Revere." History.com. 2009. Web. Accessed 24 Apr. 2018.

"Paul Revere." *Encyclopædia Britannica*. 14 July 2017. Web. Accessed 24 Apr. 2018.

Klein, Christopher. "The Midday Ride of Paul Revere." Smithsonian.com. 12 Dec. 2011. Web. Accessed 24 Apr. 2018.

Longfellow, Henry Wadsworth. "Paul Revere's Ride." Poets.org. 09 June 2017. Web. Accessed 24 Apr. 2018.

John Chapman
"John Chapman." Ohiohistorycentral.org. Web. Accessed 24 Apr. 2018.

Geiling, Natasha. "The Real Johnny Appleseed Brought Apples—and Booze—to the American Frontier." Smithsonian.com. 10 Nov. 2014. Web. Accessed 24 Apr. 2018.

Joe Strummer and the Mescaleros. "Johnny Appleseed." Hellcat Records, 2001.

Ferdinand Magellan
"The Ages of Exploration: Ferdinand Magellan." Exploration. marinersmuseum.org. Web. Accessed 24 Apr. 2018.

Charles Darwin
"iWonder—Charles Darwin: Evolution and the Story of Our Species." *BBC*. Web. Accessed 24 Apr. 2018.

Darwin, Charles, and Bynum, W. F. *On the Origin of Species: By Means of Natural Selection, or, The Preservation of Favoured Races in the Struggle for Life*. Penguin Classics, 2009. Print.

Sulloway, Frank J. "The Evolution of Charles Darwin." Smithsonian. com. 01 Dec 2005. Web. Accessed 24 Apr. 2018.

Townley, K. A. "Biography— Charles Robert Darwin." Australian Dictionary of Biography. Web. Accessed 24 Apr. 2018.

Ibn Battuta
"Ibn Battuta." Famousscientists.org. Web. Accessed 24 Apr. 2018.

Brown, Cynthia Stokes. "Ibn Battuta." Khanacademy.org. Web. Accessed 24 Apr. 2018.

Erik Thorvaldsson
"The Ages of Exploration: Erik the Red." Exploration.marinersmuseum .org. Web. Accessed 24 Apr. 2018.

Sturluson, Snurri. *The Prose Edda*. Milford, 1916. Print.

Wallace, Birgitta. "Erik the Red." *Encyclopædia Britannica*. 16 Feb. 2017. Web. Accessed 24 Apr. 2018.

John Cabot
"History—John Cabot." *BBC*. 2014. Web. Accessed 24 Apr. 2018.

"John Cabot." History.com. 2009. Web. Accessed 24 Apr. 2018.

Hiller, James, and Higgins, Jenny. "John Cabot." *Heritage: Newfoundland and Labrador*. 1997. Web. Accessed 24 Apr. 2018.

Thor Heyerdahl

"Thor Heyerdahl." *Encyclopædia Britannica*. 03 Jan. 2017. Web. Accessed 24 Apr. 2018.

Klein, Christopher. "Thor Heyerdahl's Kon-Tiki Voyage." History.com. 06 Oct. 2014. Web. Accessed 24 Apr. 2018.

Jacques Piccard

"How Much Water Is in the Ocean?" Oceanservice.noaa.gov. 01 June 2013. Web. Accessed 25 Apr. 2018.

"Soundings, Sea-Bottom, and Geophysics." Oceanservice.noaa.gov. Web. Accessed 25 Apr. 2018.

Knight, J.D. "Jacques Piccard." Seasky .org. Web. Accessed 25 Apr. 2018.

Piccard, Jacques, and Dietz, Robert S. *Seven Miles Down: The Story of the Bathyscaph Trieste*. Scientific Book Club, 1963. Print.

Strickland, Eliza. "Don Walsh Describes the Trip to the Bottom of the Mariana Trench." Spectrum.ieee .org. 29 Feb. 2012. Web. Accessed 25 Apr. 2018.

Jacques Cousteau

"Jacques Cousteau." Famousscientists .org. Web. Accessed 25 Apr. 2018.

"Sport: Poet of the Depths." *Time*. 28 Mar. 1960.

Jonas, Gerald. "Jacques Cousteau, Oceans' Impresario, Dies." *New York Times*. 25 June 1997. Web. Accessed 25 Apr. 2018.

Jeanne Baré

Cohen, Jennie. "First Woman to Circle the Globe Honored at Last." History.com. 03 Jan. 2012. Web. Accessed 25 Apr. 2018.

Helferich, Gerard. "Incredible Voyage." *Wall Street Journal*. 24 Jan. 2011. Web. Accessed 25 Apr. 2018.

Krulwich, Robert. "The First Woman To Go 'Round the World Did It as a Man." *NPR*. 24 Jan. 2012. Web. Accessed 25 Apr. 2018.

Ridley, Glynis. "A Female Explorer Discovered on the High Seas." *NPR*. 26 Dec. 2010. Web. Accessed 25 Apr. 2018.

Marco Polo

"Marco Polo." History.com. 2012. Web. Accessed 25 Apr. 2018.

Maraini, Fosco. "Marco Polo." *Encyclopædia Britannica*. 23 June 2017. Web. Accessed 25 Apr. 2018.

Polo, Marco, et al. *The Travels of Marco Polo: The Venetian*. Nabu Press, 2013. Print.

Francisco Pizarro

"Francisco Pizarro." History.com. 2009. Web. Accessed 25 Apr. 2018.

"The Ages of Exploration: Francisco Pizarro." Exploration.marinersmuseum.org. Web. Accessed 25 Apr. 2018.

Prescott, William Hickling. *History of the Conquest of Peru*. Baudrys European Library, 1847. Print.

Mel Fisher

"1622 Fleet." Melfisher.org/1622.
Web. Accessed 25 Apr. 2018.

"Treasure Hunter Mel Fisher Dies."
CBS News. 20 Dec. 1998. Web.
Accessed 25 Apr. 2018.

Pace, Eric. "Mel Fisher, 76, a Treasure
Hunter Who Got Rich Undersea."
New York Times. 20 Dec. 1998. Web.
Accessed 25 Apr. 2018.

Giovanni Battista Belzoni

"Giovanni Battista Belzoni."
Encyclopædia Britannica. 29 Jan.
2015. Web. Accessed 25 Apr. 2018.

"Giovanni Battista Belzoni." *New
World Encyclopedia*. 22 June 2017.
Web. Accessed 25 Apr. 2018.

Norden, Frederik Ludvig. *Travels in
Egypt and Nubia*. Davis & Reymers,
1757. Print.

Parsons, Marie. "Giovanni Belzoni,
Circus Giant and Collector of
Egyptian Antiquities." Touregypt
.net/featurestories/belzoni.htm.

Ernest Hemingway

Hemingway, Ernest. *A Moveable
Feast*. Vintage, 2011. Print.

Plimpton, George. "Ernest
Hemingway, The Art of Fiction No.
21." *The Paris Review*. Spring 1958.
Web. Accessed 25 Apr. 2018.

Stoppard, Tom. "Ernest Hemingway."
PBS. 13 Jan. 2009. Web. Accessed 25
Apr. 2018.

Young, Philip. "Ernest Hemingway."
Encyclopædia Britannica. 05 Oct.
2017. Web. Accessed 25 Apr. 2018.

Christopher Columbus

"Christopher Columbus." History
.com. 2009. Web. Accessed 25
Apr. 2018.

Columbus, Christopher, et al.
*Journal of the First Voyage: Diaro del
Primer Viaje, 1492*. Aris & Phillips,
1990. Print.

Flint, Valerie I.J. "Christopher
Columbus." *Encyclopædia Britannica*.
20 Dec. 2017. Web. Accessed 25
Apr. 2018.

Lane, Kris. "Five Myths About
Christopher Columbus." *Washington
Post*. 08 Oct. 2015. Web. Accessed 25
Apr. 2018.

Lynne Cox

Cox, Lynne. *Grayson*. Mariner Books,
2015. Print.

Watts, Simon. "Swim That Broke
Cold War Ice Curtain." *BBC News*.
08 Aug. 2012. Web. Accessed 25
Apr. 2018.

Cox, Lynne. *Swimming to Antarctica:
Tales of a Long-Distance Swimmer*.
Phoenix, 2006. Print.

Zheng He

Brown, Cynthia Stokes. "Zheng He."
Khanacademy.com. Web. Accessed
25 Apr. 2018.

Lo, Jung-pang. "Zheng He."
Encyclopædia Britannica. 30 Nov.
2017. Web. Accessed 25 Apr. 2018.

Mendis, Patrick. *Peaceful War: How
the Chinese Dream and the American
Destiny Create a Pacific New World
Order*. University Press of America,
2014. Print.

Bartolomeu Dias

"Bartolomeu Dias." History.com. 2009. Web. Accessed 25 Apr. 2018.

"The Ages of Exploration: Bartolomeu Dias." Exploration .marinersmuseum.org. Web. Accessed 25 Apr. 2018.

Livermore, Harold V. "Bartolomeu Dias." *Encyclopædia Britannica*. 09 Oct. 2017. Web. Accessed 25 Apr. 2018.

Otto of Freising, and Brundage, James. *The Crusades: A Documentary History*. Marquette University Press, 1962. Sourcebooks.fordham.edu. Web. Accessed 25 Apr. 2018.

Owen Chase

"Tragedy of the Whaleship Essex." *National Geographic*. 20 Nov. 2014. Web. Accessed 25 Apr. 2018.

King, Gilbert. "The True-Life Horror That Inspired Moby-Dick." Smithsonian.com. 01 Mar. 2013. Web. Accessed 25 Apr. 2018.

Melville, Herman, et al. *Moby-Dick*. W.W. Norton, 2002. Print.

Nickerson, Thomas, et al. *The Loss of the Ship Essex, Sunk by a Whale*. Penguin, 2000. Print.

Blackbeard

"Blackbeard: History of the Dreaded Pirate." Qaronline.org. Web. Accessed 25 Apr. 2018.

"Blackbeard Killed off North Carolina." History.com. Web. Accessed 25 Apr. 2018.

Powell, William S. "Blackbeard the Pirate." NCpedia.org. Web. Accessed 25 Apr. 2018.

Louise Boyd

"Louise Arner Boyd." Americanpolar .org. Web. Accessed 25 Apr. 2018.

"Louise Arner Boyd Dies at 84; Led Expeditions to the Arctic." *New York Times*. 17 Sept. 1972. Web. Accessed 25 Apr. 2018.

Amidon, Audrey. "Women of the Polar Archives: The Films and Stories of Marie Peary Stafford and Louise Boyd." Archives.gov. Summer 2010. Web. Accessed 25 Apr. 2018.

Platt, Raye. "Louis Arner Boyd." *Encyclopedia Arctica 15: Biographies*. Collections.dartmouth.edu. Web. Accessed 25 Apr. 2018.

Amerigo Vespucci

"Ages of Exploration: Amerigo Vespucci." Exploration .marinersmuseum.org. Web. Accessed 25 Apr. 2018.

"Amerigo Vespucci." History.com. 2009. Web. Accessed 25 Apr. 2018.

"Letter of Amerigo Vespucci to Pier Soderini 1497." Let.rug.nl. Web. Accessed 25 Apr. 2018.

Donald Crowhurst

Ed, Caesar. "Drama on the Waves: The Life and Death of Donald Crowhurst." *The Independent*. 27 Oct. 2006. Web. Accessed 25 Apr. 2018.

McCrum, Robert. "Robert McCrum Meets the Family of the Infamous 'Lone Sailor,' Donald Crowhurst." *The Observer*. 04 Apr. 2009. Web. Accessed 25 Apr. 2018.

Tomalin, Nicholas, and Hall, Ron. *The Strange Last Voyage of Donald Crowhurst*. Quercus, 2017. Print.

Napoleon Bonaparte
"Napoleon Bonaparte." History.com. 2009. Web. Accessed 25 Apr. 2018.

"Napoleon: The Man and the Myth." *PBS*. Web. Accessed 25 Apr. 2018.

Bonaparte, Napoleon. *The Mind of Napoleon: A Selection from His Written and Spoken Words*. Columbia University Press, 1969. Print.

Godechot, Jacques. "Napoleon I." *Encyclopædia Britannica*. 03 Jan. 2018. Web. Accessed 25 Apr. 2018.

Selin, Shannon. "How Did Napoleon Escape from Elba?" Shannonselin.com. 10 Nov. 2017. Web. Accessed 25 Apr. 2018.

Madison Washington
Brown, William Wells. "Story of the Week: Madison Washington." Storyoftheweek.loa.org. 21 Feb. 2014. Web. Accessed 25 Apr. 2018.

Brown, William Wells. *Black Man: His Antecedents, His Genius, and His Achievements*. Hardpress Ltd, 2013. Print.

Proyect, Louis. "Madison Washington and the Creole Rebellion." Louisproyect.org. 28 Oct. 2014. Web. Accessed 25 Apr. 2018.

Williams, Michael Paul. "Brig Creole Slaves." *Richmond Times-Dispatch*. 11 Feb. 2002. Web. Accessed 25 Apr. 2018.

Frederick Douglass
"Africans in America: Frederick Douglass." *PBS*. Web. Accessed 26 Apr. 2018.

"Frederick Douglass." *History.com*. 2009. Web. Accessed 26 Apr. 2018.

"Slavery in America." *History.com*. 2009. Web. Accessed 26 Apr. 2018.

Douglass, Frederick, and Davis, Angela Y. *Narrative of the Life of Frederick Douglass: An American Slave: Written by Himself*. City Lights Books, 2010. Print.

Douglass, Frederick. "What to the Slave is the Fourth of July?" Corinthian Hall, Rochester, NY. Keynote address. 05 July 1852.

Leif Erikson
"Leif Eriksson." History.com. 2010. Web. Accessed 26 Apr. 2018.

"Leif Ericson Facts & Biography." Famous-explorers.org. 2013. Web. Accessed 26 Apr. 2018.

Ashliman, D.L., editor, and Bray, Olive, translator. *Hávamál: The Words of Odin the High One from the Elder or Poetic Edda*. Pitt.edu. 28 Mar. 2003. Web. Accessed 26 Apr. 2018.

Phillis Wheatley
"Africans in America: Phillis Wheatley ." *PBS*. Web. Accessed 26 Apr. 2018.

"Phillis Wheatley, the First African-American Published Book of Poetry." Americaslibrary.gov. Web. Accessed 26 Apr. 2018.

O'Neale, Sondra. "Phillis Wheatley." Poetryfoundation.org. Web. Accessed 26 Apr. 2018.

Wheatley, Phillis. *Poems on Various Subjects, Religious and Moral*. Pantianos Classics, 2017. Print.

Sir Robert Hart
"Sir Robert Hart, 1st Baronet." *Encyclopædia Britannica*. 14 Oct. 2014. Web. Accessed 26 Apr. 2018.

Lynn, Martin. "Robert Hart: A Man of Two Worlds." Sacu.org. Web. Accessed 26 Apr. 2018.

Yi, Xing. "The Story of Sir Robert Hart." *The Telegraph*. 22 May 2017. Web. Accessed 26 Apr. 2018.

Octavie Coudreau
Leroy, Michele. "Octavie Coudreau (1867–1938): A Woman in Green Hell." HenriCoudreau.fr. Web. Accessed 26 Apr. 2018.

Olsen, Kirstin. *Chronology of Women's History*. Greenwood Press, 1994. Print.

Jacques Cartier
"Cartier's First Voyage." *CBC News*. Web. Accessed 26 Apr. 2018.

"Jacques Cartier." History.com. 2009. Web. Accessed 26 Apr. 2018.

"The Ages of Exploration: Jacques Cartier." Exploration. marinersmuseum.org. Web. Accessed 26 Apr. 2018.

"The Explorers: Jacques Cartier 1534–1542." Historymuseum.ca. Web. Accessed 26 Apr. 2018.

Ada Blackjack
Buck, Stephanie. "Stranded for Two Years on an Arctic Island, This Woman Miraculously Survived by Shooting Seals." *Timeline*. 29 Aug. 2017. Web. Accessed 26 Apr. 2018.

Niven, Jennifer. "The Female Robinson Crusoe: Who Was Ada Blackjack?" *National Geographic*. 15 Jan. 2004. Web. Accessed 26 Apr. 2018.

Stefansson, Vilhjalmur, et al. *The Adventure of Wrangel Island*. Jonathan Cape, 1926. Print.

Charles Lightoller
"Dunkirk Evacuation." *Encyclopædia Britannica*. 21 Sept. 2017. Web. Accessed 26 Apr. 2018.

"The Before, The Reality, The Aftermath: Sundowner." Dunkirk1940.org. Web. Accessed 26 Apr. 2018.

"The Life of Titanic Officer Charles Lightoller." Premierexhibitions.com. 2014. Web. Accessed 26 Apr. 2018.

Fowler, David. "Titanic Quotes." Titanicfacts.net. Web. Accessed 26 Apr. 2018.

Hernán Cortés
"Hernan Cortes." History.com. 2009. Web. Accessed 26 Apr. 2018.

"History—Hernando Cortés." *BBC*. Web. Accessed 26 Apr. 2018.

Hammond, George Peter, and Agapito, Rey. *Narratives of the Coronado Expedition, 1540–1542.* AMS, 1977. Print.

Innes, Ralph Hammond. "Hernán Cortés, Marqués del Valle de Oaxaca." *Encyclopædia Britannica.* 27 June 2017.

Peterson, Keith. "Conquistador: Hernan Cortés, King Montezuma, and the Last Stand of the Aztecs." *Washington State Magazine.* Web. Accessed 26 Apr. 2018.

Theodore Roosevelt
"Theodore Roosevelt." History.com. 2009.

Andrews, Evan. "The Amazonian Expedition That Nearly Killed Theodore Roosevelt." History.com. 26 Jan. 2017. Web. Accessed 26 Apr. 2018.

Roosevelt, Theodore. *Theodore Roosevelt: An Autobiography.* Bibliobazaar, 2007. Print.

Estevanico
"Estevanico." Elizabethan-era.org.uk. Web. Accessed 26 Apr. 2018.

"History of Estevanico." Humanities .uci.edu. Spring 2001. Web. Accessed 26 Apr. 2018.

Mason, Clifford. *The African-American Bookshelf: 50 Must-Reads from Before The Civil War Through Today.* Citadel Press, 2003. Print.

Abubakari II
Baxter, Joan. "Africa's 'Greatest Explorer.'" *BBC News.* 13 Dec. 2000. Web. Accessed 26 Apr. 2018.

ya Kama, Lisapo. "Mansa Abubakari II, the Emperor of Mali Who Travelled to America." En.lisapoyakama.org. 08 Jan. 2018. Web. Accessed 26 Apr. 2018.

Juan Garrido
"Juan Garrido, Early Black Explorer Born." Aaregistry.org. Web. Accessed 26 Apr. 2018.

Escamilla, Luis. "The Black Past : Garrido, Juan (c. 1480–c.1550)." Blackpast.org. Web. Accessed 26 Apr. 2018.

Goldschein, Eric. "The 10 Most Important Crops in the World." *Business Insider.* 20 Sept. 2011. Web. Accessed 26 Apr. 2018.

Mike Fink
"Mike Fink." *Encyclopædia Britannica.* 12 Aug. 2013. Web. Accessed 26 Apr. 2018.

"Mike Fink; an American Anti-Hero." NBCNews.com. 30 Aug. 2004. Web. Accessed 26 Apr. 2018.

Blair, Walter, and Meine, Franklin J. *Mike Fink: King of Mississippi Keelboatmen.* Greenwood Press, 1971. Print.

Field, Timothy. "Mike Fink: The Last of the Boatmen." Xroads.virginia.edu. Web. Accessed 26 Apr. 2018.

Schweikart, Larry, and Allen, Michael. "Mike Fink, King of the River." Patriotshistoryusa.com. Web. Accessed 26 Apr. 2018.

Matthew Webb
"Captain Webb Swims English Channel." History.com. Web. Accessed 26 Apr. 2018.

Martin, Douglas. "Des Renford, 72, Channel Swimmer, Is Dead." *New York Times*. 01 Feb. 2000. Web. Accessed 26 Apr. 2018.

Mason, Paul. "Heroes of Swimming: Captain Matthew Webb." *The Guardian*. 10 Oct. 2013. Web. Accessed 26 Apr. 2018.

Wooldridge, Christopher Frederick, and Everard, Cyril Ernest. "English Channel." *Encyclopædia Britannica*. 13 Feb. 2014. Web. Accessed 26 Apr. 2018.

Lord Byron
"Lord Byron Swims the Hellespont." History.com. Web. Accessed 26 Apr. 2018.

"Lord Byron (George Gordon)." Poetryfoundation.org. Web. Accessed 26 Apr. 2018.

"On Dylan Thomas." Poets.org. 01 Feb. 2015. Web. Accessed 26 Apr. 2018.

Byron, George Gordon. *The Works of Byron*. Fleischer, 1819. Print.

Horsbrugh, Becky. "The Hellespont Swim: Following in Byron's Wake." *The Guardian*. 06 May 2010. Web. Accessed 26 Apr. 2018.

Smith, Roff. "Greatest Swims: Five Epic Swims in the Wake of Nyad's Feat." *National Geographic.* 11 Nov. 2015. Web. Accessed 26 Apr. 2018.

Nellie Bly
"Around the World in 72 Days." *National Geographic Society*. 12 Dec. 2014. Web. Accessed 26 Apr. 2018.

Bly, Nellie. *Around the World in Seventy-Two Days*. Dodo Press, 2008. Print.

Bly, Nellie. *Ten Days in a Mad-House*. The Perfect Library, 2017. Print.

Dame Freya Madeline Stark
"Dame Freya Stark, Travel Writer, Is Dead at 100." *New York Times*. 10 May 1993. Web. Accessed 26 Apr. 2018.

"Freya Stark." *Encyclopædia Britannica*. 14 Feb. 2011. Web. Accessed 26 Apr. 2018.

Ruthven, Malise. "Obituary: Dame Freya Stark." *The Independent*. 10 May 1993. Web. Accessed 26 Apr. 2018.

Stark, Freya. *Baghdad Sketches*. Tauris Parke Paperbacks, 2011. Print.

Isabella Bird
"Isabella Bird." Encyclopedia.com. Web. Accessed 26 Apr. 2018.

"Isabella Bird's 1873 Visit to Rocky Mountain National Park." National Parks Service. Web. Accessed 26 Apr. 2018.

Stoddart, Anna M. *Life of Isabella Bird*. Cambridge University Press, 2011. Print.

Bird, Isabella L. *A Lady's Life in the Rocky Mountains*. Putnams, 1894. Print.

Evelyn Waugh
"About Evelyn Waugh."
Evelynwaughsociety.org. Web.
Accessed 26 Apr. 2018.

Meyers, Jeffrey. "Abyssinia out of the
Shadows." *History Today*. Nov. 2015.
Web. Accessed 26 Apr. 2018.

Waugh, Evelyn, and Davie, Michael.
The Diaries of Evelyn Waugh.
Phoenix, 2009. Print.

Mike Horn
"Pole 2 Pole." Mikehorn.com. Web.
Accessed 26 Apr. 2018.

Aimée Crocker
"Aimee Crocker." *The Paris Review*.
Web. Accessed 26 Apr. 2018.

Purves, Libby. "The Exhausting and
Exhilarating Tale of Aimée Crocker."
The Times Literary Supplement.
29 Mar. 2017. Web. Accessed 26
Apr. 2018.

Jan Morris
George, Donald W. *Tales from
Nowhere*. Lonely Planet Global,
2016. Print.

Johns, Derek. "Jan Morris at 90:
She Has Shown Us the World."
The Guardian. 02 Oct. 2016. Web.
Accessed 26 Apr. 2018.

McSmith, Andy. "Love Story: Jan
Morris—Divorce, the Death of a
Child and a Sex Change ... but Still
Together." *The Independent*. 03 June
2008. Web. Accessed 26 Apr. 2018.

Gertrude Bell
Buchan, James. "The Extraordinary
Life of Gertrude Bell." *The Guardian*.
11 Mar. 2003.

Hitchens, Christopher. "The Woman
Who Made Iraq." *The Atlantic*.
01 June 2007. Web. Accessed 26
Apr. 2018.

Muhanna, Elias. "What Gertrude
Bell's Letters Remind Us About
the Founding of Iraq." *New Yorker*.
18 June 2017. Web. Accessed 26
Apr. 2018.

Bell, Gertrude Lowthian. *Safar
Nameh: Persian Pictures: A Book of
Travel*. Cambridge University Press,
2012. Print.

Ida Pfeiffer
Pfeiffer, Ida. *A Woman's Journey
Round the World*. Tredition,
2011. Print.

Pfeiffer, Ida. *The Story of Ida
Pfeiffer and Her Travels in Many
Lands*. Thomas Nelson and Sons,
1993. Print.

Isabelle Eberhardt
"Isabelle Eberhardt" Goodreads.com.
Web. Accessed 26 Apr. 2018.

Eberhardt, Isabelle, and Kabbani,
Rana. *The Passionate Nomad: The
Diary of Isabelle Eberhardt*. Virago,
1987. Print.

Ross, Ailsa. "The Cross-Dressing
Heiress Who Decamped to the
Algerian Desert." *Atlas Obscura*.
21 June 2016. Web. Accessed 26
Apr. 2018.

Wilmers, Mary-Kay. "She Was a
Desert Cavalier." *New York Times*.
22 Apr. 1989. Web. Accessed 26
Apr. 2018.

T. E. Lawrence
"T. E. Lawrence." *PBS*. Web. Accessed 26 Apr. 2018.

Anderson, Scott. "The True Story of Lawrence of Arabia." Smithsonian .com. 01 July 2014. Web. Accessed 26 Apr. 2018.

Lawrence, T. E. *Lawrence of Arabia: Seven Pillars of Wisdom*. Easton Press, 1992. Print.

Weintraub, Stanley. "T. E. Lawrence." *Encyclopædia Britannica*. 15 Nov. 2017. Web. Accessed 26 Apr. 2018.

Lady Hester Stanhope
"Stanhope, Hester (1776–1839)." Encyclopedia.com. Web. Accessed 27 Apr. 2018.

Heinrich Schliemann
"Heinrich Schliemann Archaeology: Troy—Mask of Agamemnon." Age-of-the-sage.org. Web. Accessed 27 Apr. 2018.

Damen, Mark. "Archaeology: Troy and Heinrich Schliemann." *Utah State University 1320: History and Civilization*. Web. Accessed 27 Apr. 2018.

Kuiper, Kathleen, and Daniel, Glyn Edmund. "Heinrich Schliemann." *Encyclopædia Britannica*. 15 Nov. 2017. Web. Accessed 27 Apr. 2018.

Schliemann, Henry. *Troy and Its Remains: A Narrative of Researches and Discoveries Made on the Site of Ilium*. Forgotten Books, 2016. Print.

Mary Kingsley
"Mary Henrietta Kingsley." *Encyclopædia Britannica*. 06 Mar. 2017. Web. Accessed 27 Apr. 2018.

Andrews, Robert. *The Concise Columbia Dictionary of Quotations*. Columbia University Press, 1992. Print.

Hanebutt, Jacob. "Mary Kingsley." Womenineuropeanhistory.org. Web. Accessed 27 Apr. 2018.

Banerjee, Jacqueline. "Mary Kingsley: Demystifying Africa." Victorianweb .org. Web. Accessed 27 Apr. 2018.

Timothy Leary
"Timothy Leary." Psychology.fas .harvard.edu. Web. Accessed 27 Apr. 2018.

Leary, Timothy, et al. *The Politics of Ecstasy*. Trieste Publishing Pty Ltd., 2017. Print.

Mansnerus, Laura. "Timothy Leary, Pied Piper of Psychedelic 60's, Dies at 75." *New York Times*. 01 June 1996. Web. Accessed 27 Apr. 2018.

William Montgomery McGovern
Danzig, Christopher. "Our Very Own Indiana Jones." *Northwestern Magazine*. Spring 2010. Web. Accessed 27 Apr. 2018.

McGovern, William Montgomery. *To Lhasa in Disguise: A Secret Expedition Through Mysterious Tibet*. Asian Educational Services, 2000. Print.

Harriet Chalmers Adams

Keefe, Alexa. "A Woman of Passion, Courage, and Style Explores the World." *National Geographic*. 07 Mar. 2016. Web. Accessed 27 Apr. 2018.

Sutton, Brook. "Harriet Chalmers Adams: The Original Adventure-Lebrity." *Adventure Journal*. 11 Feb. 2016. Web. Accessed 27 Apr. 2018.

Rothenberg, Tamar. "Adams, Harriet Chalmers." Anb.org. 16 June 2017. Web. Accessed 27 Apr. 2018.

Edith Durham

Aslanyan, Anna. "Albania's Mountain Queen: Edith Durham and the Balkans by Marcus Tanner." *The Independent*. 12 June 2014. Web. Accessed 27 Apr. 2018.

Durham, Mary E. *High Albania*. Arno Pr. u.a., 1971. Print.

Elsie, Robert. "The Photo Collection of Edith Durham." Albanianphotography.net. Web. Accessed 27 Apr. 2018.

Alexandrine Tinné

"Alexandrine-Pieternella-Françoise Tinné." *Encyclopædia Britannica*. 09 Dec. 2014. Web. Accessed 27 Apr. 2018.

Johnston, Harry. *The Nile Quest: A Record of the Exploration of the Nile and Its Basin*. Negro History Press, 1970. Print.

Willink, Joost. *The Fateful Journey: The Expedition of Alexine Tinné and Theodor von Heuglin in Sudan (1863–1864): A Study of Their Travel Accounts and Ethnographic Collections*. Amsterdam University Press, 2011. Print.

Marianne North

"Marianne North (1830–1890)." Kew.org. Web. Accessed 27 Apr. 2018.

Hughes, Kathryn. "Marianne North: The Flower Huntress." *The Telegraph*. 20 Mar. 2009. Web. Accessed 27 Apr. 2018.

North, Marianne. *Recollections of a Happy Life: Being the Autobiography of Marianne North*. Cambridge University Press, 2011. Print.

Kirk, Jay. "Wrestling Leopards, Felling Apes: A Life in Taxidermy." *NPR*. 04 Dec. 2010. Web. Accessed 27 Apr. 2018.

Quayle, Catherine. "Keys to the Kingdom: The Story of a Revolutionary Taxidermist." *PBS*. 15 Nov. 2010. Web. Accessed 27 Apr. 2018.

Kira Salak

"Learn More About Kira Salak." *National Geographic*. Web. Accessed 27 Apr. 2018.

Salak, Kira. *Four Corners: A Journey into the Heart of Papua New Guinea*. ReadHowYouWant, 2013. Print.

Salak, Kira. "Kira's Comments on 'The White Mary.'" Kirasalak.com. 2008. Web. Accessed 27 Apr. 2018.

Fridtjof Nansen
"Fridtjof Nansen." *Nobelprize.org*.
Web. Accessed 27 Apr. 2018.

Nansen, Fridtjof. *Farthest North*.
Hansebooks, 2016. Print.

Sir John Mandeville
"Sir John Mandeville." Encyclopedia
.com. Web. Accessed 27 Apr. 2018.

"Sir John Mandeville." *Encyclopædia
Britannica*. 13 May 2012. Web.
Accessed 27 Apr. 2018.

Mandeville, John. *Travels of Sir John
Mandeville: The Version of the Cotton
Manuscript in Modern Spelling*.
Forgotten Books, 2015. Print.

Strabo
"Strabo." En.wikiquote.org. 16 Dec.
2016. Web. Accessed 27 Apr. 2018.

Lasserre, François. "Strabo."
Encyclopædia Britannica. 07 May
2014. Web. Accessed 27 Apr. 2018.

Lendering, Jona. "Strabo of Amasia."
Livius.org. 2015. Web. Accessed 27
Apr. 2018.

Christopher McCandless
"Christopher McCandless, Whose
Alaskan Odyssey Ended in Death."
New York Times. 30 Aug. 2016. Web.
Accessed 27 Apr. 2018.

Krakauer, Jon. *Into the Wild*. Anchor
Books, 2007. Print.

AFRICA.
Agi:
lymba.
Targa
Digir
Berdoa
Albaili
Borno
Cano
Guangara
Benin
Cago
Alafar
Nubia
Antonio
C. Bone
NW
NE
E
SE
S
SW
W

INDEX

Arabia
Mecha
Zebit
Melinde
Mel
nde.
Quiloa
Mozambique
Vasco de Acuna
S. Francesco
Adarno
Baixos de Nazaret
Mascarenas
Don galopes
S. Apollonia
S. Laurenty
Iuan de
Lisboa
Pomeri
Los Romeros
Punta de
Maria
di Mal
diuar
Brana

Index

Berdoa

Aeg

Hair Zarga

Digir

Albaili

Ge

AFRICA.

Nubia

oden

Borno

Nu

Agi:

Cano

Guan-

guara

Iymba.

Benin

Ambia

Cago

Alna

Blafar

Ab

Mellegete

gala

Gaga

con:

Helena

MN

NE

M

E

MS

S

SE

de S.
Antonio

Corra

Carne:
eu

Tristan de

C. Bone Iber

About the Author:

DANIEL GROGAN grew up in upstate New York, currently lives in Astoria, Queens, and walks everywhere. He is a writer and editor, and is also the author of *Famous Last Lines*.

Great ideas grow over time. From seed to harvest, Appleseed Press brings fine reading and entertainment together between the covers of its creatively crafted books. Our grove bears fruit twice a year, publishing a new crop of titles each Spring and Fall.

Visit us online at
www.appleseedpressbooks.com
or write to us at
68 North Street
Kennebunkport, Maine 04046

NEW YORK CITY, NEW YORK

Whalen Book Works is a book packaging company that combines top-notch design, unique formats, and fresh content to create truly innovative gift books. We plant one tree for every 10 books we print, and your purchase supports a tree in the Rocky Mountain National Park.

Visit us online at
www.whalenbooks.com
or write to us at
338 E 100 Street, Suite 5A
New York, NY 10029